ADOBE® PHOTOSHOP® CS5
CLASSROOM IN A BOOK®

The official training workbook from Adobe Systems

www.adobepress.com

Adobe Press books are published by Peachpit, a division of Pearson Education located in Berkeley, California. For the latest on Adobe Press books, go to www.adobepress.com. To report errors, please send a note to errata@peachpit.com. For information on getting permission for reprints and excerpts, contact permissions@peachpit.com.

Printed and bound in the United States of America

ISBN-13: 978-0-321-70176-3

ISBN-10: 0-321-70176-3

9 8 7 6 5 4 3 2 1

WHAT'S ON THE DISC

Here is an overview of the contents of the Classroom in a Book disc

The *Adobe Photoshop CS5 Classroom in a Book* disc includes the lesson files that you'll need to complete the exercises in this book, as well as other content to help you learn more about Adobe Photoshop CS5 and use it with greater efficiency and ease. The diagram below represents the contents of the disc, which should help you locate the files you need.

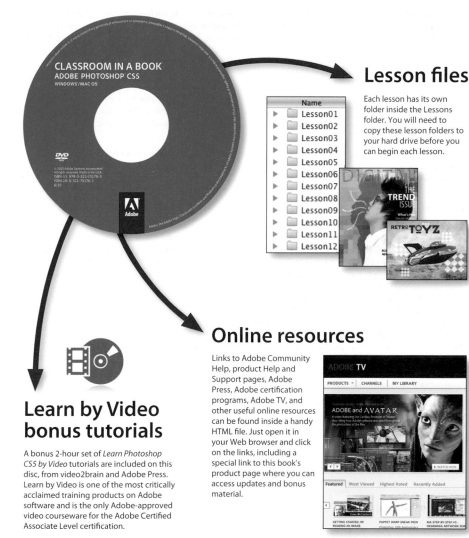

Lesson files

Each lesson has its own folder inside the Lessons folder. You will need to copy these lesson folders to your hard drive before you can begin each lesson.

Learn by Video bonus tutorials

A bonus 2-hour set of *Learn Photoshop CS5 by Video* tutorials are included on this disc, from video2brain and Adobe Press. Learn by Video is one of the most critically acclaimed training products on Adobe software and is the only Adobe-approved video courseware for the Adobe Certified Associate Level certification.

Online resources

Links to Adobe Community Help, product Help and Support pages, Adobe Press, Adobe certification programs, Adobe TV, and other useful online resources can be found inside a handy HTML file. Just open it in your Web browser and click on the links, including a special link to this book's product page where you can access updates and bonus material.

CONTENTS

GETTING STARTED

Adobe® Photoshop® CS5, the benchmark for digital imaging excellence, provides strong performance, powerful image-editing features, and an intuitive interface. Adobe Camera Raw, included with Photoshop CS5, offers flexibility and control as you work with raw images, as well as TIFF and JPEG images. Photoshop CS5 pushes the boundaries of digital image editing and helps you turn your dreams into designs more easily than ever before.

About Classroom in a Book

Adobe Photoshop CS5 Classroom in a Book® is part of the official training series for Adobe graphics and publishing software, developed with the support of Adobe product experts. The lessons are designed to let you learn at your own pace. If you're new to Adobe Photoshop, you'll learn the fundamental concepts and features you'll need to master the program. And if you've been using Adobe Photoshop for a while, you'll find that Classroom in a Book teaches many advanced features, including tips and techniques for using the latest version of the application and preparing images for the web.

Although each lesson provides step-by-step instructions for creating a specific project, there's room for exploration and experimentation. You can follow the book from start to finish, or do only the lessons that match your interests and needs. Each lesson concludes with a review section summarizing what you've covered.

What's new in this edition

This edition covers many new features in Adobe Photoshop CS5, such as bristle tips, which create realistic painting effects; the Mixer Brush tool, which blends paint on the brush with color already on the page; and content-aware fill, an almost-magical feature that replaces a selected area with content consistent with its surroundings. In addition, these lessons introduce you to Puppet Warp, Mini Bridge, straightening images with the Ruler tool, the Color Replacement tool, enhancements to the Refine Edge dialog box, the ability to merge exposures with HDR Pro, and the ability to extrude text and objects using the Repoussé feature in Photoshop Extended.

New exercises and lessons cover:

- Using the Mixer Brush tool and bristle tip options to achieve realistic paint strokes.

- Manipulating an image using the Puppet Warp feature.

- Previewing and accessing images using the Mini Bridge panel within Photoshop.

- Replacing unwanted objects in an image using content-aware fill.

- Capturing complex edges in a mask using the Refine Edge dialog box.

This edition is also chock-full of extra information on Photoshop features and how best to work with this robust application. You'll learn best practices for organizing, managing, and showcasing your photos, as well as how to optimize images for the web. And throughout this edition, look for tips and techniques from one of Adobe's own experts, Photoshop evangelist Julieanne Kost.

What's in Photoshop Extended

This edition of *Adobe Photoshop CS5 Classroom in a Book* works with many of the features in Adobe Photoshop CS5 Extended—a version with additional functions for professional, technical, and scientific users, intended for those creating special effects in video or in architectural, scientific, or engineering images.

Photoshop Extended features include:

- The ability to import 3D images and video, and to edit individual frames or image sequence files by painting, cloning, retouching, or transforming them.

- Support for 3D files including the U3D, 3DS, OBJ, KMZ, and Collada file formats, created by programs such as Adobe Acrobat® 9 Professional and Google Earth. See Lesson 12, "Working with 3D Images," to learn about these features.

- Image stacks, stored as Smart Objects, that let you combine a group of images with a similar frame of reference, and then process the multiple images to produce a composite view, for example, to eliminate unwanted content or noise.

- Animation features that show the frame duration and animation properties for document layers in Timeline mode, and that let you navigate through frames, edit them, and adjust the frame duration for layers.

- Support for specialized file formats, such as DICOM, the most common standard for receiving medical scans; MATLAB, a high-level technical computing language and interactive environment for developing algorithms, visualizing and analyzing data, and computing numbers; and 32-bit high-resolution images, including a special HDR Color Picker and the capability to paint and layer these 32-bit HDR images.

Prerequisites

Before you begin to use *Adobe Photoshop CS5 Classroom in a Book*, you should have a working knowledge of your computer and its operating system. Make sure that you know how to use the mouse and standard menus and commands, and also how to open, save, and close files. If you need to review these techniques, see the documentation included with your Microsoft® Windows® or Apple® Mac® OS X documentation.

Installing Adobe Photoshop

Before you begin using *Adobe Photoshop CS5 Classroom in a Book*, make sure that your system is set up correctly and that you've installed the required software and hardware. You must purchase the Adobe Photoshop CS5 software separately. For system requirements and complete instructions on installing the software, see the Adobe Photoshop CS5 Read Me file on the application DVD or on the web at www.adobe.com/support. Note that some Photoshop CS5 Extended features, including many 3D features, require a video card that supports OpenGL 2.0.

Photoshop and Bridge use the same installer. You must install these applications from the Adobe Photoshop CS5 application DVD onto your hard disk; you cannot run the programs from the DVD. Follow the onscreen instructions.

Make sure that your serial number is accessible before installing the application.

Starting Adobe Photoshop

You start Photoshop just as you do most software applications.

To start Adobe Photoshop in Windows: Choose Start > All Programs > Adobe Photoshop CS5.

To start Adobe Photoshop in Mac OS: Open the Applications/Adobe Photoshop CS5 folder, and double-click the Adobe Photoshop program icon.

Copying the Classroom in a Book files

The *Adobe Photoshop CS5 Classroom in a Book* DVD includes folders containing all the electronic files for the lessons in the book. Each lesson has its own folder; you must copy the folders to your hard disk to complete the lessons. To save room on your disk, you can install only the folder necessary for each lesson as you need it, and remove it when you're done.

To install the lesson files, do the following:

1 Insert the *Adobe Photoshop CS5 Classroom in a Book* DVD into your disc drive.

2 Browse the contents and locate the Lessons folder.

3 Do one of the following:

- To copy all the lesson files, drag the Lessons folder from the DVD onto your hard disk.

- To copy only individual lesson files, first create a new folder on your hard disk, and name it **Lessons**. Then, drag the lesson folder or folders that you want to copy from the DVD into the Lessons folder on your hard disk.

● **Note:** As you complete each lesson, you will preserve the start files. In case you overwrite them, you can restore the original files by recopying the corresponding Lesson folder from the *Adobe Photoshop CS5 Classroom in a Book* DVD to the Lessons folder on your hard drive.

Restoring default preferences

The preferences files stores information about panel and command settings. Each time you quit Adobe Photoshop, the positions of the panels and certain command settings are recorded in the respective preferences file. Any selections you make in the Preferences dialog box are also saved in the preferences file.

To ensure that what you see onscreen matches the images and instructions in this book, you should restore the default preferences as you begin each lesson. If you prefer to preserve your preferences, be aware that the tools, panels, and other settings in Photoshop CS5 may not match those described in this book.

If you have custom-calibrated your monitor, save the calibration settings before you start work on this book. To save your monitor-calibration settings, follow the simple procedure described below.

To save your current color settings:

1 Start Adobe Photoshop.

2 Choose Edit > Color Settings.

3 Note what is selected in the Settings menu:

- If it is anything other than Custom, write down the name of the settings file, and click OK to close the dialog box. You do not need to perform steps 4–6 of this procedure.

- If Custom is selected in the Settings menu, click Save (*not* OK).

The Save dialog box opens. The default location is the Settings folder, which is where you want to save your file. The default file extension is .csf (color settings file).

4 In the File Name field (Windows) or Save As field (Mac OS), type a descriptive name for your color settings, preserving the .csf file extension. Then click Save.

5 In the Color Settings Comment dialog box, type any descriptive text that will help you identify the color settings later, such as the date, specific settings, or your workgroup.

6 Click OK to close the Color Settings Comment dialog box, and again to close the Color Settings dialog box.

To restore your color settings:

1 Start Adobe Photoshop.

2 Choose Edit > Color Settings.

3 In the Settings menu in the Color Settings dialog box, select the settings file you noted or saved in the previous procedure, and click OK.

Additional resources

Adobe Photoshop CS5 Classroom in a Book is not meant to replace documentation that comes with the program or to be a comprehensive reference for every feature. Only the commands and options used in the lessons are explained in this book. For comprehensive information about program features and tutorials, refer to these resources:

Adobe Community Help: Community Help brings together active Adobe product users, Adobe product team members, authors, and experts to give you the most useful, relevant, and up-to-date information about Adobe products. Whether you're looking for a code sample or an answer to a problem, have a question about the software, or want to share a useful tip or recipe, you'll benefit from Community Help. Search results will show you not only content from Adobe, but also from the community.

With Adobe Community Help you can:

- Access up-to-date definitive reference content online and offline
- Find the most relevant content contributed by experts from the Adobe community, on and off Adobe.com
- Comment on, rate, and contribute to content in the Adobe community
- Download Help content directly to your desktop for offline use
- Find related content with dynamic search and navigation tools

To access Community Help: If you have any Adobe CS5 product, then you already have the Community Help application. To invoke Help, press F1 or choose Help > Photoshop Help. This companion application lets you search and browse Adobe and community content, plus you can comment on and rate any article just like you would in the browser. However, you can also download Adobe Help and language reference content for use offline. You can also subscribe to new content updates (which can be automatically downloaded) so that you'll always have the most up-to-date content for your Adobe product at all times. You can download the application from www.adobe.com/support/chc/index.html

Adobe content is updated based on community feedback and contributions. You can contribute in several ways: add comments to content or forums, including links to web content; publish your own content using Community Publishing; or contribute Cookbook Recipes. Find out how to contribute: www.adobe.com/community/publishing/download.html

See http://community.adobe.com/help/profile/faq.html for answers to frequently asked questions about Community Help.

Adobe Photoshop Help and Support: www.adobe.com/support/photoshop, where you can find and browse Help and Support content on Adobe.com.

Adobe TV: http://tv.adobe.com is an online video resource for expert instruction and inspiration about Adobe products, including a How To channel to get you started with your product.

Adobe Design Center: www.adobe.com/designcenter offers thoughtful articles on design and design issues, a gallery showcasing the work of top-notch designers, tutorials, and more.

Adobe Developer Connection: www.adobe.com/devnet is your source for technical articles, code samples, and how-to videos that cover Adobe developer products and technologies.

Resources for educators: www.adobe.com/education includes three free curricula that use an integrated approach to teaching Adobe software and can be used to prepare for the Adobe Certified Associate exams.

Also check out these useful links:

Adobe Forums: http://forums.adobe.com lets you tap into peer-to-peer discussions, questions, and answers on Adobe products.

Adobe Marketplace & Exchange: www.adobe.com/cfusion/exchange is a central resource for finding tools, services, extensions, code samples, and more to supplement and extend your Adobe products.

Adobe Photoshop CS5 product home page: www.adobe.com/products/photoshop

Adobe Labs: http://labs.adobe.com gives you access to early builds of cutting-edge technology, as well as forums where you can interact with both the Adobe development teams building that technology and other like-minded members of the community.

Adobe certification

The Adobe training and certification programs are designed to help Adobe customers improve and promote their product-proficiency skills. There are four levels of certification:

- Adobe Certified Associate (ACA)
- Adobe Certified Expert (ACE)
- Adobe Certified Instructor (ACI)
- Adobe Authorized Training Center (AATC)

The Adobe Certified Associate (ACA) credential certifies that individuals have the entry-level skills to plan, design, build, and maintain effective communications using different forms of digital media.

The Adobe Certified Expert program is a way for expert users to upgrade their credentials. You can use Adobe certification as a catalyst for getting a raise, finding a job, or promoting your expertise.

If you are an ACE-level instructor, the Adobe Certified Instructor program takes your skills to the next level and gives you access to a wide range of Adobe resources.

Adobe Authorized Training Centers offer instructor-led courses and training on Adobe products, employing only Adobe Certified Instructors. A directory of AATCs is available at http://partners.adobe.com.

For information on the Adobe Certified programs, visit www.adobe.com/support/ certification/main.html.

Accelerate your workflow with Adobe CS Live

Adobe CS Live is a set of online services that harness the connectivity of the web and integrate with Adobe Creative Suite 5 to simplify the creative review process, speed up website compatibility testing, deliver important web user intelligence, and more, allowing you to focus on creating your most impactful work. CS Live services are complimentary for a limited time* and can be accessed online or from within Creative Suite 5 applications.

Adobe BrowserLab is for web designers and developers who need to preview and test their web pages on multiple browsers and operating systems. Unlike other browser-compatibility solutions, BrowserLab renders screenshots virtually on demand with multiple viewing and diagnostic tools, and can be used with Dreamweaver CS5 to preview local content and different states of interactive pages. Being an online service, BrowserLab has fast development cycles, with greater flexibility for expanded browser support and updated functionality.

Adobe CS Review is for creative professionals who want a new level of efficiency in the creative review process. Unlike other services that offer online review of creative content, only CS Review lets you publish a review to the web directly from within InDesign, Photoshop, Photoshop Extended, and Illustrator and view reviewer comments back in the originating Creative Suite application.

Acrobat.com is for creative professionals who need to work with a cast of colleagues and clients in order to get a creative project from creative brief to final product. Acrobat.com is a set of online services that includes web conferencing, online file-sharing and workspaces. Unlike collaborating via email and attending time-consuming in-person meetings, Acrobat.com brings people to your work instead of sending files to people, so you can get the business side of the creative process done faster, together, from any location.

Adobe Story is for creative professionals, producers, and writers working on or with scripts. Story is a collaborative script-development tool that turns scripts into metadata that can be used with the Adobe CS5 Production Premium tools to streamline workflows and create video assets.

SiteCatalyst NetAverages is for web and mobile professionals who want to optimize their projects for wider audiences. NetAverages provides intelligence on how users are accessing the web, which helps reduce guesswork early in the creative process. You can access aggregate user data such as browser type, operating system, mobile device profile, screen resolution, and more, which can be shown over time. The data is derived from visitor activity to participating Omniture SiteCatalyst customer sites. Unlike other web intelligence solutions, NetAverages innovatively displays data using Flash, creating an engaging experience that is robust yet easy to follow.

You can access CS Live three different ways:

1   Set up access when you register your Creative Suite 5 products, and get complimentary access that includes all of the features and workflow benefits of using CS Live with CS5.

2   Set up access by signing up online, and get complimentary access to CS Live services for a limited time. Note that this option does not give you access to the services from within your products.

3   Desktop product trials include a 30-day trial of CS Live services.

CS Live services are complimentary for a limited time. See www.adobe.com/go/cslive for details.

1 GETTING TO KNOW THE WORK AREA

Lesson overview

In this lesson, you'll learn how to do the following:

- Open Adobe Photoshop files.

- Select and use some of the tools in the Tools panel.

- Set options for a selected tool using the options bar.

- Use various methods to zoom in on and out from an image.

- Select, rearrange, and use panels.

- Choose commands in panel and context menus.

- Open and use a panel docked in the panel well.

- Undo actions to correct mistakes or to make different choices.

- Customize the workspace.

- Find topics in Photoshop Help.

 This lesson will take about 90 minutes to complete. Copy the Lesson01 folder into the Lessons folder that you created on your hard drive for these projects (or create it now), if you haven't already done so. As you work on this lesson, you'll preserve the start files. If you need to restore the start files, copy them from the *Adobe Photoshop CS5 Classroom in a Book* DVD.

As you work with Adobe Photoshop, you'll discover that you can often accomplish the same task several ways. To make the best use of the extensive editing capabilities in Photoshop, you must first learn to navigate the work area.

Starting to work in Adobe Photoshop

The Adobe Photoshop work area includes menus, toolbars, and panels that give you quick access to a variety of tools and options for editing and adding elements to your image. You can also add commands and filters to the menus by installing third-party software known as *plug-ins*.

Photoshop works with bitmapped, digitized images (that is, continuous-tone images that have been converted into a series of small squares, or picture elements, called *pixels*). You can also work with vector graphics, which are drawings made of smooth lines that retain their crispness when scaled. You can create original artwork in Photoshop, or you can import images from many sources, such as:

* Photographs from a digital camera

* Commercial CDs of digital images

* Scans of photographs, transparencies, negatives, graphics, or other documents

* Captured video images

* Artwork created in drawing programs

Starting Photoshop and opening a file

To begin, you'll start Adobe Photoshop and reset the default preferences.

1 On the desktop, double-click the Adobe Photoshop icon to start Adobe Photoshop, and then immediately hold down Ctrl+Alt+Shift (Windows) or Command+Option+Shift (Mac OS) to reset the default settings.

If you don't see the Photoshop icon on your desktop, choose Start > All Programs > Adobe Photoshop CS5 (Windows) or look in either the Applications folder or the Dock (Mac OS).

2 When prompted, click Yes to confirm that you want to delete the Adobe Photoshop Settings file.

Note: Typically, you won't need to reset defaults when you're working on your own projects. However, you'll reset the preferences before working on each lesson in this book to ensure that what you see onscreen matches the descriptions in the lessons. For more information, see "Restoring default preferences" on page 5.

The Photoshop work area appears as shown in the following illustration.

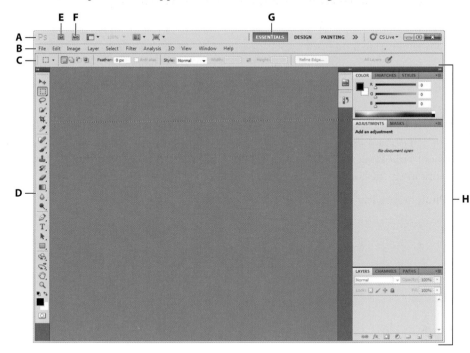

A. Application bar
B. Menu bar
C. Options bar
D. Tools panel
E. Adobe Bridge button
F. Mini Bridge button
G. Workspaces menu
H. Panels

⬤ **Note:** This illustration shows the Windows version of Photoshop. On Mac OS, the menu bar is above the Application bar. Otherwise, the arrangement is the same, but operating system styles may vary.

The default workspace in Photoshop consists of the Application bar, menu bar, and options bar at the top of the screen, the Tools panel on the left, and several open panels in the panel dock on the right. When you have documents open, one or more image windows also appear, and you can display them at the same time using the tabbed interface. The Photoshop user interface is very similar to the one in Adobe Illustrator®, Adobe InDesign®, and Adobe Flash®—so learning how to use the tools and panels in one application means that you'll know how to use them in the others.

There are a few differences between the Photoshop work area on Windows and that on Mac OS:

- On Windows, the menu bar is combined with the Application bar, if your screen resolution makes it possible to fit them on the same line.

- On Mac OS, you can work with an application frame, which contains the Photoshop application's windows and panels within a frame that is distinct from other applications you may have open; only the menu bar is outside the application frame. The application frame is disabled by default; to enable the application frame, choose Window > Application Frame. Additionally, you can enable and disable the Application bar. This book assumes you are using the Application bar, which is enabled by default.

On Mac OS, the application frame keeps the image, panels, and Application bar together.

3 Choose File > Open, and navigate to the Lessons/Lesson01 folder that you copied to your hard drive from the *Adobe Photoshop CS5 Classroom in a Book* DVD.

4 Select the 01A_End.psd file, and click Open. Click OK if you see the Embedded Profile Mismatch dialog box.

The 01A_End.psd file opens in its own window, called the *image window*. The end files in this book show you what you are creating in each project. In this file, an image of a vintage car has been enhanced without overexposing the headlight.

5 Choose File > Close, or click the close button on the title bar of the image window. (Do not close Photoshop.)

Opening a file with Adobe Bridge

In this book, you'll work with different start files in each lesson. You may make copies of these files and save them under different names or locations, or you may work from the original start files and then copy them from the DVD again if you want a fresh start. This lesson includes three start files.

In the previous exercise, you used the Open command to open a file. Now you'll open another file using Adobe Bridge, a visual file browser that helps take the guesswork out of finding the image file that you need.

1 Click the Launch Bridge button () in the Application bar. If you're prompted to enable the Photoshop extension in Bridge, click OK.

Note: You can also open Adobe Bridge by choosing File > Browse In Bridge.

Adobe Bridge opens, displaying a collection of panels, menus, and buttons.

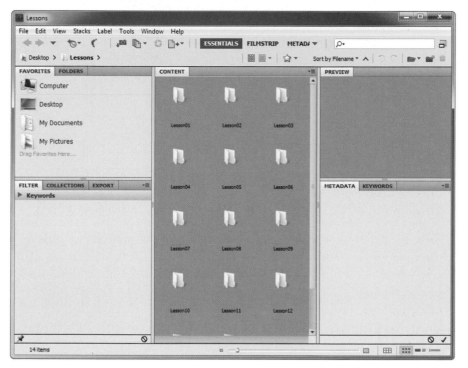

2 From the Folders panel in the upper-left corner, browse to the Lessons folder you copied from the DVD onto your hard disk. The Lessons folder appears in the Content panel.

3 Select the Lessons folder, and choose File > Add To Favorites. Adding files, folders, application icons, and other assets that you use often to the Favorites panel lets you access them quickly.

4 Select the Favorites tab to open the panel, and click the Lessons folder to open it. Then, in the Content panel, double-click the Lesson01 folder.

Thumbnail previews of the folder contents appear in the Content panel.

5 Double-click the 01A_Start.psd thumbnail in the Content panel to open the file, or select the thumbnail and choose File > Open.

The 01A_Start.psd image opens in Photoshop. Leave Bridge open; you'll use it to locate and open files later in this lesson.

Using the tools

Photoshop provides an integrated set of tools for producing sophisticated graphics for print, web, and mobile viewing. We could easily fill the entire book with details on the wealth of Photoshop tools and tool configurations. While that would certainly be a useful reference, it's not the goal of this book. Instead, you'll start gaining experience by configuring and using a few tools on a sample project. Every lesson will introduce you to more tools and ways to use them. By the time you finish all the lessons in this book, you'll have a solid foundation for further explorations of the Photoshop toolset.

Selecting and using a tool from the Tools panel

● **Note:** For a complete list of the tools in the Tools panel, see the Tools panel overview at the end of this lesson.

The Tools panel—the long, narrow panel on the far left side of the work area—contains selection tools, painting and editing tools, foreground- and background-color selection boxes, and viewing tools. In Photoshop Extended, it also includes 3D tools.

You'll start by using the Zoom tool, which also appears in many other Adobe applications, including Illustrator, InDesign, and Acrobat.

1   Click the double arrows just above the Tools panel to toggle to a double-column view. Click the arrow again to return to a single-column Tools panel and use your screen space more efficiently.

2   Examine the status bar at the bottom of the work area (Windows) or image window (Mac OS), and notice the percentage listed on the far left. This represents the current enlargement view of the image, or zoom level.

3   Move the pointer over the Tools panel, and hover it over the magnifying-glass icon until a tool tip appears. The tool tip displays the tool's name (Zoom tool) and keyboard shortcut (Z).

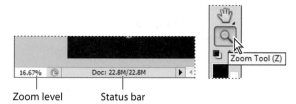

Zoom level   Status bar

4   Click the Zoom tool (🔍) in the Tools panel, or press Z to select it.

5   Move the pointer over the image window. The pointer now looks like a tiny magnifying glass with a plus sign (+) in the center of the glass.

6   Click anywhere in the image window.

The image enlarges to a preset percentage level, which replaces the previous value in the status bar. The location you clicked when you used the Zoom tool is centered in the enlarged view. If you click again, the zoom advances to the next preset level, up to a maximum of 3200%.

7   Hold down the Alt key (Windows) or Option key (Mac OS) so that the Zoom tool pointer appears with a minus sign (-) in the center of the magnifying glass, and then click anywhere in the image. Then release the Alt or Option key.

Now the view zooms out to a lower preset magnification, so that you can see more of the image, but in less detail.

8   If Scrubby Zoom is selected in the options bar, click anywhere on the image and drag the Zoom tool to the right. The image enlarges. Drag the Zoom tool to the left to zoom out. When Scrubby Zoom is selected in the options bar, you can drag the Zoom tool across the image to zoom in and out.

● **Note:** You can use other methods to zoom in and out. For example, when the Zoom tool is selected, you can select the Zoom In or Zoom Out mode on the options bar. You can choose View > Zoom In or View > Zoom Out. Or, you can type a new percentage in the status bar and press Enter or Return.

● **Note:** Scrubby Zoom is available only if OpenGL is enabled in the Photoshop Preferences panel.

9 Deselect Scrubby Zoom in the options bar if it's selected. Then, using the Zoom tool, drag a rectangle to enclose the area of the image that includes the headlight.

The image enlarges so that the area you enclosed in your rectangle now fills the entire image window.

You have now used four methods with the Zoom tool to change the magnification in the image window: clicking, holding down a keyboard modifier while clicking, dragging to zoom in and out, and dragging to define a magnification area. Many of the other tools in the Tools panel can be used with keyboard combinations and options, as well. You'll have opportunities to use these techniques in various lessons in this book.

Selecting and using a hidden tool

Photoshop has many tools you can use to edit image files, but you will probably work with only a few of them at a time. The Tools panel arranges some of the tools in groups, with only one tool shown for each group. The other tools in the group are hidden behind that tool.

A small triangle in the lower-right corner of a button is your clue that other tools are available but hidden under that tool.

1 Position the pointer over the second tool from the top in the Tools panel until the tool tip appears. The tool tip identifies the Rectangular Marquee tool (⬚) with the keyboard shortcut M. Select that tool.

2 Select the Elliptical Marquee tool (◯), which is hidden behind the Rectangular Marquee tool, using one of the following methods:

- Press and hold the mouse button over the Rectangular Marquee tool to open the pop-up list of hidden tools, and select the Elliptical Marquee tool.

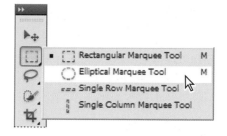

- Alt-click (Windows) or Option-click (Mac OS) the tool button in the Tools panel to cycle through the hidden marquee tools until the Elliptical Marquee tool is selected.

- Press Shift+M, which switches between the Rectangular and Elliptical Marquee tools.

3 Move the pointer over the image window, to the upper-left side of the head-light. When the Elliptical Marquee tool is selected, the pointer becomes cross-hairs (+).

4 Drag the pointer down and to the right to draw an ellipse around the headlight, and then release the mouse button.

An animated dashed line indicates that the area inside it is *selected*. When you select an area, it becomes the only editable area of the image. The area outside the selection is protected.

5 Move the pointer inside your elliptical selection so that the pointer appears as an arrow with a small rectangle (▸▫).

6 Drag the selection so that it is accurately centered over the headlight.

When you drag the selection, only the selection border moves, not pixels in the image. When you want to move the pixels in the image, you'll need to use a different technique. You'll learn more about making different kinds of selections and moving the selection contents in Lesson 3, "Working with Selections."

Using keyboard combinations with tool actions

Many tools can operate under certain constraints. You usually activate these modes by holding down specific keys as you move the tool with the mouse. Some tools have modes that you choose in the options bar.

The next task is to make a fresh start at selecting the headlight. This time, you'll use a keyboard combination that constrains the elliptical selection to a circle that you'll draw from the center outward instead of from the outside inward.

1 Make sure that the Elliptical Marquee tool (◯) is still selected in the Tools panel, and then deactivate the current selection by doing one of the following:

- In the image window, click anywhere outside the selected area.

- Choose Select > Deselect.

- Use the keyboard shortcut Ctrl+D (Windows) or Command+D (Mac OS).

2 Position the pointer in the center of the headlight.

3 Press Alt+Shift (Windows) or Option+Shift (Mac OS) and drag outward from the center of the headlight until the circle completely encloses the headlight. The Shift key constrains the ellipse to a perfect circle.

4 Carefully release first the mouse button and then the keyboard keys.

If you aren't satisfied with the selection circle, you can move it: Place the pointer inside the circle and drag, or click outside the selection circle to deselect it, and then try again.

5   In the Tools panel, double-click the Zoom tool (🔍) to switch to 100% view. If the entire image doesn't fit in the image window, click the Fit Screen button in the options bar.

Notice that the selection remains active even after you use the Zoom tool.

Applying a change to a selected area

In most cases, you'd change the area within the selection. But in order to spotlight the headlight, you'll want to darken the rest of the image, not the area inside the current selection. To protect that area, you'll invert the selection, so that everything *but* the headlight is selected in the image.

1   Choose Select > Inverse.

Although the animated selection border around the headlight looks the same, notice that a similar border appears all around the edges of the image. Now the rest of the image is selected and can be edited, while the area within the circle is not selected. The unselected area (the headlight) cannot be changed while the selection is active.

A. Selected (editable) area
B. Unselected (protected) area

● **Note:** If you accidentally release the Alt or Option key prematurely, the tool reverts to its normal behavior (drawing from the edge). If, however, you haven't yet released the mouse button, you can just press the key down again, and the selection changes back. If you have released the mouse button, simply start again at step 1.

▶ **Tip:** The keyboard shortcut for this command, Ctrl+Shift+I (Windows) or Command+Shift+I (Mac OS), appears by the command name in the Select menu. In the future, you can just press that keyboard combination to invert a selection.

2   In the Adjustments panel, click the Curves icon to add a Curves adjustment layer. The Curves options appear in the Adjustments panel.

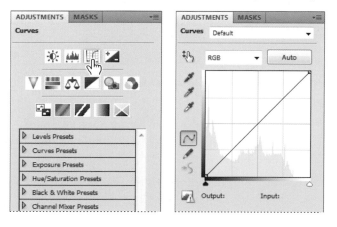

3 In the Curves panel, drag the control point in the upper-right corner of the graph straight across to the left until the Input value is approximately **204**. The Output value should remain 255.

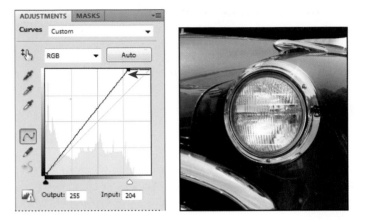

As you drag, highlights are brightened in the selected area of the image.

4 Adjust the Input value up or down until you are satisfied with the results.

5 In the Layers panel, examine the Curves adjustment layer. (If the Layers panel isn't open, click its tab or choose Window > Layers.)

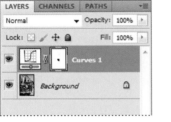

Adjustment layers let you make changes to your image, such as adjusting the brightness of the highlights in this car, without affecting the actual pixels. Because you've used an adjustment layer, you can always return to the original image by hiding or deleting the adjustment layer—and you can edit the adjustment layer at any time. You'll learn more about adjustment layers in Lessons 5 and 9.

6 Do one of the following:

- To save your changes, choose File > Save, and then choose File > Close.

- To revert to the unaltered version of the file, choose File > Close, and click No or Don't Save when you're asked if you want to save your changes.

- To save your changes without affecting the original file, choose File > Save As, and then either rename the file or save it to a different folder on your computer, and click OK. Then choose File > Close.

You don't have to deselect, because closing the file cancels the selection.

Congratulations! You've just finished your first Photoshop project. Although a Curves adjustment layer is actually one of the more sophisticated methods of altering an image, it isn't difficult to use, as you have seen. You'll learn more about making adjustments to images in many other lessons in this book. Lessons 2, 6, and 10, in particular, address techniques like those used in classic darkroom work, such as adjusting for exposure, retouching, and correcting colors.

Zooming and scrolling with the Navigator panel

The Navigator panel is another speedy way to make large changes in the zoom level, especially when the exact percentage of magnification is unimportant. It's also a great way to scroll around in an image, because the thumbnail shows you exactly what part of the image appears in the image window. To open the Navigator panel, choose Window > Navigator.

The slider under the image thumbnail in the Navigator panel enlarges the image when you drag to the right (toward the large mountain icon) and reduces it when you drag to the left.

The red rectangular outline represents the area of the image that appears in the image window. When you zoom in far enough that the image window shows only part of the image, you can drag the red outline around the thumbnail area to see other areas of the image. This is also an excellent way to verify which part of an image you're working on when you work at very high zoom levels.

Using the options bar and other panels

You've already had some experience with the options bar. When you selected the Zoom tool in the previous project, you saw that the options bar contained options that change the view of the current image window. Now you'll learn more about setting tool properties in the options bar, as well as using panels and panel menus.

Previewing and opening another file

The next project involves a promotional postcard for a community project. First, preview the end file to see what you're aiming to do.

1 Click the Launch Mini Bridge button ([Br]) in the Application bar to open the Mini Bridge panel.

You can access many of the features of Adobe Bridge without leaving Photoshop. The Mini Bridge panel lets you browse, select, open, and import files while you're working with your image in Photoshop.

2 Click Browse Files in the Mini Bridge panel to display the Navigation area.

3 Select Favorites in the Navigation area, and then select the Lessons folder. Double-click the Lesson01 folder in the Content area of the Mini Bridge panel.

4 Select the 01B_End.psd file in the Content area, and press the spacebar to see a full-screen preview of the image.

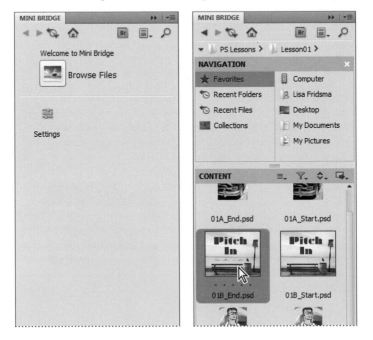

Notice the text that is set against the sandy area across the lower part of the image.

5   Press the spacebar again to return to the thumbnail view.

Beach photo: Amana Stock Photography

6   Scroll to the 01B_Start.psd file in the Content area, and then double-click it to open it in Photoshop.

7   Click the double arrow at the top of the Mini Bridge panel to collapse it to an icon so you can see the image window clearly.

Setting tool properties in the options bar

With the 01B_Start.psd file open in Photoshop, you're ready to select the text properties and then to type your message.

1   In the Tools panel, select the Horizontal Type tool (T).

The buttons and menus in the options bar now relate to the Type tool.

2   In the options bar, select a font you like from the first pop-up menu. (We used Garamond, but you can use another font if you prefer.)

3   Specify **38 pt** for the font size.

You can specify 38 points by typing directly in the font-size text box and pressing Enter or Return, or by scrubbing the font-size menu label. You can also choose a standard font size from the font-size pop-up menu.

4   Click once anywhere on the left side of the image, and type **Monday is Beach Cleanup Day.**

The text appears with the font and font size that you selected.

▶ **Tip:** You can place the pointer over the labels of most numeric settings in the tool options bar, in panels, and in dialog boxes in Photoshop, to display a "scrubby slider." Dragging the pointing-finger slider to the right increases the value; dragging to the left decreases the value. Alt-dragging (Windows) or Option-dragging (Mac OS) changes the values in smaller increments; Shift-dragging changes them in larger increments.

5   In the Tools panel, select the Move tool (⊕). It's the first tool.

6   Position the Move tool pointer over the text you typed, and drag the text onto the sand, centering it over the bench.

Using panels and panel menus

The text color in your image is the same as the Foreground Color swatch in the Tools panel, which is black by default. The text in the end-file example was a magenta shade that made the text stand out. You'll color the text by selecting it and then choosing another color.

1   In the Tools panel, select the Horizontal Type tool (T).

2   Drag the Horizontal Type tool across the text to select all the words.

3   Click the Swatches tab to bring that panel forward, if it's not already visible.

Note: When you move the pointer over the swatches, it temporarily changes into an eyedropper. Set the tip of the eyedropper on the swatch you want, and click to select it.

4   Select any swatch. The color you select appears in three places: as the Foreground Color in the Tools panel, in the text color swatch in the options bar, and in the text you selected in the image window. (Select any other tool in the Tools panel to deselect the text so that you can see the color applied to it.)

That's how easy it is to select a color, although there are other methods in Photoshop. However, you'll use a specific color for this project, and it's easier to find it if you change the Swatches panel display.

5   Select another tool in the Tools panel, such as the Move tool (▶✛), to deselect the Horizontal Type tool. Then, click the menu button (▾≣) on the Swatches panel to open the panel menu, and choose the Small List command.

6   Select the Type tool and reselect the text, as you did in steps 1 and 2.

7   In the Swatches panel, scroll about halfway down the list to find the Pastel Violet Magenta swatch, and then select it.

Now the text appears in the lighter violet color.

8   Select the Hand tool (✋) to deselect the text. Then click the Default Foreground And Background Colors button in the Tools panel to make Black the foreground color.

Resetting the default colors does not change the color of the text in the image, because that text is no longer selected.

9   You've finished the task, so close the file. You can either save it, close it without saving, or save it under a different name or location.

It's as simple as that—you've completed another project. Nice job!

Undoing actions in Photoshop

In a perfect world, you'd never make a mistake. You'd never click the wrong object. You'd always perfectly anticipate how specific actions would bring your design ideas to life exactly as you imagined them. You'd never have to backtrack.

For the real world, Photoshop gives you the power to step back and undo actions so that you can try other options. The next project provides you with an opportunity to experiment freely, knowing that you can reverse the process.

This project also introduces you to layering, which is one of the fundamental and most powerful features in Photoshop. Photoshop features many kinds of layers, some of which contain images, text, or solid colors, and others that simply interact with layers below them. The file for this next project has both kinds of layers. You don't have to understand layers to complete this project successfully, so don't worry about that right now. You'll learn more about layers in Lesson 4, "Layer Basics," and Lesson 9, "Advanced Layering."

Undoing a single action

Even beginning computer users quickly come to appreciate the familiar Undo command. Once again, you'll begin this project by looking at the final result.

1 Click the Launch Bridge button (⬛), and navigate to the Lesson01 folder.

2 Select the 01C_End.psd file, press Shift, and select the 01C_Start.psd file. Both files appear in the Preview panel. In the start file, the tie is solid; in the end file, it is patterned.

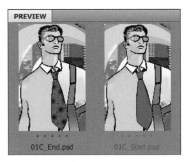

3 In the Content panel, deselect the 01C_End.psd file thumbnail, and then double-click the 01C_Start.psd file thumbnail to open it in Photoshop.

4 In the Layers panel, select the Tie Designs layer.

Notice the listings in the Layers panel. The Tie Designs layer is a clipping mask. A clipping mask works somewhat like a selection in that it restricts the area of the image that can be altered. With the clipping mask in place, you can paint a design over the tie without worrying about any stray brush strokes disturbing the rest of the image. You've selected the Tie Designs layer because it's the layer you'll be editing now.

5 In the Tools panel, select the Brush tool (✎), or press B to select it by its keyboard shortcut.

6 In the options bar, click the brush size to display brush options. Then, move the Size slider to 65 pixels. In the list of brushes, select the Soft Round Pressure Size brush. (The name will appear as a tool tip if you hover the pointer over a brush.)

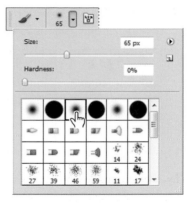

If you want to try a different brush, that's OK, but select a brush that's reasonably close to 65 pixels—preferably between 45 and 75 pixels.

7 Move the pointer over the image so that it appears as a circle the same diameter as the brush. Then draw a stripe anywhere in the orange tie. You don't have to worry about staying within the lines, because the brush won't paint anything outside the tie clipping mask.

Oops! Your stripe may be very nice, but the design calls for dots, so you'll need to remove that stripe you just painted.

Illustration: Pamela Hobbs

8 Choose Edit > Undo Brush Tool, or press Ctrl+Z (Windows) or Command+Z (Mac OS) to undo the Brush tool action.

The tie is again a solid orange color, with no stripe.

● **Note:** You'll get more experience with clipping masks in Lesson 6, "Masks and Channels," Lesson 7, "Typographic Design," and Lesson 9, "Advanced Layering."

Undoing multiple actions

The Undo command reverses only one step. This is a practicality, because Photoshop files can be very large, and maintaining multiple Undo steps can tie up a lot of memory, which tends to degrade performance. You could use the Step Backward command to undo additional steps one at a time. However, it's faster and easier to step back through multiple actions using the History panel.

1 Using the same Brush tool settings, click once over the (unstriped) orange tie to create a soft dot.

2 Click several more times in different areas on the tie to create a pattern of dots.

3 Choose Window > History to open the History panel. Then drag a corner of the History panel to resize it so that you can see more steps.

The History panel records the recent actions you've performed in the image. The current state is selected, at the bottom of the list.

4 Click an earlier action in the History panel, and notice how the image changes. Several previous actions are undone.

5 In the image window, create a new dot on the tie with the Brush tool.

Notice that the History panel has removed the dimmed actions that were listed after the selected history state and has added a new one.

6 Choose Edit > Undo Brush Tool or press Ctrl+Z (Windows) or Command+Z (Mac OS) to undo the dot you created in step 5.

Now the History panel restores the earlier listing of dimmed actions.

7 Select the state at the bottom of the History panel list.

The image is restored to the condition it was in when you finished step 2 of this exercise.

By default, the Photoshop History panel retains only the last 20 actions. This is a compromise, striking a balance between flexibility and performance. You can change the number of levels in the History panel by choosing Edit > Preferences > Performance (Windows) or Photoshop > Preferences > Performance (Mac OS) and entering a different value for History States.

Using a context menu

Context menus are short menus that contain commands and options appropriate to specific elements in the work area. They are sometimes referred to as "right-click" or "shortcut" menus. Usually, the commands on a context menu are also available in some other area of the user interface, but using the context menu can save time.

1 If the Brush tool ( ) is not still selected in the Tools panel, select it now.

2 In the image window, right-click (Windows) or Control-click (Mac OS) anywhere in the image to open the Brush tool context menu.

Context menus vary with their context, of course, so what appears can be a menu of commands or a panel-like set of options, which is what happens in this case.

3 Select a finer brush, such as the Hard Round brush, and change the size to 9 pixels. You may need to scroll up or down the list in the context menu to find the right brush.

4 In the image window, use the selected brush to create smaller dots on the tie.

Note: Clicking anywhere in the work area closes the context menu. If the tie area is hidden behind the Brush tool context menu, click another area or double-click your selection in the context menu to close it.

5 As it suits you, use the Undo command and the History panel to backtrack through your painting actions to correct mistakes or make different choices.

When you finish making changes to your tie design, give yourself a pat on the back for finishing another project. You can choose File > Save if you want to save your results, choose File > Save As if you want to save the file in another location or with a different name, or close the file without saving.

More about panels and panel locations

Photoshop panels are powerful and varied. Rarely would you need to see all panels simultaneously. That's why they're in panel groups, and why the default configurations leave some panels unopened.

The complete list of panels appears in the Window menu, with check marks by the names of the panels that are open at the front of their panel groups. You can open a closed panel or close an open one by selecting the panel name in the Window menu.

You can hide all panels at once—including the options bar and Tools panel—by pressing the Tab key. To reopen them, press Tab again.

You already used panels in the panel dock when you used the Layers and Swatches panels. You can drag panels to or from the panel dock. This is convenient for bulky panels or ones that you use only occasionally but want to keep handy.

You can arrange panels in other ways, as well:

- To move an entire panel group, drag the title bar to another location in the work area.

- To move a panel to another group, drag the panel tab into that panel group so that a blue highlight appears inside the group, and then release the mouse button.

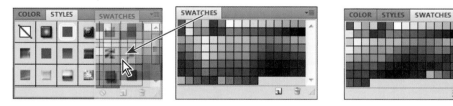

- To dock a panel or panel group, drag the title bar or panel tab onto the top of the dock.

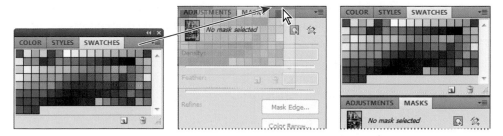

- To undock a panel or panel group so that it becomes a floating panel or panel group, drag its title bar or panel tab away from the dock.

Expanding and collapsing panels

You can also resize panels to use screen space more efficiently and to see fewer or more panel options, either by dragging or clicking to toggle between preset sizes:

- To collapse open panels to icons, click the double arrow in the title bar of the dock or panel group. To expand a panel, click its icon or the double arrow.

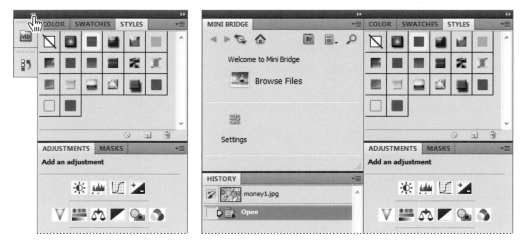

- To change the height of a panel, drag its lower-right corner.
- To change the width of the dock, position the pointer on the left edge of the dock until it becomes a double-headed arrow, and then drag to the left to widen the dock, or to the right to narrow it.

- To resize a floating panel, move the pointer over the right, left, or bottom edge of the panel until it becomes a double-headed arrow, and then drag the edge in or out. You can also pull the lower-right corner in or out.

Note: You can collapse, but not resize, the Color, Character, and Paragraph panels.

- To collapse a panel group so that only the dock header bar and tabs are visible, double-click a panel tab or panel title bar. Double-click again to restore it to the expanded view. You can open the panel menu even when the panel is collapsed.

Notice that the tabs for the panels in the panel group and the button for the panel menu remain visible after you collapse a panel.

Special notes about the Tools panel and options bar

The Tools panel and the options bar share some characteristics with other panels:

- You can drag the Tools panel by its title bar to a different location in the work area. You can move the options bar to another location by dragging the grab bar at the far left end of the panel.
- You can hide the Tools panel and options bar.

However, some panel features are not available or don't apply to the Tools panel or options bar:

- You cannot group the Tools panel or options bar with other panels.
- You cannot resize the Tools panel or options bar.
- You cannot stack the Tools panel or options bar in the panel dock.
- The Tools panel and options bar do not have panel menus.

Customizing the workspace

Note: If you closed 01C_Start.psd at the end of the previous exercise, open it—or open any other image file—to complete the following exercise.

It's great that Photoshop offers so many ways to control the display and location of the options bar and its many panels, but it can be time-consuming to drag panels around the screen so that you can see some panels for certain projects and other panels for other projects. That's why Photoshop lets you customize your workspace, controlling which panels, tools, and menus are available at any time. In fact, it comes with a few preset workspaces suitable for different types of workflows— tone and color correction, painting and retouching, and so on. You'll experiment with them.

1 Choose Window > Workspace > Painting. If prompted, click Yes to apply the workspace.

If you've been experimenting with opening, closing, and moving panels, you'll notice that Photoshop closes some panels, opens others, and stacks them neatly in the dock along the right edge of the workspace.

2 Choose Window > Workspace > Design. If prompted, click Yes to apply the workspace. Different panels are open in the dock.

3 Click the Workspace Switcher in the Application bar, and choose Essentials. Photoshop returns to the default workspace.

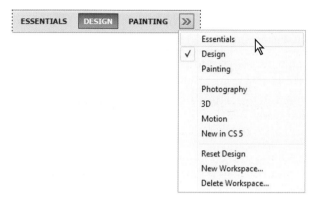

You can choose workspaces from the Window menu or from the pop-up menu in the Application bar.

For times when presets don't suit your purposes, you can customize the workspace to your specific needs. Say, for example, that you do lots of web design, but no digital video work. You can specify which menu items to display in the workspace.

4 Click the View menu, and choose Pixel Aspect Ratio to see the submenu.

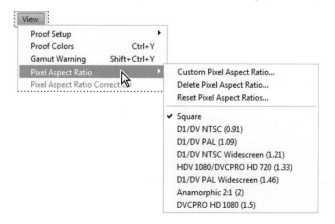

This submenu includes several DV formats that many print and web designers don't need to use.

5 Choose Window > Workspace > Keyboard Shortcuts And Menus.

The Keyboard Shortcuts And Menus dialog box lets you control which application and panel menu commands are available, as well as create custom keyboard shortcuts for menus, panels, and tools. You can hide commands that you use infrequently, or highlight commonly used commands to make them easier to see.

6 Click the Menus tab in the Keyboard Shortcuts And Menus dialog box, and then choose Application Menus from the Menu For pop-up menu.

7 Expand the View menu commands by clicking the triangle next to View.

Photoshop displays the View menu commands and subcommands.

8 Scroll down to Pixel Aspect Ratio, and click the eye icon to turn off visibility for all of the DV and video formats—there are seven of them, beginning with D1/DV NTSC (0.91) and ending with DVCPro HD 1080 (1.5). Photoshop removes them from the menu for this workspace.

9 Expand the Image menu commands.

10 Scroll down to the Image > Mode > RGB Color command, and click None in the Color column. Choose Red from the pop-up menu to highlight this command in red.

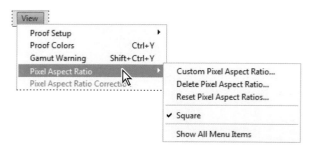

11 Click OK to close the Keyboard Shortcuts And Menus dialog box.

12 Choose Image > Mode. RGB Color is now highlighted in red.

13 Choose View > Pixel Aspect Ratio. The DV and video formats are no longer included in this submenu.

14 To save a workspace, choose Window > Workspace > New Workspace. In the New Workspace dialog box, give your workspace a name, select the Menus and Keyboard Shortcuts options, and then click Save.

The custom workspace you save is listed in the Window > Workspace submenu and in the Workspace Switcher on the Application bar.

For now, return to the default workspace configuration.

15 Choose Essentials from the Workspace pop-up menu on the Application bar. Don't save the changes in the current workspace.

Congratulations again; you've finished Lesson 1.

Now that you're acquainted with the basics of the Photoshop work area, you can begin learning how to create and edit images. Once you know the basics, you can complete the *Adobe Photoshop CS5 Classroom in a Book* lessons either in sequential order or according to the subjects you find most interesting.

Finding resources for using Photoshop

For complete and up-to-date information about using Photoshop panels, tools, and other application features, visit the Adobe website. To search for information in Photoshop Help and support documents, as well as other websites relevant to Photoshop users, choose Help > Photoshop Help. You can narrow your search results to view only Adobe Help and support documents, as well.

For additional resources, such as tips and techniques and the latest product information, check out the Adobe Community Help page at community.adobe.com/help/main.

Checking for updates

Adobe periodically provides updates to software. You can easily obtain these updates through Adobe Application Manager, as long as you have an active Internet connection.

1 In Photoshop, choose Help > Updates. Adobe Application Manager automatically checks for updates available for your Adobe software.

2 In the Adobe Application Manager dialog box, select the updates you want to install, and then click to install them.

Note: To set your preferences for future updates, click Preferences in the Adobe Application Manager. Select whether you want to be notified of updates, and which applications you want the Adobe Application Manager to check for. Click Done to accept the new settings.

Tools panel overview

Photoshop CS5
Tools panel

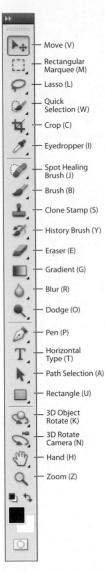

- Move (V)
- Rectangular Marquee (M)
- Lasso (L)
- Quick Selection (W)
- Crop (C)
- Eyedropper (I)
- Spot Healing Brush (J)
- Brush (B)
- Clone Stamp (S)
- History Brush (Y)
- Eraser (E)
- Gradient (G)
- Blur (R)
- Dodge (O)
- Pen (P)
- Horizontal Type (T)
- Path Selection (A)
- Rectangle (U)
- 3D Object Rotate (K)
- 3D Rotate Camera (N)
- Hand (H)
- Zoom (Z)

The Move tool moves selections, layers, and guides.

The marquee tools make rectangular, elliptical, single row, and single column selections.

The lasso tools make free-hand, polygonal (straight-edged), and magnetic (snap-to) selections.

The Quick Selection tool lets you quickly "paint" a selection using an adjustable round brush tip.

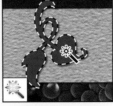

The Magic Wand tool selects similarly colored areas.

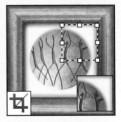

The Crop tool trims images.

The Eyedropper tool samples colors in an image.

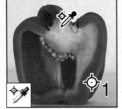

The Color Sampler tool samples up to four areas of the image.

The Ruler tool measures distances, locations, and angles.

The Note tool makes notes that can be attached to an image.

The Count tool counts objects in an image.

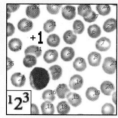

The Slice tool creates slices.

The Slice Select tool selects slices.

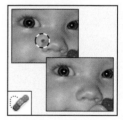

The Spot Healing Brush tool quickly removes blemishes and imperfections from photographs with a uniform background.

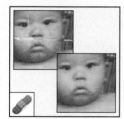

The Healing Brush tool paints with a sample or pattern to repair imperfections in an image.

The Patch tool repairs imperfections in a selected area of an image using a sample or pattern.

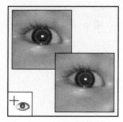

The Red Eye tool removes red eye in flash photos with one click.

The Brush tool paints brush strokes.

The Pencil tool paints hard-edged strokes.

The Color Replacement tool substitutes one color for another.

The Mixer Brush tool blends sampled color with an existing color.

Tools panel overview (continued)

The Clone Stamp tool paints with a sample of an image.

The Pattern Stamp tool paints with a part of an image as a pattern.

The History Brush tool paints a copy of the selected state or snapshot into the current image window.

The Art History Brush tool paints stylized strokes that simulate the look of different paint styles, using a selected state or snapshot.

The Eraser tool erases pixels and restores parts of an image to a previously saved state.

The Background Eraser tool erases areas to transparency by dragging.

The Magic Eraser tool erases solid-colored areas to transparency with a single click.

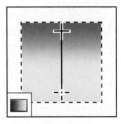

The Gradient tool creates straight-line, radial, angle, reflected, and diamond blends between colors.

The Paint Bucket tool fills similarly colored areas with the foreground color.

The Blur tool blurs hard edges in an image.

The Sharpen tool sharpens soft edges in an image.

The Smudge tool smudges data in an image.

The Dodge tool lightens areas in an image.

The Burn tool darkens areas in an image.

The Sponge tool changes the color saturation of an area.

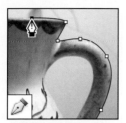

The pen tools draw smooth-edged paths.

The type tools create type on an image.

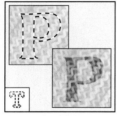

The type mask tools create a selection in the shape of type.

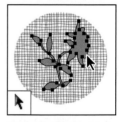

The path selection tools make shape or segment selections showing anchor points, direction lines, and direction points.

The shape tools and Line tool draw shapes and lines in a normal layer or shape layer.

The Custom Shape tool makes customized shapes selected from a custom shape list.

The Hand tool moves an image within its window.

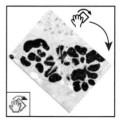

The Rotate View tool nondestructively rotates the canvas.

The Zoom tool magnifies and reduces the view of an image.

3D tools overview (Photoshop Extended)

The 3D Object Rotate tool rotates a 3D model around its x-axis or y-axis.

The 3D Object Roll tool rotates a 3D model around its z-axis.

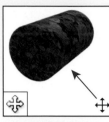

The 3D Object Pan tool moves the model in the x or y direction.

The 3D Object Slide tool moves the 3D model along the z-axis, so that it appears closer or farther away.

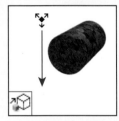

The 3D Object Scale tool resizes the 3D model.

The 3D Rotate Camera tool orbits the camera in the x or y direction.

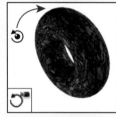

The 3D Roll Camera tool rotates the camera around the z-axis.

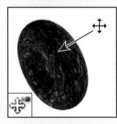

The 3D Pan Camera tool pans the camera in the x or y direction.

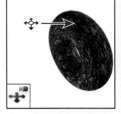

The 3D Walk Camera tool walks the camera.

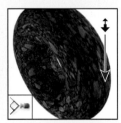

The 3D Zoom Camera tool changes the field of view closer or farther away.

Review questions

1 Describe two types of images you can open in Photoshop.

2 How do you open image files using Adobe Bridge?

3 How do you select tools in Photoshop?

4 Describe two ways to change your view of an image.

5 What are two ways to get more information about Photoshop?

Review answers

1 You can scan a photograph, transparency, negative, or graphic into the program; capture a digital video image; or import artwork created in a drawing program. You can also import digital photos.

2 Click the Launch Bridge button in the Photoshop Application bar to jump to Bridge. Then, locate the image file you want to open, and double-click its thumbnail to open it in Photoshop.

3 Click a tool in the Tools panel, or press the tool's keyboard shortcut. A selected tool remains active until you select a different tool. To select a hidden tool, either use a keyboard shortcut to toggle through the tools, or hold down the mouse button on the tool in the Tools panel to open a pop-up menu of the hidden tools.

4 Choose commands from the View menu to zoom in or out of an image, or to fit it onscreen, or use the zoom tools and click or drag over an image to enlarge or reduce the view. You can also use keyboard shortcuts or the Navigator panel to control the display of an image.

5 The Photoshop Help system includes full information about Photoshop features plus keyboard shortcuts, task-based topics, and illustrations. Photoshop also includes a link to the Adobe Systems Photoshop web page for additional information on services, products, and tips pertaining to Photoshop.

2 BASIC PHOTO CORRECTIONS

Lesson overview

In this lesson, you'll learn how to do the following:

- Understand image resolution and size.

- Open and edit an image in Camera Raw.

- Adjust the tonal range of an image.

- Straighten and crop an image.

- Paint over a color with the Color Replacement tool.

- Adjust the saturation of isolated areas of an image using the Sponge tool.

- Use the Clone Stamp tool to eliminate an unwanted part of an image.

- Use the Spot Healing Brush tool to repair part of an image.

- Use content-aware fill to remove blemishes.

- Apply the Unsharp Mask filter to finish retouching photos.

- Save an image file for use in a page layout application.

 This lesson will take about an hour to complete. Copy the Lesson02 folder onto your hard drive if you haven't already done so. As you work on this lesson, you'll preserve the start files. If you need to restore the start files, copy them from the *Adobe Photoshop CS5 Classroom in a Book* DVD.

Adobe Photoshop includes a variety of tools and commands for improving the quality of a photographic image. This lesson steps you through the process of acquiring, resizing, and retouching a photo intended for a print layout. The same basic workflow applies to web images.

Strategy for retouching

How much retouching you do depends on the image you're working on and your goals for it. For many images, you can achieve your desired outcome with just a few clicks in Adobe Camera Raw, which is installed with Adobe Photoshop. For others, you may start in Camera Raw to adjust the white point, for example, and then move on to Photoshop for more advanced retouching, such as applying filters to selected parts of an image.

Organizing an efficient sequence of tasks

Most retouching procedures follow these general steps:

- Duplicating the original image or scan (Working in a copy of the image file makes it easy to recover the original later if necessary.)

- Ensuring that the resolution is appropriate for the way you'll use the image

- Cropping the image to final size and orientation

- Repairing flaws in scans of damaged photographs (such as rips, dust, or stains)

- Adjusting the overall contrast or tonal range of the image

- Removing any color casts

- Adjusting the color and tone in specific parts of the image to bring out highlights, midtones, shadows, and desaturated colors

- Sharpening the overall focus of the image

● **Note:** In Lesson 1, you used an adjustment layer, which gives you great flexibility to experiment with different correction settings without risking damage to the original image.

Usually, you should complete these processes in the order listed. Otherwise, the results of one process may cause unintended changes to other aspects of the image, making it necessary for you to redo some of your work.

Adjusting your process for different intended uses

The retouching techniques you apply to an image depend in part on how you'll use the image. Whether an image is intended for black-and-white publication on newsprint or for full-color online distribution affects everything from the resolution of the initial scan to the type of tonal range and color correction that the image requires. Photoshop supports the CMYK color mode for preparing an image to be printed using process colors, as well as RGB and other color modes for web and mobile authoring.

To illustrate one application of retouching techniques, this lesson takes you through the steps of correcting a photograph intended for four-color print publication.

For more information about CMYK and RGB color modes, see Lesson 14, "Producing and Printing Consistent Color."

Resolution and image size

The first step in retouching a photograph in Photoshop is to make sure that the image has an appropriate resolution. The term *resolution* refers to the number of small squares, known as *pixels,* that describe an image and establish its detail. Resolution is determined by *pixel dimensions*, or the number of pixels along the width and height of an image.

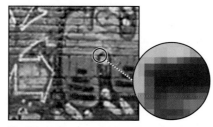

Pixels in a photographic image

In computer graphics, there are different types of resolution:

The number of pixels per unit of length in an image is called the *image resolution*, usually measured in pixels per inch (ppi). An image with a high resolution has more pixels (and therefore a larger file size) than an image of the same dimensions with a low resolution. Images in Photoshop can vary from high resolution (300 ppi or higher) to low resolution (72 ppi or 96 ppi).

The number of pixels per unit of length on a monitor is the *monitor resolution*, also usually measured in pixels per inch (ppi). Image pixels are translated directly into monitor pixels. In Photoshop, if the image resolution is higher than the monitor resolution, the image appears larger onscreen than its specified print dimensions. For example, when you display a 1x1-inch, 144-ppi image on a 72-ppi monitor, the image fills a 2x2-inch area of the screen.

4 x 6 inches at 72 ppi; file size 364.5 KB

100% onscreen view

4 x 6 inches at 200 ppi; file size 2.75 MB

100% onscreen view

● **Note:** It's important to understand what "100% view" means when you work onscreen. At 100%, one image pixel = one monitor pixel. Unless the resolution of your image is exactly the same as the resolution of the monitor, the image size (in inches, for example) onscreen may be larger or smaller than the image size will be when printed.

The number of ink dots per inch (dpi) produced by a platesetter or laser printer is the *printer,* or *output, resolution*. Higher resolution images output to higher resolution printers generally produce the best quality. The appropriate resolution for a printed image is determined both by the printer resolution and by the *screen frequency,* or lines per inch (lpi), of the halftone screens used to reproduce images.

Keep in mind that the higher the image resolution, the larger the file size, and the longer the file takes to download from the web.

For more information on resolution and image size, see Photoshop Help.

Getting started

In this lesson, you'll prepare a scanned photograph to be placed in an Adobe InDesign layout for a fictitious magazine. The final image size in the print layout will be 3.5x2.5 inches.

You'll start the lesson by comparing the original scan to the finished image.

1   Start Adobe Bridge CS5 by choosing Start > All Programs > Adobe Bridge CS5 (Windows) or double-clicking Adobe Bridge CS5 in the Applications folder (Mac OS).

2   In the Favorites panel in the upper-left corner of Bridge, click the Lessons folder. Then, in the Content panel, double-click the Lesson02 folder to see its contents..

3   Compare the 02Start.jpg and 02End.psd files. To enlarge the thumbnails in the Content panel, drag the Thumbnail slider at the bottom of the Bridge window to the right.

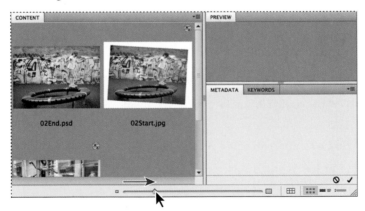

In the 02Start.jpg file, notice that the image is crooked, the colors are relatively dull, and the image has a red color cast. The dimensions are also larger than needed for the requirements of the magazine. You'll fix all of these problems in this lesson, starting with the color and tone of the image.

4   Select the 02Start.jpg thumbnail, and choose File > Open In Camera Raw.

The image opens in Camera Raw. As you make changes to the image, Camera Raw saves those changes in a separate file that is associated with your original image file. You can return to the original at any time when working in Camera Raw.

Adjusting the color in Camera Raw

You'll start by removing the color cast and adjusting the color and tone in the image.

● **Note:** You'll work with Camera Raw more extensively in Lesson 5.

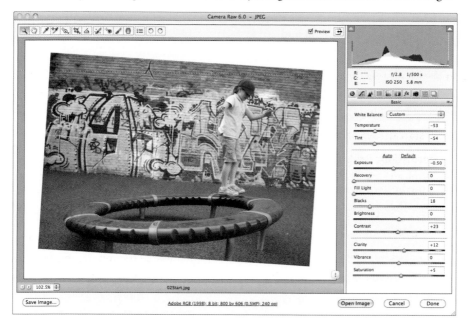

1 Select the White Balance tool (✏) at the top of the Camera Raw dialog box.

Adjusting the white balance changes all the colors in the image. To set an accurate white balance, select an area that should be white or gray.

2 Click a white area of the graffiti. The color tone of the image changes dramatically.

3 Click the girl's white shoe. The color tone changes again.

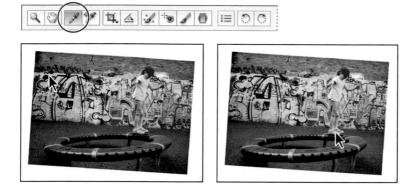

In some images, adjusting the white balance is enough to remove a color cast and correct the tone of the image. Selecting a white balance is a good start. You'll use settings in the Basic panel to fine-tune the tone.

4 In the Basic panel, move the Temperature slider to **-53** and the Tint slider to **-54**.

5 In the next section of the Basic panel, move the sliders to the following values:

- Exposure: **-.50**
- Blacks: **18**
- Contrast: **+23**

6 In the bottom section of the Basic panel, move the sliders to the following values:

- Clarity: **+12**
- Vibrance: **+25**
- Saturation: **+5**

7 Deselect Preview at the top of the Camera Raw window to compare the edited version with the original image. Select Preview again to see how the changes affected it.

You're ready to move the image into Photoshop to continue retouching it.

8 Click Open Image at the bottom of the Camera Raw window to open the image in Photoshop.

9 In Photoshop, choose File > Save As, rename the file **02Working.psd**, and click Save to save it in the Lesson02 folder.

Remember, when you're making permanent corrections to an image file, it's always wise to work on a copy rather than on the original. Then, if something goes horribly wrong, at least you'll be able to start over on a fresh copy of the original image.

Straightening and cropping the image in Photoshop

You'll use the Ruler tool to straighten the image, which was scanned at an angle. Then, you'll use the Crop tool to trim and scale the photograph so that it fits the space designed for it. You can use either the Crop tool or the Crop command to crop an image. Both methods permanently delete all the pixels outside the crop selection area.

1 In the Tools panel, select the Ruler tool (⬚), hidden behind the Eyedropper tool (✎).

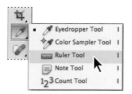

2 With the Ruler tool, click on the upper-left corner of the photo, where it meets the white space. Drag the tool to the upper-right corner of the photo, and click again.

3 Click the Straighten button in the options bar (at the top of the work area).

Photoshop straightens the photograph.

4 In the Tools panel, select the Crop tool (⬚). Then, in the options bar, enter the dimensions (in inches) of the finished image. For Width, type **3.5 in**, and for Height type **2.5 in**.

5 Draw a crop marquee around the image. Don't worry about which part of the image is included, because you'll adjust the marquee in a moment. As you drag, the marquee retains the same proportion as the dimensions you specified for the target size (3.5 x 2.5 inches).

When you release the mouse button, a *cropping shield* covers the area outside the cropping selection, and the options bar displays choices about the cropping shield.

6 Place the pointer inside the crop marquee, and drag the marquee until it contains the portion of the picture you want shown to produce an artistically pleasing result. If you need to adjust the size of the marquee, drag one of the corner handles. You can also use the arrow keys on the keyboard to adjust the marquee in 1-pixel increments.

7 Press Enter or Return. The image is now cropped, and the cropped image now fills the image window, straightened, sized, and cropped according to your specifications.

▶ **Tip:** You can choose Image > Trim to discard a border area around the edge of the image, based on transparency or edge color.

8 Choose File > Save to save your work.

Replacing colors in an image

Use the Color Replacement tool to paint over one color with another. When you start painting with the Color Replacement tool, it analyzes the first pixels you paint over. Because it then only replaces pixels of a similar color, you don't have to be terribly precise as you paint. You can select settings that determine whether the tool paints over contiguous or discontiguous pixels, and how much color difference the tool accepts.

You'll use the Color Replacement tool to change the color of the child's cap in the image of the playground.

1 Zoom in to see the child's cap clearly.

2 Select the Color Replacement tool (🖌) in the Tools panel, hidden behind the Brush tool (🖌).

3 Click the Foreground Color swatch in the Tools panel. In the Color Picker, select a color of green. We selected an RGB color with the values R=49, G=184, and B=6.

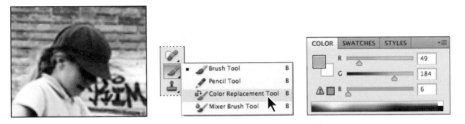

You'll paint the foreground color over the red hat.

4   In the options bar, open the Brush pop-up panel to view brush options.

5   Move the Size slider to **15** pixels, the Hardness slider to **40%**, and the Spacing slider to **25%**. Choose Off from the Size and Tolerance menus.

6   Click outside the Brush pop-up panel to close it.

7   In the options bar, choose Hue from the Mode menu. Then click Sampling: Continous (🖌) (the button next to the Hue menu). Choose Find Edges from the Limits menu, and set the Tolerance to **32%**. Make sure Anti-Alias is selected.

8   Begin painting in the middle of the hat, and paint out toward the edges.

9   Choose a smaller brush, if you like, and continue painting out towards the edges of the hat. You can zoom in if needed.

10 When the hat is green, save the file.

Adjusting saturation with the Sponge tool

When you change the saturation of a color, you adjust its strength or purity. The Sponge tool is useful for making subtle saturation changes to specific areas of an image. You'll use the Sponge tool to saturate the color of some of the graffiti.

1   Zoom out or scroll, if necessary, to see the colorful graffiti.

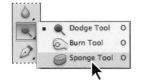

2   Select the Sponge tool (●), hidden under the Dodge tool (🔍).

3   In the options bar, do the following:

   •   In the Brush pop-up panel, move the Size slider to 150 px, and then move the Hardness slider to **0**%.

   •   Choose Saturate from the Mode menu.

   •   For Flow, enter **40%**. The Flow value determines the intensity of the saturation effect.

4   Drag the sponge back and forth over the graffiti to the left of the girl to increase its saturation. The more you drag over an area, the more saturated the color becomes. Be careful not to oversaturate the graffiti.

5   Select the Move tool (▸⊕) to ensure you don't accidentally add saturation elsewhere.

6   Save your work.

Repairing areas with the Clone Stamp tool

The Clone Stamp tool uses pixels from one area of an image to replace the pixels in another part of the image. Using this tool, you can not only remove unwanted objects from your images, but you can also fill in missing areas in photographs you scan from damaged originals.

You'll start by replacing a bright white area of the wall—a hot spot—with cloned bricks from another area of the picture.

1 Select the Clone Stamp tool (🖋) in the Tools panel.

2 In the options bar, open the Brush pop-up menu, and set the size to **21** and the Hardness to **0%**. Then, make sure that the Aligned option is selected.

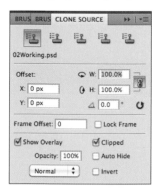

3 Choose Window > Clone Source to open the Clone Source panel. This panel gives you greater control over the area you're cloning from (in this case, the bricks).

4 Select Show Overlay and Clipped in the Clone Source panel. Then, make sure Opacity is set to **100**%. The overlay lets you see what you're cloning before you stamp it.

5 Move the Clone Stamp tool over the darker bricks just to the right of the hot spot on the wall. (You may want to zoom in to see the area better.)

6 Alt-click (Windows) or Option-click (Mac OS) to start sampling that part of the image. (When you press Alt or Option, the pointer appears as target cross-hairs.)

7 Starting at the area just to the right of the girl's hat, drag the Clone Stamp tool to the right, over the hot spot on the bricks. The clone overlay lets you see what will appear there. This is particularly useful for keeping the bricks in a straight line.

● **Note:** When the Aligned option is not selected, each time you make a stroke, you begin sampling from the same source point, regardless of where you place the tool.

8 Release the mouse button and move the pointer to another area in the hot spot, and then start dragging again.

Each time you click the Clone Stamp tool, it begins again with a new source point, in the same relationship to the tool as the first stroke you made. That is, if you begin painting further right, it samples from bricks that are further right than the original source point. That's because Aligned is selected in the options bar.

9 Continue cloning the bricks until the entire hot spot is filled in.

If necessary to help make the bricks appear to blend in naturally with the rest of the image, you can adjust your cloning by resetting the sample area (as you did in step 6) and recloning. Or, you can try deselecting the Aligned option and cloning again.

10 When you're satisfied with the appearance of the bricks, close the Clone Source panel, and choose File > Save.

Using the Spot Healing Brush tool

The next task is to clean up some dark spots in the wall. You could do this with the Clone Stamp tool (⟁), but instead you'll use another technique. You'll use the Spot Healing Brush to clean up the wall.

The Spot Healing Brush tool quickly removes blemishes and other imperfections from photos. It paints with sampled pixels from an image or pattern and matches the texture, lighting, transparency, and shading of the sampled pixels to the pixels being healed. Unlike the Clone Stamp tool, the Spot Healing Brush doesn't require you to specify a sample spot. It automatically samples from around the retouched area.

The Spot Healing Brush is excellent for retouching blemishes in portraits, but will also work nicely in this image in the dark area of the wall, because the wall has a uniform, muted appearance to the right of the dark areas.

Note: The Healing Brush tool works similarly to the Spot Healing Brush tool, except that it requires you to sample source pixels before retouching an area.

1   Zoom in or scroll to see the dark areas on the upper-left corner of the image.

2   In the Tools panel, select the Spot Healing Brush tool (✐).

3   In the options bar, open the Brush pop-up panel, and specify a **100%** hard brush that is about **40** px in diameter.

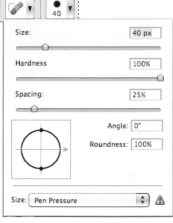

4   In the image window, drag the Spot Healing Brush from right to left across the dark spots in the upper-left corner of the image. You can use as many or as few strokes as you like; paint until you're satisfied with the results. As you drag, the stroke at first appears black, but when you release the mouse, the painted area is "healed."

5   Choose File > Save.

Using content-aware fill

Content-aware fill takes blending a few steps further. Photoshop fills a selection with pixels that match the surroundings. Applying content-aware fill isn't like cloning, because you aren't copying part of the image to another part. Really, it's more like magic. You can fill any selection with content similar to the content around it, as if the object you've selected never existed. You'll get a chance to see it for yourself as you touch up the brick wall, removing the large crack and the dark areas of the wall on the left. Because the wall varies in color, texture, and lighting, it would be challenging to successfully use the Clone Stamp tool to touch up these areas. Fortunately, the content-aware fill feature make this process easy.

1   In the Tools panel, select the Quick Selection tool (✎).

2   In the options bar, open the Brush pop-up menu, and set the brush size to **3 px**.

3   Drag the Quick Selection tool around the crack in the wall to select it.

4   Choose Edit > Fill.

5   In the Fill dialog box, choose Content-Aware from the Use menu, and click OK.

The selection changes to match the area around it.

6   Choose Select > Deselect.

7   Use the Quick Selection tool to select the darker area on the left edge of the wall.

8   Choose Edit > Fill, choose Content-Aware from the Use menu, and click OK.

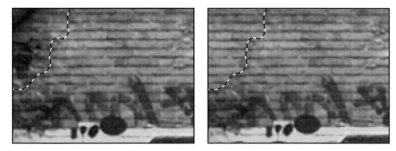

9   Choose Select > Deselect.

Applying the Unsharp Mask filter

The last task you might want to do when retouching a photo is to apply the Unsharp Mask filter. The Unsharp Mask filter adjusts the contrast of the edge detail and creates the illusion of a more focused image.

1 Choose Filter > Sharpen > Unsharp Mask.

2 In the Unsharp Mask dialog box, make sure that Preview is selected so you can see the effect of settings you adjust in the image window.

You can drag inside the preview window in the dialog box to see different parts of the image, or use the plus and minus buttons below the thumbnail to zoom in and out.

3 Drag the Amount slider to about **70%** to sharpen the image.

4 Drag the Radius slider to determine the number of pixels surrounding the edge pixels that will affect the sharpening. The higher the resolution, the higher the Radius setting should be. (We used the default value, 1.0 pixel.)

5 (Optional) Adjust the Threshold slider. This determines how different the sharpened pixels must be from the surrounding area before they are considered edge pixels and subsequently sharpened by the Unsharp Mask filter. The default Threshold value of 0 sharpens all pixels in the image. Try a different value, such as 2 or 3.

6 When you're satisfied with the results, click OK to apply the Unsharp Mask filter.

7 Choose File > Save.

▶ **Tip:** As you try different settings, toggle the Preview option on and off to see how your changes affect the image. Or, you can click and hold the mouse button on the preview window in the dialog box to temporarily toggle the filter off in the preview window. If your image is large, using the preview window can be more efficient, because only a small area is redrawn.

About unsharp masking

Unsharp masking, or USM, is a traditional film-compositing technique used to sharpen edges in an image. The Unsharp Mask filter corrects blurring introduced during photographing, scanning, resampling, or printing. It's useful for images intended for both print and online viewing.

Unsharp Mask locates pixels that differ from surrounding pixels by the threshold you set and increases the pixels' contrast by the amount you specify. In addition, you can adjust the radius of the region to which each pixel is compared.

The effects of the Unsharp Mask filter are far more pronounced onscreen than they are in high-resolution output. If your final destination is print, experiment to determine which settings work best for your image.

Saving the image for four-color printing

Before you save a Photoshop file for use in a four-color publication, you must change the image to CMYK color mode. You'll use the Mode command to change the image color mode.

For more information about converting between color modes, see Photoshop Help.

Tip: Most images include more than one layer. Choose Layer > Merge Visible before you change the color mode to ensure that all the changes you made are included in the CYMK image.

1 Choose File > Save As, and save the file as **02_CMYK.psd**. It's a good idea to save a copy of your original file before changing color modes, so that you can make changes in the original later, if necessary.

2 Choose Image > Mode > CMYK Color. Click OK when Photoshop displays an alert about the color management profile.

If you were preparing this image for a real publication, you'd want to confirm that you were using the appropriate CMYK profile. See Lesson 14, "Producing and Printing Consistent Color," to learn about color management.

3 If you use Adobe InDesign to create your publications, simply choose File > Save. InDesign can import native Photoshop (PSD) files, so there is no need to convert the image to TIFF.

If you're using another layout application, choose File > Save As, and then proceed to step 4 to save the image as a TIFF file.

4 In the Save As dialog box, choose TIFF from the Format menu.

5 Click Save.

6 In the TIFF Options dialog box, select your operating system for the Byte Order, and click OK.

The image is now fully retouched, saved, and ready for placement in a page layout application.

For more information about file formats, see Photoshop Help.

You can combine Photoshop images with other elements in a layout application such as Adobe InDesign.

Extra Credit

You can get great results converting a color image to black and white (with or without a tint) in Photoshop or Camera Raw.

In Photoshop:

1 Choose File > Open, and navigate to the bike.jpg file in the Lesson02 folder. Click Open.

2 If the file opens in Camera Raw, click Open Image to open it in Photoshop.

3 In the Adjustments panel, click the Black & White button to add a Black & White adjustment layer.

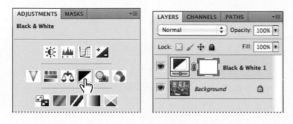

4 Adjust the color sliders to change the saturation of color channels. You can also experiment with options from the preset menu, such as Darker or Infrared. Or, select the tool in the upper-left corner of the Adjustments panel, and then drag it across the image to adjust the colors associated with that area. (We darkened the bike itself and made the background areas lighter.)

5 If you want to add a tint to the photo, select Tint. Then, click the color swatch and select a tint color (we used R=227, G=209, and B=198).

In Camera Raw:

1 In Bridge, select the bike.jpg file, and choose File > Open In Camera Raw.

2 In Camera Raw, click the HSL/Grayscale tab.

3 Select Convert To Grayscale, and then adjust the color sliders to in the Hue, Saturation, and Luminance panes to change the intensity of the shades.

Review questions

1 What does *resolution* mean?

2 What does the Crop tool do?

3 How can you adjust the tone and color of an image in Camera Raw?

4 What tools can you use to remove blemishes in an image?

5 What effect does the Unsharp Mask filter have on an image?

Review answers

1 The term *resolution* refers to the number of pixels that describe an image and establish its detail. *Image resolution* and *monitor resolution* are measured in pixels per inch (ppi). *Printer,* or *output, resolution* is measured in ink dots per inch (dpi).

2 You can use the Crop tool to trim or scale an image.

3 Use the White Balance tool to adjust the color temperature. Then fine-tune the color and tone using sliders in the Basic panel.

4 The Healing Brush, Spot Healing Brush, and Clone Stamp tools, as well as content-aware fill, let you replace unwanted portions of an image with other areas of the image. The Clone Stamp tool copies the source area exactly; the Healing Brush and Spot Healing Brush tools blend the area with the surrounding pixels. The Spot Healing Brush tool doesn't require a source area at all; it "heals" areas to match the surrounding pixels. Content-aware fill replaces a selection with content that matches the surrounding area.

5 The Unsharp Mask filter adjusts the contrast of the edge detail and creates the illusion of a more focused image.

3

WORKING WITH SELECTIONS

Lesson overview

In this lesson, you'll learn how to do the following:

- Make specific areas of an image active using selection tools.

- Reposition a selection marquee.

- Move and duplicate the contents of a selection.

- Use keyboard-mouse combinations that save time and hand motions.

- Deselect a selection.

- Constrain the movement of a selected area.

- Adjust the position of a selected area using the arrow keys.

- Add to and subtract from a selection.

- Rotate a selection.

- Use multiple selection tools to make a complex selection.

- Erase pixels within a selection.

 This lesson will take about an hour to complete. Copy the Lesson03 folder onto your hard drive if you haven't already done so. As you work on this lesson, you'll preserve the start files. If you need to restore the start files, copy them from the *Adobe Photoshop CS5 Classroom in a Book* DVD.

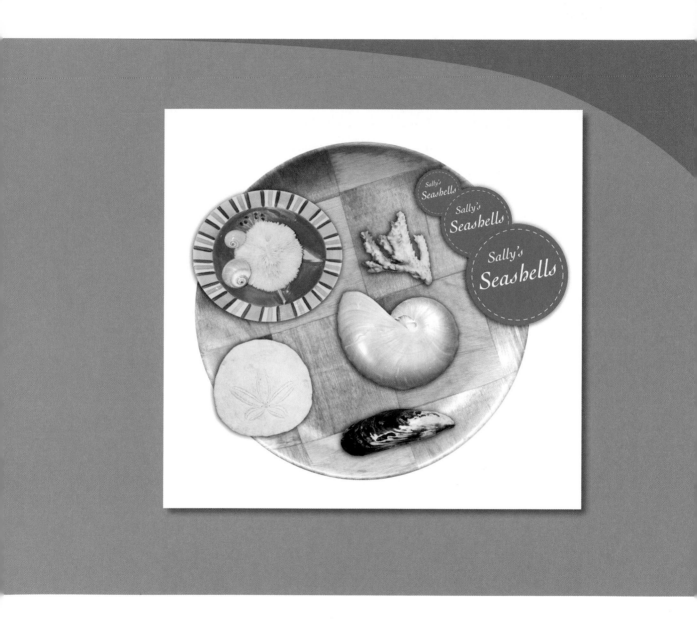

Learning how to select areas of an image is of primary importance—you must first select what you want to affect. Once you've made a selection, only the area within the selection can be edited.

About selecting and selection tools

● **Note:** You'll learn how to select vector areas using the pen tools in Lesson 8, "Vector Drawing Techniques."

Making changes to an area within an image in Photoshop is a two-step process. You first select the part of an image you want to change with one of the selection tools. Then, you use another tool, filter, or other feature to make changes, such as moving the selected pixels to another location or applying a filter to the selected area. You can make selections based on size, shape, and color. The selection process limits changes to within the selected area. Other areas are unaffected.

The best selection tool for a specific area often depends on the characteristics of that area, such as shape or color. There are four types of selections:

Geometric selections The Rectangular Marquee tool (▢) selects a rectangular area in an image. The Elliptical Marquee tool (◯), which is hidden behind the Rectangular Marquee tool, selects elliptical areas. The Single Row Marquee tool (▭) and Single Column Marquee tool (▯) select either a 1-pixel-high row or a 1-pixel-wide column, respectively.

Freehand selections Drag the Lasso tool (◯) around an area to trace a freehand selection. Using the Polygonal Lasso tool (⋎), click to set anchor points in straight-line segments around an area. The Magnetic Lasso tool (⧖) works something like a combination of the other two lasso tools, and works best when good contrast exists between the area you want to select and its surroundings.

Edge-based selections The Quick Selection tool (✐) quickly "paints" a selection by automatically finding and following defined edges in the image.

Color-based selections The Magic Wand tool (✺) selects parts of an image based on the similarity in color of adjacent pixels. It is useful for selecting odd-shaped areas that share a specific range of colors.

Getting started

First, you'll look at the image you will create as you explore the selection tools in Adobe Photoshop.

1   Start Photoshop, and then immediately hold down Ctrl+Alt+Shift (Windows) or Command+Option+Shift (Mac OS) to restore the default preferences. (See "Restoring default preferences" on page 5.)

2   When prompted, click Yes to confirm that you want to delete the Adobe Photoshop Settings file.

3   Click the Launch Bridge button (▣) in the Application bar to open Adobe Bridge.

4   In the Favorites panel, click the Lessons folder. Then, double-click the Lesson03 folder in the Content panel to see its contents.

5   Study the 03End.psd file. Move the thumbnail slider to the right if you want to see the image in more detail.

The project is a collage of objects, including a piece of coral, a sand dollar, a mussel, a nautilus, a bowl of small shells, a wooden plate, and the "Sally's Seashells" logo. The challenge in this lesson is to arrange these elements, which were scanned together on the single page you see in the 03Start.psd file. The ideal composition is up to you, so this lesson won't describe precise locations. There is no right or wrong position for any of the objects.

6   Double-click the 03Start.psd thumbnail to open the image file in Photoshop.

7   Choose File > Save As, rename the file **03Working.psd**, and click Save. By saving another version of the start file, you don't have to worry about overwriting the original.

Using the Quick Selection tool

The Quick Selection tool provides one of the easiest ways to make a selection. You simply paint an area of an image, and the tool automatically finds the edges. You can add or subtract areas of the selection until you have exactly the area you want.

The image of the sand dollar in the 03Working.psd file has clearly defined edges, making it an ideal candidate for the Quick Selection tool. You'll select just the sand dollar, not the shadow or background behind it.

1 Select the Zoom tool in the Tools panel, and then zoom in so that you can see the sand dollar well.

2 Select the Quick Selection tool (✐) in the Tools panel.

3 Click on an off-white area near the outside edge of the sand dollar. The Quick Selection tool finds the full edge automatically, selecting the entire sand dollar.

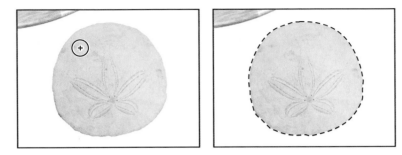

Leave the selection active so that you can use it in the next exercise.

Moving a selected area

Once you've made a selection, any changes you make apply exclusively to the pixels within the selection. The rest of the image is not affected by those changes.

To move the selected area to another part of the composition, you use the Move tool. This image has only one layer, so the pixels you move will replace the pixels beneath them. This change is not permanent until you deselect the moved pixels, so you can try different locations for the selection you're moving before you make a commitment.

1 If the sand dollar is not still selected, repeat the previous exercise to select it.

2 Zoom out so you can see both the wooden plate and the sand dollar.

3 Select the Move tool (▸+). Notice that the sand dollar remains selected.

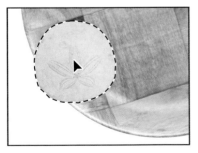

4 Drag the selected area (the sand dollar) to the left area of the collage so that the sand dollar overlaps the lower-left edge of the wooden plate.

5 Choose Select > Deselect, and then choose File > Save.

In Photoshop, it's not easy to lose a selection. Unless a selection tool is active, clicking elsewhere in the image will not deselect the active area. To deliberately deselect a selection, you can choose Select > Deselect, press Ctrl+D (Windows) or Command+D (Mac OS), or click outside the selection with any selection tool to start a different selection.

Julieanne Kost is an official Adobe Photoshop evangelist.

Tool tips from the Photoshop evangelist

Move tool tip

If you're moving objects in a multilayer file with the Move tool and you suddenly need to select one of the layers, try this: With the Move tool selected, move the pointer over any area of an image and right-click (Windows) or Control-click (Mac OS). The layers that are under the pointer appear in the context menu. Choose the one you'd like to make active.

Manipulating selections

You can reposition selections as you create them, move them, and even duplicate them. In this section, you'll learn several ways to manipulate selections. Most of these methods work with any selection, but you'll use them here with the Elliptical Marquee tool, which lets you select ovals or perfect circles.

One of the best things about this section is the introduction of keyboard shortcuts that can save you time and arm motions.

Repositioning a selection marquee while creating it

Selecting ovals and circles can be tricky. It's not always obvious where you should start dragging, so sometimes the selection will be off-center, or the ratio of width to height won't match what you need. In this exercise, you'll learn techniques for managing those problems, including two important keyboard-mouse combinations that can make your Photoshop work much easier.

As you perform this exercise, be very careful to follow the directions about keeping the mouse button or specific keys pressed. If you accidentally release the mouse button at the wrong time, simply start the exercise again from step 1.

1   Select the Zoom tool (🔍), and click the bowl of shells on the right side of the image window to zoom in to at least 100% view (use 200% view if the entire bowl of shells will still fit in the image window on your screen).

2   Select the Elliptical Marquee tool (⬭), hidden under the Rectangular Marquee tool (⬚).

3   Move the pointer over the bowl of shells, and drag diagonally across the oval bowl to create a selection, but *do not release the mouse button*. It's OK if your selection does not match the bowl shape yet.

If you accidentally release the mouse button, draw the selection again. In most cases—including this one—the new selection replaces the previous one.

4   Still holding down the mouse button, press the spacebar, and continue to drag the selection. Instead of resizing the selection, now you're moving it. Position it so that it more closely aligns with the bowl.

● **Note:** You don't have to include every pixel in the bowl of shells, but the selection should be the shape of the bowl, and should contain the shells comfortably.

5   Carefully release the spacebar (but not the mouse button) and continue to drag, trying to make the size and shape of the selection match the oval bowl of shells as closely as possible. If necessary, hold down the spacebar again and drag to move the selection marquee into position around the bowl of shells.

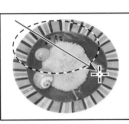 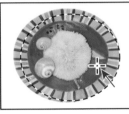 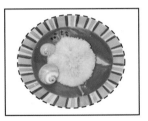

Begin dragging a selection.   Press the spacebar to move it.   Complete the selection.

6   When the selection border is positioned appropriately, release the mouse button.

7   Choose View > Zoom Out or use the slider in the Navigator panel to reduce the zoom view so that you can see all of the objects in the image window.

Leave the Elliptical Marquee tool and the selection active for the next exercise.

Moving selected pixels with a keyboard shortcut

Now you'll use a keyboard shortcut to move the selected pixels onto the wooden plate. The shortcut temporarily switches the active tool to the Move tool, so you don't need to select it from the Tools panel.

1   If the bowl of shells is not still selected, repeat the previous exercise to select it.

2 With the Elliptical Marquee tool (○) selected in the Tools panel, press Ctrl (Windows) or Command (Mac OS), and move the pointer within the selection. The pointer icon now includes a pair of scissors (✂) to indicate that the selection will be cut from its current location.

3 Drag the bowl of shells onto the wooden plate so that it overlaps the upper left edge of the wooden plate. (You'll use another technique to nudge the oval bowl into the exact position in a minute.)

4 Release the mouse button, but don't deselect the bowl of shells.

● **Note:** You can release the Ctrl or Command key after you start dragging, and the Move tool remains active. Photoshop reverts to the previously selected tool when you deselect, whether you click outside the selection or use the Deselect command.

Moving with the arrow keys

You can make minor adjustments to the position of selected pixels by using the arrow keys. You can nudge the selection in increments of either one pixel or ten pixels.

When a selection tool is active in the Tools panel, the arrow keys nudge the selection border, but not the contents. When the Move tool is active, the arrow keys move the selection border and its contents.

You'll use the arrow keys to nudge the bowl of shells. Before you begin, make sure that the bowl of shells is still selected in the image window.

1 Press the Up Arrow key (⬆) on your keyboard a few times to move the oval upward.

Notice that each time you press the arrow key, the bowl of shells moves one pixel. Experiment by pressing the other arrow keys to see how they affect the selection.

2 Hold down the Shift key as you press an arrow key.

When you hold down the Shift key, the selection moves ten pixels every time you press an arrow key.

Sometimes the border around a selected area can distract you as you make adjustments. You can hide the edges of a selection temporarily without actually deselecting, and then display the selection border once you've completed the adjustments.

3 Choose View > Show > Selection Edges or View > Extras.

Either command hides the selection border around the bowl of shells.

4 Use the arrow keys to nudge the bowl of shells until it's positioned where you want it. Then choose View > Show > Selection Edges to reveal the selection border again.

Hidden selection edges

Visible selection edges

5 Choose Select > Deselect, or press Ctrl+D (Windows) or Command+D (Mac OS).

6 Choose File > Save to save your work so far.

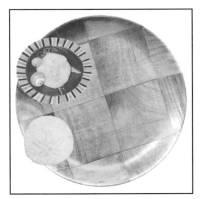

Selecting from a center point

In some cases, it's easier to make elliptical or rectangular selections by drawing a selection from the center point. You'll use this technique to select the logo graphic.

1 Select the Zoom tool (🔍), and zoom in on the logo to a magnification of about 300%. Make sure that you can see the entire Sally's Seashells graphic in your image window.

2 Select the Elliptical Marquee tool (◯) in the Tools panel.

3 Move the pointer to the approximate center of the Sally's Seashells graphic.

4 Click and begin dragging. Then, without releasing the mouse button, press Alt (Windows) or Option (Mac OS) as you continue dragging the selection to the outer edge of the Sally's Seashells graphic.

The selection is centered over its starting point.

5 When you have the entire Sally's Seashells graphic selected, release the mouse button first, and then release Alt or Option (and the Shift key if you used it). Do not deselect, because you'll use this selection in the next exercise.

▶ **Tip:** To select a perfect circle, press Shift as you drag. Hold down Shift while dragging the Rectangular Marquee tool to select a perfect square.

6 If necessary, reposition the selection border using one of the methods you learned earlier. If you accidentally released the Alt or Option key before you released the mouse button, try selecting the Sally's Seashells graphic again.

Moving and changing the pixels in a selection

Now you'll move the Sally's Seashells graphic to the upper-right corner of the wooden plate. Then, you'll change its color for a dramatic effect.

Before you begin, make sure that the Sally's Seashells graphic is still selected. If it's not, reselect it by completing the previous exercise.

1 Choose View > Fit On Screen so that the entire image fits within the image window.

2 Select the Move tool (▶+) in the Tools panel.

3 Position the pointer within the Sally's Seashells graphic selection. The pointer becomes an arrow with a pair of scissors (▶✂), which indicates that dragging the selection will cut it from its current location and move it to the new location.

4 Drag the Sally's Seashells graphic onto the upper-right corner of the plate. If you want to adjust the position after you stop dragging, simply start dragging again. The Sally's Seashells graphic remains selected throughout the process.

5 Choose Image > Adjustments > Invert.

The colors making up the Sally's Seashells graphic are inverted so that now it's effectively a color negative of itself.

6 Leaving the Sally's Seashells graphic selected, choose File > Save to save your work.

Moving and duplicating a selection simultaneously

You can move and duplicate a selection at the same time. You'll make a copy of the logo graphic. If the logo graphic image is no longer selected, reselect it now, using the techniques you learned earlier.

1 With the Move tool (⊹) selected, press Alt (Windows) or Option (Mac OS) as you position the pointer inside the Sally's Seashells graphic selection. The pointer becomes a double arrow, which indicates that a duplicate will be made when you move the selection.

2 Continue holding down the Alt or Option key as you drag a duplicate of the graphic down and to the right. The two copies of the graphic can overlap. Release the mouse button and the Alt or Option key, but don't deselect the duplicate graphic.

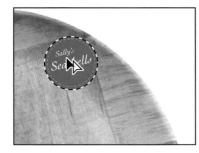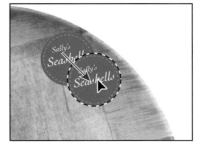

3 Choose Edit > Transform > Scale. A bounding box appears around the selection.

4 Press Shift as you drag one of the corner points to enlarge the graphic so that it becomes about 50% larger than the original. Then press Enter or Return to commit the change and remove the transformation bounding box.

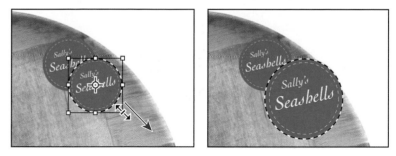

As you resize the object, the selection marquee resizes, too. The duplicate graphic remains selected. Pressing the Shift key as you resize the selection constrains the proportions so that the enlarged object isn't distorted.

5 Hold down Alt+Shift (Windows) or Option+Shift (Mac OS), and drag a new copy of the second Sally's Seashells graphic down and to the right.

Pressing the Shift key as you move a selection constrains the movement horizontally or vertically in 45-degree increments.

6 Repeat steps 3 and 4 for the third Sally's Seashells graphic, making it about twice the size of the first one.

7 When you're satisfied with the size and position of the third Sally's Seashells graphic, press Enter or Return to confirm the scale, choose Select > Deselect, and then choose File > Save.

▶ **Tip:** Choose Edit > Transform > Again to duplicate the logo and enlarge it by twice as much as the last transformation.

For information on working with the center point in a transformation, see "Set or move the reference point for a transformation" in Photoshop Help.

Copying selections or layers

You can use the Move tool to copy selections as you drag them within or between images, or you can copy and move selections using the Copy, Copy Merged, Cut, and Paste commands. Dragging with the Move tool saves memory because the clipboard is not used as it is with the Copy, Copy Merged, Cut, and Paste commands.

Photoshop has several copy and paste commands:

- Copy copies the selected area on the active layer.
- Copy Merged creates a merged copy of all the visible layers in the selected area.
- Paste pastes a cut or copied selection into another part of the image or into another image as a new layer.
- Paste Into pastes a cut or copied selection inside another selection in the same or a different image. The source selection is pasted onto a new layer, and the destination selection border is converted into a layer mask.

Keep in mind that when a selection or layer is pasted between images with different resolutions, the pasted data retains its pixel dimensions. This can make the pasted portion appear out of proportion to the new image. Use the Image Size command to make the source and destination images the same resolution before copying and pasting.

Using the Magic Wand tool

The Magic Wand tool selects all the pixels of a particular color or color range. It's most useful for selecting an area of similar colors surrounded by areas of very different colors. As with many of the selection tools, after you make the initial selection, you can add or subtract areas of the selection.

The Tolerance option sets the sensitivity of the Magic Wand tool. This value limits or extends the range of pixel similarity. The default tolerance value of 32 selects the color you click plus 32 lighter and 32 darker tones of that color. You may need to adjust the tolerance level up or down depending on the color ranges and variations in the image.

If a multicolored area that you want to select is set against a background of a different color, it can be much easier to select the background than the area itself. In this procedure, you'll use the Rectangular Marquee tool to select a larger area, and then use the Magic Wand tool to subtract the background from the selection.

1 Select the Rectangular Marquee tool (▦), hidden behind the Elliptical Marquee tool (◯).

2 Drag a selection around the piece of coral. Make sure that your selection is large enough so that a margin of white appears between the coral and the edges of the marquee.

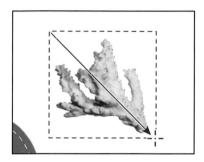

At this point, the coral and the white background area are selected. You'll subtract the white area from the selection so that only the coral remains in the selection.

3 Select the Magic Wand tool (✎), hidden under the Quick Selection tool (✐).

4 In the options bar, confirm that the Tolerance value is **32**. This value determines the range of colors the wand selects.

5 Select the Subtract From Selection button (▣) in the options bar. A minus sign appears next to the wand in the pointer icon. Anything you select now will be subtracted from the initial selection.

6 Click in the white background area within the selection marquee.

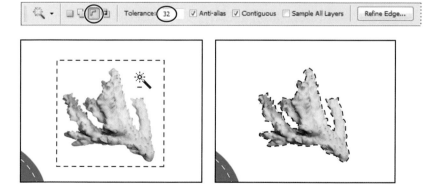

The Magic Wand tool selects the entire background, subtracting it from the selection. Now all the white pixels are deselected, leaving the coral perfectly selected.

7 Select the Move tool (✛), and drag the coral to the wooden plate, a little to the right and above the center of the plate.

8 Choose Select > Deselect, and then save your work.

Selecting with the lasso tools

Photoshop includes three lasso tools: the Lasso tool, the Polygonal Lasso tool, and the Magnetic Lasso tool. You can use the Lasso tool to make selections that require both freehand and straight lines, using keyboard shortcuts to move back and forth between the Lasso tool and the Polygonal Lasso tool. You'll use the Lasso tool to select the mussel. It takes a bit of practice to alternate between straight-line and freehand selections—if you make a mistake while you're selecting the mussel, simply deselect and start again.

1 Select the Zoom tool (🔍), and click the mussel until the view enlarges to 100%. Make sure you can see the entire mussel in the window.

2 Select the Lasso tool (𝒫). Starting at the lower-left section of the mussel, drag around the rounded end of the mussel, tracing the shape as accurately as possible. *Do not release the mouse button.*

3 Press the Alt (Windows) or Option (Mac OS) key, and then release the mouse button so that the lasso pointer changes to the polygonal lasso shape (𝇇). *Do not release the Alt or Option key.*

4 Begin clicking along the end of the mussel to place anchor points, following the contours of the mussel. Be sure to hold down the Alt or Option key throughout this process.

Drag with the Lasso tool.

Click with the Polygonal Lasso tool.

The selection border automatically stretches like a rubber band between anchor points.

5 When you reach the tip of the mussel, hold down the mouse button as you release the Alt or Option key. The pointer again appears as the lasso icon.

6 Carefully drag around the tip of the mussel, holding the mouse button down.

7 When you finish tracing the tip and reach the lower side of the mussel, first press Alt or Option again, and then release the mouse button. Click along the lower side of the mussel with the Polygonal Lasso tool as you did on the top. Continue to trace the mussel until you arrive back at the starting point of your selection near the left end of the image.

8 Click at the start of the selection, and then release the Alt or Option key. The mussel is now entirely selected. Leave the mussel selected for the next exercise.

Rotating a selection

So far, you've moved, resized, duplicated, and inverted the color of selected areas. In this exercise, you'll see how easy it is to rotate a selected object.

Before you begin, make sure that the mussel is still selected.

1 Choose View > Fit On Screen to resize the image window to fit on your screen.

2 Press Ctrl (Windows) or Command (Mac OS) as you drag the mussel to the lower section of the wooden plate. The pointer changes to the Move tool icon.

3 Choose Edit > Transform > Rotate. The mussel and selection marquee are enclosed in a bounding box.

4 Move the pointer outside the bounding box so that it becomes a curved, double-headed arrow (↻). Drag to rotate the mussel to a –15-degree angle. You can verify the angle in the Rotate box in the options bar. Press Enter or Return to commit the transformation changes.

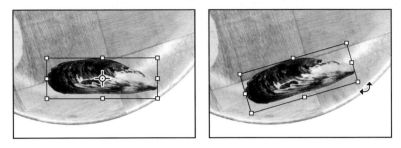

5 If necessary, select the Move tool (▸₊) and drag to reposition the mussel. When you're satisfied, choose Select > Deselect.

6 Choose File > Save.

Selecting with the Magnetic Lasso tool

You can use the Magnetic Lasso tool to make freehand selections of areas with high-contrast edges. When you draw with the Magnetic Lasso tool, the selection border automatically snaps to the edge between areas of contrast. You can also control the selection path by occasionally clicking the mouse to place anchor points in the selection border.

You'll use the Magnetic Lasso tool to select the nautilus so that you can move it to the center of the plate.

1   Select the Zoom tool ($\mathbb{Q}$), and click the nautilus to zoom in to at least 100%.

2   Select the Magnetic Lasso tool ($\mathbb{P}$), hidden under the Lasso tool ($\wp$).

3   Click once along the left edge of the nautilus, and then move the Magnetic Lasso tool along the edge to trace its outline.

▶ **Tip:** In low-contrast areas, you may want to click to place your own fastening points. You can add as many as you need. To remove the most recent fastening point, press Delete, and then move the mouse back to the remaining fastening point and continue selecting.

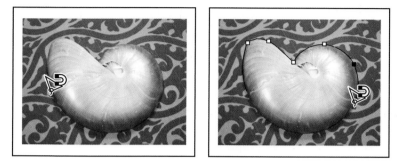

Even though you're not holding down the mouse button, the tool snaps to the edge of the nautilus and automatically adds fastening points.

4   When you reach the left side of the nautilus again, double-click to return the Magnetic Lasso tool to the starting point, closing the selection. Or you can move the Magnetic Lasso tool over the starting point and click once.

5   Double-click the Hand tool ($\mathbb{m}$) to fit the image in the image window.

6   Select the Move tool ($\triangleright_{+}$), and drag the nautilus onto the plate.

7   Choose Select > Deselect, and then choose File > Save.

Cropping an image and erasing within a selection

Now that your composition is in place, you'll crop the image to a final size and clean up some of the background scraps left behind when you moved selections. You can use either the Crop tool or the Crop command to crop an image.

1 Select the Crop tool (✝), or press C to switch from the current tool to the Crop tool. Then, drag diagonally across the collage composition to select the area you want to keep. Photoshop dims the area outside the crop border.

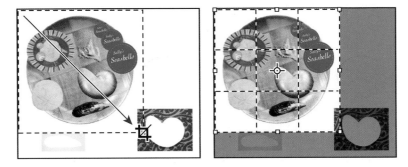

2 Adjust the crop area, as necessary:

- To reposition the crop border, position the pointer inside the cropping area and drag.

- To resize the crop area, drag a handle.

3 When you're satisfied with the position of the crop area, press Enter or Return to crop the image.

The cropped image may include some scraps of the background from which you selected and removed shapes. You'll fix that next.

4 If a scrap of background color or leftover drop shadow protrudes into the composition, use the Rectangular Marquee tool (▭) or the Lasso tool (⟡) to select it. Be careful not to include any part of the image that you want to keep.

5 Select the Eraser tool ( ) in the Tools panel, and then make sure that the foreground and background color swatches in the Tools panel are set to the defaults: black in the foreground and white in the background.

6 In the options bar, open the Brushes pop-up panel, and specify an **80**-pixel brush with **100%** hardness.

7 Drag the Eraser tool across the area you want to remove. You can erase quickly, because the Eraser tool affects only the selected area.

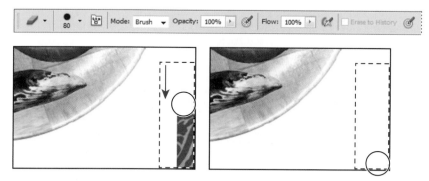

8 Repeat steps 4–7 to remove any other unwanted scraps of background.

9 Choose File > Save to save your work.

Softening the edges of a selection

To smooth the hard edges of a selection, you can apply anti-aliasing or feathering, or use the Refine Edge option.

Anti-aliasing smooths the jagged edges of a selection by softening the color transition between edge pixels and background pixels. Since only the edge pixels change, no detail is lost. Anti-aliasing is useful when cutting, copying, and pasting selections to create composite images.

Anti-aliasing is available for the Lasso, Polygonal Lasso, Magnetic Lasso, Elliptical Marquee, and Magic Wand tools. (Select the tool to display its options in the options bar.) To apply anti-aliasing, you must select the option before making the selection. Once a selection is made, you cannot add anti-aliasing to it.

Feathering blurs edges by building a transition boundary between the selection and its surrounding pixels. This blurring can cause some loss of detail at the edge of the selection.

You can define feathering for the marquee and lasso tools as you use them, or you can add feathering to an existing selection. Feathering effects become apparent when you move, cut, or copy the selection.

Once you have a selection, you can use the Refine Edge option to smooth the outline, feather it, or contract or expand it. You'll use the Refine Edge option later in this lesson.

- To use anti-aliasing, select a lasso tool, or the Elliptical Marquee or Magic Wand tool, and select Anti-alias in the options bar.

- To define a feathered edge for a selection tool, select any of the lasso or marquee tools. Enter a Feather value in the options bar. This value defines the width of the feathered edge and can range from 1 to 250 pixels.

- To define a feathered edge for an existing selection, choose Select > Modify > Feather. Enter a value for the Feather Radius, and click OK.

Refining the edge of a selection

Sometimes you'll get better results if you feather a selection edge to soften it, increase the edge's contrast, or expand or contract the edge to capture wisps of hair or other detail. The Refine Edge option improves the quality of a selection's edge, and lets you see the edge more clearly by removing it from context and placing it against different backgrounds.

In this composition, the coral has more complicated edges than the other elements. You'll select it and then fine-tune its edges.

1 Select the Quick Selection tool (🖌), hidden beneath the Magic Wand tool (🪄) in the Tools panel.

2 Drag from the upper-left corner of the coral to select it with part of the brown background. Use a size 6 brush to get a more precise selection.

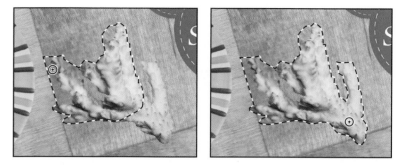

3 In the options bar, click the Subtract From Selection button (🖌).

4 Click throughout the brown portion of the selection, until only the coral is selected.

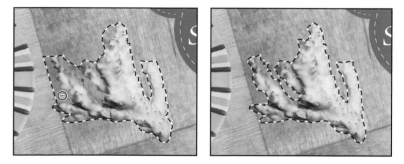

5 Click Refine Edge in the options bar.

The Refine Edge dialog box contains options to improve the selection edges by softening, feathering, or expanding them, or increasing their contrast. You can also view the selection edges as if masked or against various backgrounds.

6 To prepare the edge for a drop shadow, set Smooth to **24**, Feather to **0.5**, Contrast to **12**, and Shift Edge to **-21**.

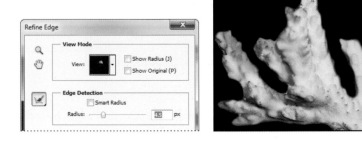

7 Select the Zoom tool in the dialog box, and then drag it across the piece of coral to zoom in on its edges.

You'll preview the shadow that you'll add to the coral against one of the mattes.

8 In the View Mode area of the dialog box, click the arrow next to the small preview, and then choose On Black from the pop-up menu. A black background appears under the selection, and the selection edges disappear. You can choose the other options to see the edges against different backgrounds.

9 Increase the Radius value to add more of a shadow around the coral edges. We used a value of 4.5 pixels.

You've gone to a lot of work to make and refine your selection. Now, so that you don't lose it, you'll save it to a new layer.

10 When you're satisfied with the adjustments, choose New Layer from the Output To menu, and then click OK.

11 In the Layers panel, double-click the new layer's name, and rename it **Coral.**

12 In the Layers panel, click the eye icon next to the Background layer to make it visible.

> ▶ **Tip:** You'll learn other ways to save selections in Lesson 6, "Masks and Channels."

Isolating and saving selections

You'll save selections of the other elements in the composition, as well. That way, your selections remain intact and easily available for editing.

1 Zoom out or scroll across the image so that you can see the nautilus shell.

2 In the Layers panel, select the Background layer.

3 Use the Quick Selection tool (📷) to select the nautilus. Increase the brush size to select it more quickly. Remember that you can add or subtract from the selection using the buttons in the options bar.

4 Choose Edit > Copy, and then choose Edit > Paste to paste a copy of the nautilus shell onto a new layer. In the Layers panel, double-click the new layer's name, and rename it **Nautilus**.

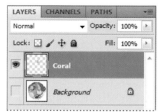

5 Repeat steps 1–4 for the bowl of shells, mussel, sand dollar, and Sally's Seashells logo, naming their new layers **Bowl**, **Mussel, Sand Dollar**, and **Logo**, respectively.

6 Choose File > Save.

It's good to save your selections on discrete layers—especially when you've spent time and effort creating them—so that you can easily retrieve them.

Creating a soft drop shadow

To complete your composition, you'll add a drop shadow behind the shells and logo. Adding the drop shadow is a simple matter of adding a layer effect.

1 In the Layers panel, select the Mussel layer.

2 At the bottom of the Layers panel, click the Add A Layer Style button (*fx*), and choose Drop Shadow from the pop-up menu.

3 In the Layer Styles dialog box, adjust the shadow settings to add a soft shadow. We used these values: Blend mode: Multiply, Opacity: **45%**, Angle: **30**, Distance: **5** px, Spread **3**%, Size: **30** px. Then click OK.

The mussel now has a soft drop shadow.

To replicate this shadow for the rest of the shells and the Sally's Seashells logo, you'll simply copy the effect to their layers.

4 In the Layers panel, position the pointer on the Drop Shadow layer effect beneath the Mussel thumbnail (the pointer turns into a pointing hand).

5 Hold down Alt (Windows) or Option (Mac OS), and drag the effect up to the Coral layer to copy it.

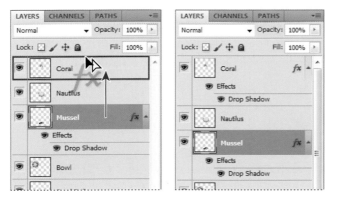

There you have it! You've copied the drop shadow.

6 Repeat step 5, Alt-dragging (Windows) or Option-dragging (Mac OS) the Drop Shadow effect onto each of the other layers except the Background layer.

7 Choose File > Save to save your work.

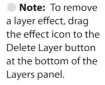

Note: To remove a layer effect, drag the effect icon to the Delete Layer button at the bottom of the Layers panel.

You've used several different selection tools to move all the seashells into place. The collage is complete!

Separating portions of an image onto different layers

To quickly create multiple images from one scan, use the Crop And Straighten Photos command. Images with a clearly delineated outline and a uniform background—such as the 03Start.psd file—work best. To try it, open the 03Start.psd file in the Lesson03 folder, and choose File > Automate > Crop And Straighten Photos. Photoshop automatically crops each image in the start file and creates individual Photoshop files for each. You can close each file without saving.

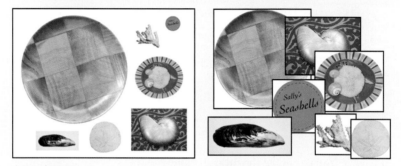

Original image   *Result*

Review questions

1 Once you've made a selection, what area of the image can be edited?

2 How do you add to and subtract from a selection?

3 How can you move a selection while you're drawing it?

4 When drawing a selection with the Lasso tool, how should you finish drawing the selection to ensure it's the shape you want?

5 What does the Quick Selection tool do?

6 How does the Magic Wand tool determine which areas of an image to select? What is tolerance, and how does it affect a selection?

Review answers

1 Only the area within an active selection can be edited.

2 To add to a selection, click the Add To Selection button in the options bar, and then click the area you want to add. To subtract from a selection, click the Subtract From Selection button in the options bar, and then click the area you want to subtract. You can also add to a selection by pressing Shift as you drag or click; to subtract, press Alt (Windows) or Option (Mac OS) as you drag or click.

3 To reposition a selection, without releasing the mouse button, hold down the spacebar and drag.

4 To make sure that the selection is the shape you want when you use the Lasso tool, end the selection by dragging across the starting point of the selection. If you start and stop the selection at different points, Photoshop draws a straight line between the start point of the selection and the end point of the selection.

5 The Quick Selection tool expands outward from where you click to automatically find and follow defined edges in the image.

6 The Magic Wand tool selects adjacent pixels based on their similarity in color. The Tolerance setting determines how many color tones the Magic Wand tool will select. The higher the tolerance setting, the more tones are selected.

4 LAYER BASICS

Lesson overview

In this lesson, you'll learn how to do the following:

- Organize artwork on layers.

- Create, view, hide, and select layers.

- Rearrange layers to change the stacking order of artwork.

- Apply blending modes to layers.

- Resize and rotate layers.

- Apply a gradient to a layer.

- Apply a filter to a layer.

- Add text and layer effects to a layer.

- Save a copy of the file with the layers flattened.

This lesson will take less than an hour to complete. Copy the Lesson04 folder onto your hard drive if you haven't already done so. As you work on this lesson, you'll preserve the start files. If you need to restore the start files, copy them from the *Adobe Photoshop CS5 Classroom in a Book* DVD.

Adobe Photoshop lets you isolate different parts of an image on *layers*. Each layer can then be edited as discrete artwork, allowing tremendous flexibility in composing and revising an image.

About layers

Every Photoshop file contains one or more *layers*. New files are generally created with a *background layer*, which contains a color or an image that shows through the transparent areas of subsequent layers. All new layers in an image are transparent until you add text or artwork (pixel values).

Working with layers is analogous to placing portions of a drawing on clear sheets of film, such as those viewed with an overhead projector: Individual sheets may be edited, repositioned, and deleted without affecting the other sheets. When the sheets are stacked, the entire composition is visible.

Getting started

You'll start the lesson by viewing an image of the final composition.

1 Start Photoshop, and then immediately hold down Ctrl+Alt+Shift (Windows) or Command+Option+Shift (Mac OS) to restore the default preferences. (See "Restoring default preferences" on page 5.)

2 When prompted, click Yes to delete the Adobe Photoshop Settings file.

3 In the Application bar, click the Launch Mini Bridge button to open the Mini Bridge panel.

4 In the Mini Bridge panel, click Browse Files.

5 In the Favorites panel, click the Lessons folder. Then, double-click the Lesson04 folder in the Content panel, and select the 04End.psd file. Press the spacebar for a full-screen view.

This layered composite represents a postcard. You will create it now, and, in doing so, learn how to create, edit, and manage layers.

6 Press the spacebar again to return to the Mini Bridge panel, and then double-click the 04Start.psd file to open it in Photoshop.

7 Choose File > Save As, rename the file **04Working.psd**, and click Save. Click OK if you see the Photoshop Format Options dialog box.

Saving another version of the start file frees you to make changes without worrying about overwriting the original.

Using the Layers panel

The Layers panel lists all the layers in an image, displaying the layer names and thumbnails of the content on each layer. You can use the Layers panel to hide, view, reposition, delete, rename, and merge layers. The layer thumbnails are automatically updated as you edit the layers.

1   If the Layers panel is not visible in the work area, choose Window > Layers.

The Layers panel lists five layers for the 04Working.psd file (from top to bottom): Postage, HAWAII, Flower, Pineapple, and Background.

2   Select the Background layer to make it active (if it's not already selected). Notice the layer thumbnail and the icons on the Background layer level:

- The lock icon (🔒) indicates that the layer is protected.

- The eye icon (👁) indicates that the layer is visible in the image window. If you click the eye, the image window no longer displays that layer.

The first task for this project is to add a photo of the beach to the postcard. First, you'll open the beach image in Photoshop.

▶ **Tip:** Use the context menu to hide or resize the layer thumbnail. Right-click (Windows) or Control-click (Mac OS) a thumbnail in the Layers panel to open the context menu, and then select No Thumbnails, Small Thumbnails, Medium Thumbnails, or Large Thumbnails.

3 In the Mini Bridge panel, double-click the Beach.psd file in the Lesson04 folder to open it in Photoshop.

The Layers panel changes to display the layer information for the active Beach.psd file. Notice that only one layer appears in the Beach.psd image: Layer 1, not Background. (For more information, see the sidebar, "About the background layer.")

About the background layer

When you create a new image with a white or colored background, the bottom layer in the Layers panel is named Background. An image can have only one background. You cannot change the stacking order of a background layer, its blending mode, or its opacity. You can, however, convert a background layer to a regular layer.

When you create a new image with transparent content, the image doesn't have a background layer. The bottom layer isn't constrained like the background layer; you can move it anywhere in the Layers panel, and change its opacity and blending mode.

To convert a background layer into a regular layer:

1 Double-click the name Background in the Layers panel, or choose Layer > New > Layer From Background.

2 Rename the layer, and set any other layer options.

3 Click OK.

To convert a regular layer into a background layer:

1 Select a layer in the Layers panel.

2 Choose Layer > New > Background From Layer.

● **Note:** To create a background layer from a regular layer, you must use the Background From Layer command; you can't create a background layer simply by renaming a regular layer Background.

Renaming and copying a layer

To add content to an image and create a new layer for it simultaneously, drag an object or layer from one file into the image window of another file. Whether you drag from the image window of the original file or from its Layers panel, only the active layer is reproduced in the destination file.

You'll drag the Beach.psd image onto the 04Working.psd file. Before you begin, make sure that both the 04Working.psd and Beach.psd files are open, and that the Beach.psd file is selected.

First, you'll give Layer 1 a more descriptive name.

1 In the Layers panel, double-click the name Layer 1, type **Beach**, and then press Enter or Return. Keep the layer selected.

2 Click the Arrange Documents button (▦) in the Application bar, and then select one of the 2 Up layouts. Photoshop displays both of the open image files. Select the Beach.psd image so that it is the active file.

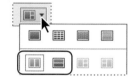

3 Select the Move tool (▶⊹), and use it to drag the Beach.psd image onto the 04Working.psd image window.

The Beach layer now appears in the 04Working.psd file image window and its Layers panel, between the Background and Pineapple layers. Photoshop always adds new layers directly above the selected layer; you selected the Background layer earlier.

Tip: If you hold down Shift as you drag an image from one file into another, the dragged image automatically centers itself in the target image window.

4   Close the Beach.psd file without saving changes to it.

Viewing individual layers

The 04Working.psd file now contains six layers. Some of the layers are visible and some are hidden. The eye icon (👁) next to a layer thumbnail in the Layers panel indicates that the layer is visible.

1   Click the eye icon (👁) next to the Pineapple layer to hide the image of the pineapple.

You can hide or show a layer by clicking this icon or clicking in its column—also called the Show/Hide Visibility column.

2 Click again in the Show/Hide Visibility column to display the pineapple.

Adding a border to a layer

Now you'll add a white border around the Beach layer to create the impression that it's a photograph.

1 Select the Beach layer. (To select the layer, click the layer name in the Layers panel.)

The layer is highlighted, indicating that it is active. Changes you make in the image window affect the active layer.

2 To make the opaque areas on this layer more obvious, hide all layers except the Beach layer: Press Alt (Windows) or Option (Mac OS) as you click the eye icon (👁) next to the Beach layer.

The white background and other objects in the image disappear, leaving only the beach image against a checkerboard background. The checkerboard indicates transparent areas of the active layer.

3 Choose Layer > Layer Style > Stroke.

The Layer Style dialog box opens. Now you'll select the options for the white stroke around the beach image.

4 Specify the following settings:

- Size: **5** px

- Position: Inside

- Blend Mode: Normal

- Opacity: **100**%

- Color: White (Click the Color box, and select white in the Color Picker.)

5 Click OK. A white border appears around the beach photo.

Rearranging layers

The order in which the layers of an image are organized is called the *stacking order*. The stacking order determines how the image is viewed—you can change the order to make certain parts of the image appear in front of or behind other layers.

You'll rearrange the layers so that the beach image is in front of another image that is currently hidden in the file.

1   Make the Postage, HAWAII, Flower, Pineapple and Background layers visible by clicking the Show/Hide Visibility column next to their layer names.

The beach image is almost entirely blocked by images on other layers.

2   In the Layers panel, drag the Beach layer up so that it is positioned between the Pineapple and Flower layers—when you've positioned it correctly, you'll see a thick line between the layers in the panel—and then release the mouse button.

The Beach layer moves up one level in the stacking order, and the beach image appears on top of the pineapple and background images, but under the flower and "HAWAII."

▶ **Tip:** You can also control the stacking order of layered images by selecting them in the Layers panel and choosing Layer > Arrange, and then choosing Bring To Front, Bring Forward, Send To Back, or Send Backward.

Changing the opacity of a layer

You can reduce the opacity of any layer to let other layers show through it. In this case, the postmark is too dark on the flower. You'll edit the opacity of the Postage layer to let the flower and other images show through.

1   Select the Postage layer, and then click the arrow next to the Opacity box to display the Opacity slider. Drag the slider to **25**%. You can also type the value in the Opacity box or scrub the Opacity label.

The Postage layer becomes partially transparent, so you can see the other layers underneath. Notice that the change in opacity affects only the image area of the Postage layer. The Pineapple, Beach, Flower and HAWAII layers remain opaque.

2   Choose File > Save to save your work.

Duplicating a layer and changing the blending mode

You can also apply different blending modes to a layer. *Blending modes* affect how the color pixels on one layer blend with pixels in the layers underneath. First you'll use blending modes to increase the intensity of the image on the Pineapple layer so that it doesn't look so dull. Then you'll change the blending mode on the Postage layer. (Currently, the blending mode for both layers is Normal.)

1   Click the eye icons next to the HAWAII, Flower, and Beach layers to hide them.

2   Right-click or Control-click the Pineapple layer, and choose Duplicate Layer from the context menu. (Make sure you click the layer name, not its thumbnail, or you'll see the wrong context menu.) Click OK in the Duplicate Layer dialog box.

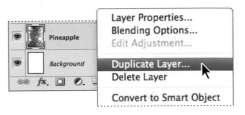

A layer called "Pineapple copy" appears above the Pineapple layer in the Layers panel.

3 With the Pineapple copy layer selected, choose Overlay from the Blending Modes menu in the Layers panel.

The Overlay blending mode blends the Pineapple copy layer with the Pineapple layer beneath it to create a vibrant, more colorful pineapple with deeper shadows and brighter highlights.

4 Select the Postage layer, and choose Multiply from the Blending Modes menu. The Multiply blending mode multiplies the colors in the underlying layers with the color in the top layer. In this case, the postmark becomes a little stronger.

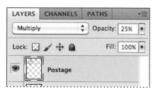

5 Choose File > Save to save your work.

▶ **Tip:** For more about blending modes, including definitions and visual examples, see Photoshop Help.

Resizing and rotating layers

You can resize and transform layers.

1 Click the Visibility column on the Beach layer to make it visible.

2 Select the Beach layer in the Layers panel, and then choose Edit > Free Transform. A Transform bounding box appears around the beach image. The bounding box has handles on each corner and each side.

First, you'll resize and angle the layer.

3 Press Shift as you drag a corner handle inward to scale the beach photo down by about 50%. (Watch the Width and Height percentages in the options bar.)

4 With the bounding box still active, position the pointer just outside one of the corner handles until it becomes a curved double arrow. Drag clockwise to rotate the beach image approximately 15 degrees. You can also enter **15** in the Set Rotation box in the options bar.

5 Click the Commit Transform button (✔) in the options bar.

6 Make the Flower layer visible. Then, select the Move tool (▸⊹), and drag the beach photo so that its corner is tucked neatly beneath the flower, as in the illustration.

7 Choose File > Save.

Using a filter to create artwork

Next, you'll create a new layer with no artwork on it. (Adding empty layers to a file is comparable to adding blank sheets of acetate to a stack of images.) You'll use this layer to add realistic-looking clouds to the sky with a Photoshop filter.

1 In the Layers panel, select the Background layer to make it active, and then click the New Layer button (⊟) at the bottom of the Layers panel.

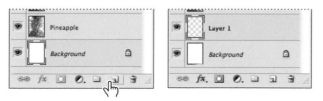

A new layer, named Layer 1, appears between the Background and Pineapple layers. The layer has no content, so it has no effect on the image.

2 Double-click the name Layer 1, type **Clouds**, and press Enter or Return to rename the layer.

3 In the Tools panel, click the Foreground Color swatch, select a sky blue color from the Color Picker, and click OK. We selected a color with the following values: R 48, G 138, and B 174. The Background Color remains white.

● **Note:** You can also create a new layer by choosing Layer > New > Layer, or by choosing New Layer from the Layers panel menu.

4 With the Clouds layer still active, choose Filter > Render > Clouds. Realistic-looking clouds appear behind the image.

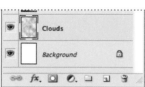

5 Choose File > Save.

Dragging to add a new layer

You can add a layer to an image by dragging an image file from the desktop, Bridge, or Explorer (Windows) or the Finder (Mac OS). You'll add another flower to the postcard now.

1 If Photoshop fills your monitor, reduce the size of the Photoshop window:

- In Windows, click the Maximize/Restore button (▣) in the upper-right corner, and then drag the lower-right corner of the Photoshop window to make it smaller.

- In Mac OS, click the green Maximize/Restore button (◉) in the upper-left corner of the image window.

2 In Photoshop, select the Pineapple copy layer in the Layers panel to make it the active layer.

3 In Explorer (Windows) or the Finder (Mac OS), navigate to the Lessons folder you copied from the Classroom in a Book DVD. Then navigate to the Lesson04 folder.

4 Select Flower2.psd, and drag it from Explorer or the Finder onto your image.

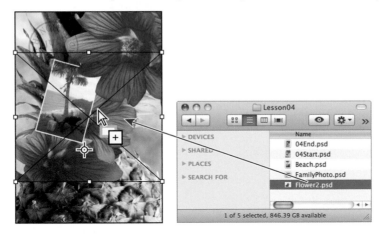

The Flower2 layer appears in the Layers panel, directly above the Pineapple copy layer. Photoshop places the image as a Smart Object, which is a layer you can edit without making permanent changes. You'll work with Smart Objects in Lessons 5 and 8.

5 Position the Flower2 layer in the lower-left corner of the postcard, so that about half of the flower is visible.

6 Click the Commit button (✔) in the options bar to accept the new layer.

Adding text

Now you're ready to create some type using the Horizontal Type tool, which places the text on its own type layer. You'll then edit the text and apply a special effect.

1 Make the HAWAII layer visible. You'll add text just below this layer, and apply special effects to both layers.

2 Choose Select > Deselect Layers, so that no layers are selected.

3 Click the Foreground Color swatch in the Tools panel, and then select a shade of grassy green in the Color Picker. Click OK to close the Color Picker.

4 In the Tools panel, select the Horizontal Type tool (T). Then, choose Window > Character to open the Character panel. Do the following in the Character panel:

- Select a serif font (we used Birch Std).

- Select a font style (we used Regular).

- Select a large font size (we used 36 points).

- Select Crisp from the Anti-aliasing menu (ᵃa).

- Select a large tracking value (ᴬⱽ) (we used 250).

- Click the All Caps button (TT).

- Click the Faux Bold button (T).

● **Note:** If you make a mistake when you click to set the type, simply click away from the type and repeat step 5.

5 Click just below the "H" in the word *HAWAII*, and type **Island Paradise**. Then click the Commit Any Current Edits button (✔) in the options bar.

The Layers panel now includes a layer named Island Paradise with a "T" thumbnail, indicating that it is a type layer. This layer is at the top of the layer stack.

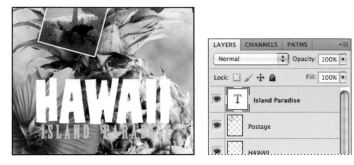

The text appears where you clicked, which probably isn't exactly where you want it to be positioned.

6 Select the Move tool (►⊕), and drag the "Island Paradise" text so that it is centered below HAWAII.

Applying a gradient to a layer

You can apply a color gradient to all or part of a layer. In this example, you'll apply a gradient to the HAWAII type to make it more colorful. First, you'll select the letters, and then you'll apply the gradient.

1 Select the HAWAII layer in the Layers panel to make it active.

2 Right-click or Control-click the thumbnail in the HAWAII layer, and choose Select Pixels. Everything on the HAWAII layer (the white lettering) is selected.

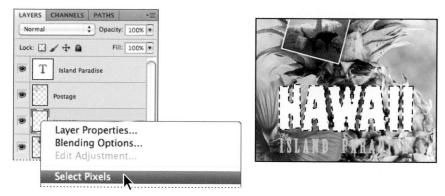

Now that you've selected the area to fill, you'll apply a gradient.

3 In the Tools panel, select the Gradient tool (▥).

4 Click the Foreground Color swatch in the Tools panel, select a bright color of orange in the Color Picker, and click OK. The Background Color should still be white.

5 In the options bar, make sure that Linear Gradient (▥) is selected.

6 In the options bar, click the arrow next to the Gradient Editor box to open the gradient picker. Select the Foreground To Background swatch (it's the first one), and then click anywhere outside the gradient picker to close it.

7 With the selection still active, drag the Gradient tool from the bottom to the top of the letters. If you want to be sure you drag straight up, press the Shift key as you drag.

▶ **Tip:** To list the gradient options by name rather than by sample, click the gradient picker menu button, and choose either Small List or Large List. Or, hover the pointer over a thumbnail until a tool tip appears, showing the gradient name.

The gradient extends across the type, starting with orange at the bottom and gradually blending to white at the top.

8 Choose Select > Deselect to deselect the HAWAII type.

9 Save the work you've done so far.

Applying a layer style

You can enhance a layer by adding a shadow, stroke, satin sheen, or other special effect from a collection of automated and editable layer styles. These styles are easy to apply and link directly to the layer you specify.

Like layers, layer styles can be hidden by clicking eye icons (👁) in the Layers panel. Layer styles are nondestructive, so you can edit or remove them at any time. You can apply a copy of a layer style to a different layer by dragging the effect onto the destination layer.

Earlier, you used a layer style to add a stroke to the beach photo. Now, you'll add drop shadows to the text to make it stand out.

▶ **Tip:** You can also open the Layer Style dialog box by clicking the Add A Layer Style button at the bottom of the Layers panel and then choosing a layer style, such as Bevel And Emboss, from the pop-up menu.

1   Select the Island Paradise layer, and then choose Layer > Layer Style > Drop Shadow.

2   In the Layer Style dialog box, make sure that the Preview option is selected, and then, if necessary, move the dialog box so that you can see the Island Paradise text in the image window.

3   In the Structure area, select Use Global Light, and then specify the following settings:

- Blend Mode: Multiply
- Opacity: **75%**
- Angle: **78** degrees
- Distance: **5** px
- Spread: **30%**
- Size: **10** px

Photoshop adds a drop shadow to the "Island Paradise" text in the image.

4   Click OK to accept the settings and close the Layer Style dialog box.

Photoshop nests the layer style in the Island Paradise layer. First it lists Effects, and then the layer styles applied to the layer. An eye icon (👁) appears next to the effect category and next to each effect. To turn off an effect, click the eye icon. Click the visibility column again to restore the effect. To hide all layer styles, click the eye icon next to Effects. To collapse the list of effects, click the arrow next to the layer.

5   Make sure that eye icons appear for both items nested in the Island Paradise layer.

6   Press Alt (Windows) or Option (Mac OS) and drag the Effects line down onto the HAWAII layer. The Drop Shadow layer style is applied to the HAWAII layer, using the same settings you applied to the Island Paradise layer.

Now you'll add a green stroke around the word HAWAII.

7   Select the HAWAII layer in the Layers panel, click the Add A Layer Style button (*fx*) at the bottom of the panel, and choose Stroke from the pop-up menu.

8   In the Structure area of the Layer Styles dialog box, specify the following settings:

- Size: **4** px

- Position: Outside

- Blend Mode: Normal

- Opacity: **100**%

- Color: Green (Select a shade that goes well with the one you used for the "Island Paradise" text.)

9 Click OK to apply the stroke.

Now you'll add a drop shadow and a satin sheen to the flower.

10 Select the Flower layer, and choose Layer > Layer Style > Drop Shadow. Then change the following settings in the Structure area: Opacity: **60**%, Distance: **13** px, Spread: **9**%. Make sure Use Global Light is selected, and that the Blend Mode is Multiply. Do not click OK.

11 With the Layer Style dialog box still open, select Satin on the left. Then make sure Invert is selected, and apply the following settings:

- Color (next to Blend Mode): Fuchsia (choose a color that complements the flower color)

- Opacity: **20**%

- Distance: **22** px

12 Click OK to apply both layer styles.

Updating layer effects

Layer effects are automatically updated when you make changes to a layer. You can edit the text and watch how the layer effect tracks the change.

1 Select the Island Paradise layer in the Layers panel.

2 In the Tools panel, select the Horizontal Type tool (T).

3 In the options bar, set the font size to **32** points, and press Enter or Return.

Although you didn't select the text by dragging the Type tool (as you would have to do in a word-processing program), "Island Paradise" now appears in 32-point type.

4 Using the Horizontal Type tool, click between "Island" and "Paradise," and type **of**.

As you edit the text, the layer styles are applied to the new text.

5 You don't actually need the word "of," so delete it.

6 Select the Move tool (⊕) and drag "Island Paradise" to center it beneath the word "HAWAII."

● **Note:** You don't have to click the Commit Any Current Edits button after making any text edits, because selecting the Move tool has the same effect.

7 Choose File > Save.

Adding a border

The Hawaii postcard is nearly done. The elements are almost all arranged correctly in the composition. You'll finish up by positioning the postmark and then adding a white postcard border.

1 Select the Postage layer, and then use the Move tool (⊕) to drag it to the middle-right of the image, as in the illustration.

2 Select the Island Paradise layer in the Layers panel, and then click the Create A New Layer button (⬛) at the bottom of the panel.

3 Choose Select > All.

4 Choose Select > Modify > Border. In the Border Selection dialog box, type **10** pixels for the Width, and click OK.

Border Selection
Width: 10 pixels   OK   Cancel

A 10-pixel border is selected around the entire image. Now, you'll fill it with white.

5 Select white for the Foreground Color, and then choose Edit > Fill.

6 In the Fill dialog box, select Foreground Color, and click OK.

7 Choose Select > Deselect.

Fill

Contents
Use: Foreground Color   OK   Cancel
Custom Pattern:

Blending
Mode: Normal
Opacity: 100 %
☐ Preserve Transparency

8 Double-click the Layer 1 name in the Layers panel, and rename the layer **Border.**

LAYERS   CHANNELS   PATHS

Normal   Opacity: 100%

Lock: ☒ ✏ ✛ 🔒   Fill: 100%

👁   Border

👁   T   Island Paradise   *fx*

Flattening and saving files

When you finish editing all the layers in your image, you can merge or *flatten* layers to reduce the file size. Flattening combines all the layers into a single background layer. However, you cannot edit layers once you've flattened them, so you shouldn't flatten an image until you are certain that you're satisfied with all your design decisions. Rather than flattening your original PSD files, it's a good idea to save a copy of the file with its layers intact, in case you need to edit a layer later.

To appreciate what flattening does, notice the two numbers for the file size in the status bar at the bottom of the image window.

● **Note:** If the sizes do not appear in the status bar, click the status bar pop-up menu arrow and choose Show > Document Sizes.

The first number represents what the file size would be if you flattened the image. The second number represents the file size without flattening. This lesson file, if flattened, would be about 2.29 MB, but the current file is actually much larger—about 29 MB. So flattening is well worth it in this case.

1 Select any tool but the Type tool (T), to be sure that you're not in text-editing mode. Then choose File > Save (if it is available) to be sure that all your changes have been saved in the file.

2 Choose Image > Duplicate.

3 In the Duplicate Image dialog box, name the file **04Flat.psd**, and click OK.

4 Leave the 04Flat.psd file open, but close the 04Working.psd file.

5 Choose Flatten Image from the Layers panel menu.

Only one layer, named Background, remains in the Layers panel.

6 Choose File > Save. Even though you chose Save rather than Save As, the Save As dialog box appears.

7 Make sure the location is the Lessons/Lesson04 folder, and then click Save to accept the default settings and save the flattened file.

You have saved two versions of the file: a one-layer, flattened copy as well as the original file, in which all the layers remain intact.

▶ **Tip:** If you want to flatten only some of the layers in a file, click the eye icons to hide the layers you don't want to flatten, and then choose Merge Visible from the Layers panel menu.

About layer comps

Layer comps provide one-click flexibility in switching between different views of a multilayered image file. A layer comp is simply a definition of the settings in the Layers panel. Once you've defined a layer comp, you can change as many settings as you please in the Layers panel and then create another layer comp to preserve that configuration of layer properties. Then, by switching from one layer comp to another, you can quickly review the two designs. The beauty of layer comps becomes apparent when you want to demonstrate a number of possible design arrangements. When you've created a few layer comps, you can review the design variations without having to tediously select and deselect eye icons or change settings in the Layers panel.

Say, for example, that you are designing a brochure, and you're producing a version in English as well as in French. You might have the French text on one layer, and the English text on another in the same image file. To create two different layer comps, you would simply turn on visibility for the French layer and turn off visibility for the English layer, and then click the Create New Layer Comp button on the Layer Comps panel. Then you'd do the inverse—turn on visibility for the English layer and turn off visibility for the French layer, and click the create New Layer Comp button—to create an English layer comp.

To view the different layer comps, you click the Apply Layer Comp box for each comp in the Layer Comps panel to view them in turn. With a little imagination, you can appreciate how much time this saves for more complex variations. Layer comps can be an especially valuable feature when the design is in flux or when you need to create multiple versions of the same image file.

You've created a colorful, attractive postcard. This lesson only begins to explore the vast possibilities and the flexibility you gain when you master the art of using Photoshop layers. You'll get more experience and try out different techniques for layers in almost every chapter as you move forward in the book, and especially in Lesson 9, "Advanced Layering."

Extra Credit

Take the blinking and bad poses out of an otherwise great family portrait with the Auto-Align Layers feature.

1 Open FamilyPhoto.psd in your Lesson04 folder.

2 In the Layers panel, turn Layer 2 on and off to see the two similar photos. When both layers are visible, Layer 2 shows the tall man in the center blinking, and the two girls in the front looking away.

You'll align the two photos, and then use the Eraser tool to brush out the parts of the photo on Layer 2 that you want to improve.

3 Make both layers visible, and Shift-click to select them. Choose Edit > Auto-Align Layers; click OK to accept the default Auto position. Now click the eye icon next to Layer 2 off and on to see that the layers are perfectly aligned.

Now for the fun part! You'll brush out the photo where you want to improve it.

4 Select the Eraser tool in the Tools panel, and pick a soft, 45-pixel brush in the options bar. Select Layer 2, and start brushing in the center of the blinking man's head to reveal the smiling face below.

Continues on next page

Continued from previous page

5 Use the Eraser tool on the two girls looking away,
revealing the image below, where they look into the camera.

You've created a natural family snapshot.

Review questions

1 What is the advantage of using layers?

2 When you create a new layer, where does it appear in the Layers panel stack?

3 How can you make artwork on one layer appear in front of artwork on another layer?

4 How can you apply a layer style?

5 When you've completed your artwork, what can you do to minimize the file size without changing the quality or dimensions?

Review answers

1 Layers let you move and edit different parts of an image as discrete objects. You can also hide individual layers as you work on other layers.

2 A new layer always appears immediately above the active layer.

3 You can make artwork on one layer appear in front of artwork on another layer by dragging layers up or down the stacking order in the Layers panel, or by using the Layer > Arrange subcommands—Bring To Front, Bring Forward, Send To Back, and Send Backward. However, you can't change the layer position of a background layer.

4 To apply a layer style, select the layer, and then click the Add A Layer Style button in the Layers panel, or choose Layer > Layer Style > [style].

5 To minimize file size, you can flatten the image, which merges all the layers onto a single background. It's a good idea to duplicate image files with layers intact before you flatten them, in case you have to make changes to a layer later.

5 CORRECTING AND ENHANCING DIGITAL PHOTOGRAPHS

Lesson overview

In this lesson, you'll learn how to do the following:

- Process a proprietary camera raw image and save your adjustments.

- Merge images of different exposures to create a high dynamic range (HDR) image.

- Make typical corrections to a digital photograph, including removing red eye and noise and bringing out shadow and highlights detail.

- Apply optical lens correction to an image.

- Align and blend two images to extend the depth of field.

- Adopt best practices for organizing, managing, and saving your images.

 This lesson will take about 1½ hours to complete. Copy the Lesson05 folder onto your hard drive if you haven't already done so. As you work on this lesson, you'll preserve the start files. If you need to restore the start files, copy them again from the *Adobe Photoshop CS5 Classroom in a Book* DVD.

Whether you have a collection of digital images amassed for clients or projects, or a personal collection that you want to refine, archive, and preserve for posterity, Photoshop has an array of tools for importing, editing, and archiving digital photographs.

Getting started

In this lesson, you'll edit several digital images using Photoshop and Adobe Camera Raw, which comes with Photoshop. You'll use a variety of techniques to touch up and improve the appearance of digital photographs. You'll start by viewing the before and after images in Adobe Bridge.

1 Start Photoshop, and then immediately hold down Ctrl+Alt+Shift (Windows) or Command+Option+Shift (Mac OS) to restore the default preferences. (See "Restoring default preferences" on page 5.)

2 When prompted, click Yes to delete the Adobe Photoshop Settings file.

3 Click the Launch Bridge button (▣) in the Application bar to open Adobe Bridge.

4 In the Favorites panel in Bridge, click the Lessons folder. Then, in the Content panel, double-click the Lesson05 folder to open it.

5 Adjust the thumbnail slider, if necessary, so that you can see the thumbnail previews clearly. Then look at the 05A_Start.crw and 05A_End.psd files.

05A_Start.crw   05A_End.psd

The original photograph of a Spanish-style church is a camera raw file, so it doesn't have the usual .psd file extension you've worked with so far in this book. It was shot with a Canon Digital Rebel camera and has the Canon proprietary .crw file extension instead. You'll process this proprietary camera raw image to make it brighter, sharper, and clearer, and then save it as a JPEG file for the web and as a PSD file so that you could work on it further in Photoshop.

6 Open the Model folder, and look at the three Camera Raw exposures (Model01.dng, Model02.dng, and Model03.dng). Compare them to the file outside the Model folder, called 05B_End.psd. You'll merge the three model exposures to create a new HDR image, and then perform color corrections and image enhancements in Photoshop to achieve the end result.

Model01.dng

05B_End.psd

7 Look at the 05C_Start.psd and 05C_End.psd thumbnail previews.

05C_Start.psd

05C_End.psd

You'll make several corrections to this portrait of a girl on the beach, including bringing out shadow and highlight detail, removing red eye, and sharpening the image.

8 Look at the 05D_Start.psd and 05D_End.psd thumbnail previews.

05D_Start.psd   05D_End.psd

The original image is distorted, with the columns appearing to be bowed. You'll correct the lens barrel distortion.

9 Look at the 05E_Start.psd and 05E_End.psd thumbnail previews.

05E_Start.psd   05E_End.psd

The first image has two layers. Depending on which layer is visible, either the glass in the foreground or the beach in the background is in focus. You'll extend the depth of field to make both clear.

About camera raw files

A *camera raw* file contains unprocessed picture data from a digital camera's image sensor. Many digital cameras can save images in camera raw format. The advantage of camera raw files is that they let the photographer—rather than the camera—interpret the image data and make adjustments and conversions. (In contrast, shooting JPEG images with your camera locks you into your camera's processing.) Because the camera doesn't do any image processing when you shoot a camera raw photo, you can use Adobe Camera Raw to set the white balance, tonal range, contrast, color saturation, and sharpening. Think of camera raw files as photo negatives. You can go back and reprocess the file any time you like to achieve the results you want.

To create camera raw files, set your digital camera to save files in its own, possibly proprietary, raw file format. When you download the file from your camera, it has a file extension such as .nef (from Nikon) or .crw (from Canon). In Bridge or Photoshop, you can process camera raw files from a myriad of supported digital cameras from Canon, Kodak, Leica, Nikon, and other makers—and even process multiple images simultaneously. You can then export the proprietary camera raw files to DNG, JPEG, TIFF, or PSD file format.

Note: The Photoshop Raw format (.raw extension) is a file format for transferring images between applications and computer platforms. Don't confuse Photoshop Raw with camera raw file formats.

You can process camera raw files obtained from supported cameras, but you can also open TIFF and JPEG images in Camera Raw, which includes some editing features that aren't in Photoshop. However, you won't have the same flexibility with white balance and other settings if you're using a TIFF or JPEG image. Although Camera Raw can open and edit a camera raw image file, it cannot save an image in camera raw format.

You used Camera Raw to edit the color and lighting in an image in Lesson 2. In this exercise, you'll take advantage of more of its features.

Processing files in Camera Raw

When you make adjustments to an image in Camera Raw, such as straightening or cropping the image, Photoshop and Bridge preserve the original file data. This way, you can edit the image as you desire, export the edited image, and keep the original intact for future use or other adjustments.

Opening images in Camera Raw

You can open Camera Raw from either Bridge or Photoshop, and you can apply the same edits to multiple files simultaneously. This is especially useful if you're working with images that were all shot in the same environment, and which therefore need the same lighting and other adjustments.

Camera Raw provides extensive controls for adjusting white balance, exposure, contrast, sharpness, tone curves, and much more. In this exercise, you'll edit one image and then apply the settings to similar images.

1 In Bridge, open the Lessons/Lesson05/Mission folder, which contains three shots of the Spanish church you previewed earlier.

2 Shift-click to select all of the images—Mission01.crw, Mission02.crw, and Mission03.crw—and then choose File > Open In Camera Raw.

A. Filmstrip
B. Toggle Filmstrip
C. Toolbar
D. Toggle Full-Screen Mode
E. RGB values
F. Image adjustment tabs
G. Histogram
H. Camera Raw Settings menu
I. Zoom levels
J. Click to display work-flow options
K. Multi-image navigation controls
L. Adjustment sliders

The Camera Raw dialog box displays a large preview of the first image, and a filmstrip down the left side displays all open images. The histogram in the upper-right corner shows the tonal range of the selected image; the workflow options link below the preview window displays the selected image's color space, bit depth, size, and resolution. Tools along the top of the dialog box let you zoom, pan, straighten, and make other adjustments to the image. Tabbed panels on the right side of the dialog box give you more nuanced options for adjusting the image: You can correct the white balance, adjust the tone, sharpen the image, remove noise, adjust color, and make other changes. You can also save settings as a preset, and then apply them later.

For the best results using Camera Raw, plan your workflow to move from left to right and top to bottom. That is, you'll often want to use the tools across the top first, and then move through the panels in order, making changes as necessary.

You will explore these controls now as you edit the first image file.

3 Click each thumbnail in the filmstrip to preview each image before you begin. Or, you can click the Forward button under the main preview window to cycle through the images. When you've seen all three images, select the Mission01.crw image again.

4 Make sure that Preview is selected at the top of the dialog box, so that you can see the effect of the adjustments you're about to make.

Adjusting white balance

An image's white balance reflects the lighting conditions under which it was captured. A digital camera records the white balance at the time of exposure; this is the value that initially appears in the Camera Raw dialog box image preview.

White balance comprises two components. The first is *temperature*, which is measured in kelvins and determines the level of "coolness" or "warmness" of the image—that is, its cool blue-green tones or warm yellow-red tones. The second component is *tint*, which compensates for magenta or green color casts in the image.

Depending on the settings you're using on your camera and the environment in which you're shooting (for example, if there's glare or uneven lighting), you may want to adjust the white balance for the image. If you plan to modify the white balance, make that the first thing you do, as it will affect all other changes in the image.

1 If the Basic panel isn't already displayed on the right side of the dialog box, click the Basic button (◉) to open it.

By default, As Shot is selected in the White Balance menu. Camera Raw applies the white balance settings that were in your camera at the time of exposure. You'll use the White Balance tool to change the temperature of the image.

2 Select the White Balance tool (✐) at the top of the Camera Raw dialog box.

To set an accurate white balance, select an object that should be white or gray. Camera Raw uses that information to determine the color of the light in which the scene was shot, and then adjusts for scene lighting automatically.

3 Click the white clouds in the image. The lighting of the image changes.

4 Click a different area of the clouds. The lighting shifts.

You can use the White Balance tool to find the best lighting for the scene quickly and easily. Clicking different areas changes the lighting without making any permanent changes to the file, so you can experiment freely.

Camera Raw also includes several White Balance presets, which you can use as a starting point to see different lighting effects.

5 In the Basics panel, choose different options from the White Balance menu, and observe how the lighting changes the image.

6 Choose Cloudy from the White Balance menu.

▶ **Tip:** To undo the settings, press Ctrl+Z (Windows) or Command+Z (Mac OS). To compare the changes you've made in the current panel with the original image, deselect Preview. Select Preview again to see the modified image.

The Cloudy preset suits this image, which was taken on a cloudy day.

Making tonal adjustments in Camera Raw

Other sliders in the Basic panel affect exposure, brightness, contrast, and saturation in the image. Exposure essentially defines the *white point*, or the lightest point of the image, so that Camera Raw adjusts everything else accordingly. Conversely, the Blacks slider sets the *black point*, or the darkest point in the image. The Fill Light slider increases detail in the shadows.

The Brightness slider determines how bright the image is, and the Contrast slider adjusts the contrast. For more nuanced contrast adjustments, you can use the Clarity slider, which adds depth to an image by increasing local contrast, especially on the midtones.

▶ **Tip:** For the best effect, increase the Clarity slider until you see halos near the edge details, and then reduce the setting slightly.

The Saturation slider adjusts the saturation of all colors in the image equally. The Vibrance slider, on the other hand, has a greater effect on undersaturated colors, so you can bring life to a background without oversaturating skin tones, for example.

You can use the Auto option to let Camera Raw attempt to correct the image tone, or you can select your own settings.

1   Click Auto in the Basic panel.

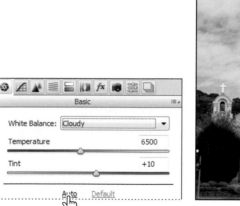

Camera Raw increases the saturation and decreases the blacks and the contrast. You could use this as a starting point. However, in this exercise, you'll return to the default settings and adjust them yourself.

2 Click Default in the Basic panel.

3 Change the sliders as follows:

- Increase Exposure to **+1.20**.
- Leave Brightness at **50**.
- Increase Contrast to **+29**.
- Decrease Clarity to **-75**.
- Decrease Saturation to **-5**.

These settings help pump up the midtones of the image, so that it looks bolder and more dimensional without being oversaturated. However, it's quite soft. You'll adjust the Clarity setting to sharpen it up a little bit.

4 Increase Clarity to **+25**.

About the Camera Raw histogram

The histogram in the upper-right corner of the Camera Raw dialog box simultaneously shows the red, green, and blue channels of the selected image, and it updates interactively as you adjust any settings. Also, as you move any tool over the preview image, the RGB values for the area under the cursor appear below the histogram.

Applying sharpening

Photoshop offers several sharpening filters, but when you need to sharpen an entire image, Camera Raw provides the best control. The sharpening controls are in the Detail panel. To see the effect of sharpening in the preview panel, you must view the image at 100% or greater.

1 Double-click the Zoom tool (🔍) on the left side of the toolbar to zoom in to 100%. Then select the Hand tool (✋), and pan the image to see the cross at the top of the mission tower.

2 Click the Detail tab (◭) to open the Detail panel.

The Amount slider determines how much sharpening Camera Raw applies. Typically, you'll want to exaggerate the amount of sharpening first, and then adjust it after you've set the other sliders.

3 Move the Amount slider to **100**.

The Radius slider determines the pixel area Camera Raw analyzes as it sharpens the image. For most images, you'll get the best results if you keep the radius low, even below one pixel, as a larger radius can begin to cause an unnatural look, almost like a watercolor.

4 Move the Radius slider to **0.9**.

The Detail slider determines how much detail you'll see. Even when this slider is set to 0, Camera Raw performs some sharpening. Typically, you'll want to keep the Detail setting relatively low.

5 Move the Detail slider to **25**, if it isn't already there.

▶ **Tip:** If you want to make an adjustment to only a specific part of an image, use the Adjustment Brush tool or the Graduated Filter tool. With the Adjustment Brush tool, you can apply Exposure, Brightness, Clarity, and other adjustments by "painting" them onto the photo. With the Graduated Filter tool, you can apply the same types of adjustments gradually across a region of a photo.

The Masking slider determines which parts of the image Camera Raw sharpens. When the Masking value is high, Camera Raw sharpens only those parts of the image that have strong edges.

Tip: Press Alt (Windows) or Option (Mac OS) as you move the Masking slider to see what Camera Raw will sharpen.

6 Move the Masking slider to **61**.

After you've adjusted the Radius, Detail, and Masking sliders, you can lower the Amount slider to finalize the sharpening.

7 Decrease the Amount slider to **50**.

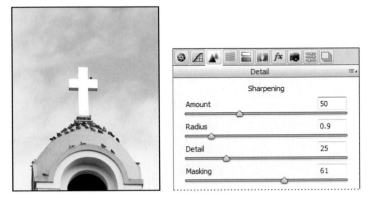

Note: If you zoom out, the image won't appear to be sharpened. You can preview sharpening effects only at zoom levels of 100% or greater.

Sharpening the image gives stronger definition to the details and edges. The Masking slider lets you target the sharpening effect to the lines in the image, so that artifacts don't appear in unfocused or background areas.

When you make adjustments in Camera Raw, the original file data is preserved. Your adjustment settings for the image are stored either in the Camera Raw database file or in "sidecar" XMP files that accompany the original image file in the same folder. These XMP files retain the adjustments you made in Camera Raw when you move the image file to a storage medium or another computer.

Synchronizing settings across images

All three of the mission images were shot at the same time under the same lighting conditions. Now that you've made the first one look stunning, you can automatically apply the same settings to the other two images. You do this using the Synchronize command.

1 In the upper-left corner of the Camera Raw dialog box, click Select All to select all of the images in the filmstrip.

2 Click the Synchronize button.

The Synchronize dialog box appears, listing all the settings you can apply to the images. By default, all options except Crop and Spot Removal are selected. You can accept the default for this project, even though you didn't change all the settings.

3 Click OK in the Synchronize dialog box.

When you synchronize the settings across all of the selected images, the thumbnails update to reflect the changes you made. To preview the images, click each thumbnail in the filmstrip.

Saving Camera Raw changes

You can save your changes in different ways for different purposes. First, you'll save the images with adjustments as low-resolution JPEG files that you can share on the web. Then, you'll save one image, Mission01, as a Photoshop file that you can continue to work with in Photoshop. You'll open the Mission01 image as a Smart Object in Photoshop so that you can return to Camera Raw at any time to make further adjustments.

1 Click Select All in the Camera Raw dialog box to select all three images.

2 Click Save Images in the lower-left corner.

3 In the Save Options dialog box, do the following:

- Choose Save In Same Location from the Destination menu.
- In the File Naming area, leave *Document Name* in the first box.
- Choose JPEG from the Format menu.

These settings will save your corrected images as smaller, downsampled JPEG files, which you can share with colleagues on the web. Your files will be named Mission01.jpg, Mission02.jpg, and Mission03.jpg.

4 Click Save.

● **Note:** Before sharing these images on the web, you would probably want to open them in Photoshop and resize them to 640 x 480 pixels. They are currently much larger, and most viewers would need to scroll to see the full-size images.

Bridge returns you to the Camera Raw dialog box, and indicates how many images have been processed until all the images have been saved. The CRW thumbnails still appear in the Camera Raw dialog box. In Bridge, however, you now also have JPEG versions as well as the original, unedited CRW image files, which you can continue to edit or leave for another time.

Now, you'll open a copy of the Mission01 image in Photoshop.

5 Select the Mission01.crw image thumbnail in the filmstrip in the Camera Raw dialog box. Then press the Shift key, and click Open Object at the bottom of the dialog box.

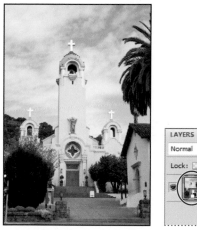

The Open Object button opens the image as a Smart Object in Photoshop, and you can return to Camera Raw to continue making adjustments at any time. If you click Open Image, the image opens as a standard Photoshop image. Pressing the Shift key changes the Open Image button to the Open Object button.

6 In Photoshop, choose File > Save As. In the Save As dialog box, choose Photoshop for the Format, rename the file **Mission_Final.psd**, navigate to the Lesson05 folder, and click Save. Click OK if a compatibility dialog box appears. Then close the file.

▶ **Tip:** To make the Open Object button the default, click the workflow options link (in blue) below the preview window, select Open In Photoshop As Smart Objects, and click OK.

About saving files in Camera Raw

Every camera model saves raw images in a unique format, but Adobe Camera Raw can process many raw file formats. Camera Raw processes the raw files with default image settings based on built-in camera profiles for supported cameras and the EXIF data.

You can save the proprietary files in DNG format (the format saved by Adobe Camera Raw), JPEG, TIFF, and PSD. All of these formats can be used to save RGB and CMYK continuous-tone, bitmapped images, and all of them except DNG are also available in the Photoshop Save and Save As dialog boxes.

- The *Adobe Digital Negative (DNG)* format contains raw image data from a digital camera and metadata that defines what the image data means. DNG is meant to be an industry-wide standard format for raw image data, helping photographers manage the variety of proprietary raw formats and providing a compatible archival format. (You can save this format only from the Camera Raw dialog box.)

- The *JPEG (Joint Photographic Experts Group)* file format is commonly used to display photographs and other continuous-tone RGB images on the web. Higher-resolution JPEG files may be used for other purposes, including high-quality printing. JPEG format retains all color information in an image, but compresses file size by selectively discarding data. The greater the compression, the lower the image quality.

- *TIFF (Tagged Image File Format)* is used to exchange files between applications and computer platforms. TIFF is a flexible format supported by virtually all paint, image-editing, and page layout applications. Also, virtually all desktop scanners can produce TIFF images.

- The *PSD format* is the Photoshop native file format. Because of the tight integration between Adobe products, other Adobe applications such as Adobe Illustrator and Adobe InDesign can directly import PSD files and preserve many Photoshop features.

Once you open a file in Photoshop, you can save it in many different formats, including Large Document Format (PSB), Cineon, Photoshop Raw, or PNG. Not to be confused with camera raw file formats, the Photoshop Raw format (RAW) is a file format for transferring images between applications and computer platforms.

For more information about file formats in Camera Raw and Photoshop, see Photoshop Help.

Merging exposures and applying advanced color correction

When you look at the world, your eyes adapt to different brightness levels, so that you can see the detail in shadows or highlights. Cameras and computer monitors, however, are more limited in the dynamic range (the ratio between dark and bright regions) they can reproduce. The ability to create high dynamic range (HDR) images in Photoshop lets you bring the brightness you can see in the real world into your images. HDR images are used mostly in movies, special effects, and other high-end photography. However, you can create an HDR image using multiple photographs, each captured at a different exposure, to bring the detail revealed in each shot into a single image.

You'll use the Merge to HDR Pro filter to combine three photos of a model, each taken at a different exposure. Then you'll use Levels, the Healing Brush tool, and other Photoshop features to further enhance the image.

Merging exposures into an HDR image

When a scene contains a more complex dynamic range than you can capture in one image, take three or more, and then merge them in Photoshop. In this exercise, you'll merge three images of the same model: one that was underexposed, one that was overexposed, and one with middle exposure.

1 In Photoshop, choose File > Automate > Merge To HDR Pro.

2 In the Merge To HDR Pro dialog box, click Browse. Then navigate to the Lesson05/Model folder, and Shift-select the Model01.dng, Model02.dng, and Model03.dng files. Click OK or Open.

3 Make sure Attempt To Automatically Align Source Images is selected, and then click OK.

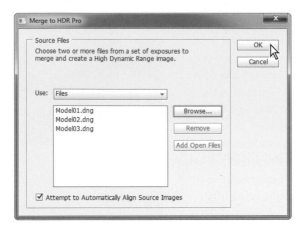

Photoshop opens each of the files briefly and merges them into a single image. That image appears in the Merge To HDR Pro dialog box, with default settings applied. The three images you merged are shown in the lower-left corner of the dialog box.

4 Adjust the following settings in the Merge To HDR Pro dialog box:

- In the Edge Glow area, move the Radius slider to **1** px and the Strength to **0.10**. These settings determine how a glow effect is applied.

- In the Tone And Detail area, change the Gamma to **2.64**, Exposure to **0.70**, Detail to **36**%, Shadow to **40**%, and Highlight to **-63**%. Each of these settings affects the overall tone of the image, and how much detail is revealed in shadows and highlights.

- In the Color area, change the Vibrance to **28**% and the Saturation to **24**% to adjust the color intensity.

These settings bring the background and the model's shirt to life. You'll enhance her face using other tools in Photoshop.

5 Click OK to accept the changes and close the Merge To HDR Pro dialog box.

6 Choose File > Save. Save the file as **05B_Working.psd** in the Lesson05 folder.

Adjusting levels

The tonal range of an image represents the amount of contrast, or detail, in the image and is determined by the image's distribution of pixels, ranging from the darkest pixels (black) to the lightest pixels (white). You were able to make most of the necessary changes to tone in the Merge To HDR Pro dialog box. You'll use a Levels adjustment layer to fine-tune the tonal range.

1 Click the Levels button (⛰) in the Adjustments panel.

Photoshop adds a Levels adjustment layer to the Layers panel. The Levels controls and a histogram appear in the Adjustments panel. The histogram displays the range of dark and light values in the image. The left (black) triangle represents the shadows; the right (white) triangle represents the highlights; and the middle (gray) triangle represents the midtones, or gamma. Unless you're aiming for a special effect, the ideal histogram has its black point at the beginning of the data and its white point at the end of the data, and the middle portion has fairly uniform peaks and valleys, representing adequate pixel data in the midtones.

2 Click the Calculate A More Accurate Histogram button (▨) on the left side of the histogram. Photoshop replaces the histogram.

There is a single line on the far left side of the histogram, representing the current black point, but the bulk of the data begins further to the right. You want to set the black point to match the beginning of that data.

3 Drag the left (black) triangle to the right to the point where the histogram indicates the darkest colors begin.

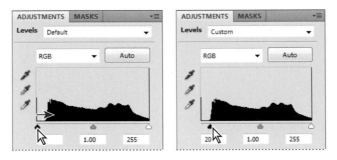

As you drag, the first Input Levels value (beneath the histogram graph) changes, and so does the image itself.

4 Pull the middle (gray) triangle a little bit to the left to slightly lighten the midtones. We moved it to a value of 1.18.

Using the Healing Brush tools to remove blemishes

Now you're ready to give the model's face some focused attention. You'll use the Healing Brush and Spot Healing Brush tools to heal blemishes and freckles, remove red veins from the eyes, and clear hair from the face.

1 In the Layers panel, select the Background layer. Then, choose Duplicate Layer from the Layers panel menu. Name the layer **Corrections**, and click OK.

Working on a duplicate layer preserves the original pixels so you can make changes later.

2   Zoom in on the model's face so that you can see it clearly. Zoom in to at least 100%.

3 Select the Spot Healing Brush tool (⌀).

4 In the options bar, select the following settings:

- Brush size: 7 px

- Mode: Normal

- Type: Content-Aware

5 With the Spot Healing Brush tool, brush out the hair across the face. Because you've selected Content-Aware in the options bar, the Spot Healing Brush tool replaces the hair with skin that is similar to that around it.

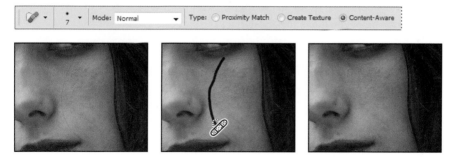

6 Paint over fine lines around the eyes and mouth. You can also brush away the red veins in the model's eyes, and freckles and spots on her face. Experiment with simply clicking, using very short strokes, and creating longer brush strokes. Remove obtrusive or distracting lines and blemishes, but leave enough that the face retains its character.

Now you'll use the Healing Brush tool to remove the darker makeup smudges under the model's eyes.

7 Select the Healing Brush tool (⌀). Select a brush with a size of **19** pixels and a hardness of **50**%.

8 Alt-click (Windows) or Option-click (Mac OS) an area just below the dark areas beneath her eyes to create the sampling source.

9 Brush beneath her eyes to remove the dark makeup. You're changing the color now. You'll smooth out the texture later.

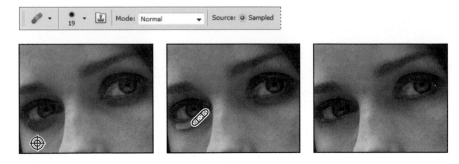

10 Choose File > Save to save your work so far.

Enhancing an image using the Dodge and Sponge tools

You'll use the Dodge tool to further lighten the color under the eyes so that it looks more natural. Then, you'll use the Sponge tool to saturate the eyes.

1 With the Corrections layer still active, select the Dodge tool (🔍).

2 In the options bar, change the brush size to **65** px and the Exposure to **30**%. Make sure Midtones is selected in the Range menu.

3 Brush the Dodge tool over the shadows under the eyes to lighten them.

4 Select the Sponge tool (🌑), hidden under the Dodge tool. In the options bar, make sure Vibrance is selected, and then select the following settings:

- Brush size: **35** px
- Brush hardness: **0**%
- Mode: Saturate
- Flow: **50**%

5 Move the Sponge tool over the irises in the eyes to increase their saturation.

6 Select the Dodge tool again, and select Shadows from the Range menu in the options bar.

7 Use the Dodge tool to lighten the eye shadow area above the eyes and the areas around the irises to bring out the color.

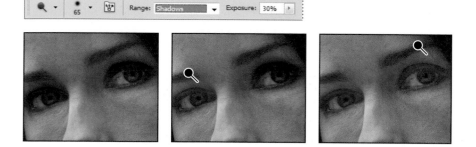

A photographer for more than 25 years, Jay Graham began his career designing and building custom homes. Today, Graham has clients in the advertising, architectural, editorial, and travel industries.

See Jay Graham's portfolio on the web at jaygraham.com.

Pro Photo Workflow

Good habits make all the difference

A sensible workflow and good work habits will keep you enthused about digital photography, help your images shine—and save you from the night terrors of losing work you never backed up. Here's an outline of the basic workflow for digital images from a professional photographer with more than 25 years' experience. To help you get the most from the images you shoot, Jay Graham offers guidelines for setting up your camera, creating a basic color workflow, selecting file formats, organizing images, and showing off your work.

Graham uses Adobe Lightroom® to organize thousands of images.

"The biggest complaint from people is they've lost their image. Where is it? What does it look like?" says Graham. "So naming is important."

Start out right by setting up your camera preferences

If your camera has the option, it's generally best to shoot in its camera raw file format, which captures all the image information you need. With one camera raw photo, says Graham, "You can go from daylight to an indoor tungsten image without degradation" when it's reproduced. If it makes more sense to shoot in JPEG for your project, use fine compression and high resolution.

Start with the best material

Get all the data when you capture—at fine compression and high resolution. You can't go back later.

Organize your files

Name and catalog your images as soon after downloading them as possible. "If the camera names files, eventually it resets and produces multiple files with the same name," says Graham. Use Adobe Lightroom to rename, rank, and add metadata to the photos you plan to keep; cull those you don't.

Graham names his files by date (and possibly subject). He would store a series of photos taken Dec. 12, 2006, at Stinson Beach in a folder named "20061212_Stinson_01"; within the folder, he names each image incrementally, and each image has a unique filename. "That way, it lines up on the hard drive real easily," he says. Follow Windows naming conventions to keep filenames usable on non-Macintosh platforms (32 characters maximum; only numbers, letters, underscores, and hyphens).

Convert raw images to Adobe Camera Raw

It may be best to convert all your camera raw images to the DNG format. Unlike many cameras' proprietary raw formats, this open-source format can be read by any device.

Keep a master image

Save your master in PSD, TIFF, or DNG format, not in JPEG. Each time a JPEG is re-edited and saved, compression is reapplied and the image quality degrades.

Show off to clients and friends

When you prepare your work for delivery, choose the appropriate color file for the destination. Convert the image to that profile, rather than assigning the profile. sRGB is generally best for viewing electronically or for printing from most online printing services. Adobe 1998 or Colormatch are the best profiles to use for RGB images destined for traditionally printed material such as brochures. Adobe 1998 or ProPhoto RGB are best for printing with inkjet printers. Use 72 dpi for electronic viewing and 180 dpi or higher for printing.

Back up your images

You've devoted a lot of time and effort to your images: don't lose them. Because the lifespan of CDs and DVDs is uncertain, it's best to back up to an external hard drive (or drives!), ideally set to back up automatically. "The question is not if your [internal] hard drive is going to crash," says Graham, reciting a common adage. "It's when."

Applying surface blur

You're almost done with the model. As a finishing touch, you'll apply the Surface Blur filter to give her a smooth appearance.

1   Select the Corrections layer, and choose Layer > Duplicate Layer. Name the layer **Surface Blur**, and click OK in the Duplicate Layer dialog box.

2   With the Surface Blur layer selected, choose Filter > Blur > Surface Blur.

3   In the Surface Blur dialog box, leave the Radius at 5 pixels, and move the Threshold to **10** levels. Then click OK.

The Surface Blur filter has left the model looking a little glassy. You'll reduce its effect by reducing its opacity.

4   With the Surface Blur layer selected, change the Opacity to **30%** in the Layers panel.

She looks more realistic now, but you can target the surface blur more precisely using the Eraser tool.

5 Select the Eraser tool. In the options bar, select a midsized brush between **10** and **50** pixels, with **10%** hardness. Set the Opacity to **90%**.

6 Brush over the eyes, eyebrows, the defining lines of the nose, and the teeth. You're erasing part of the blurred layer to let the sharper layer below show through in these areas.

7 Increase the brush size to 400 pixels, and then lightly sweep across the background, the shirt, and the hair to bring those areas back to their full sharpness. Now only the model's face has the surface blur.

8 Save your work, and close the image.

Correcting digital photographs in Photoshop

As you've seen, Photoshop provides many features to help you easily improve the quality of digital photographs. These include the ability to bring out details in the shadow and highlight areas of an image, gracefully remove red eye, reduce unwanted noise, and sharpen targeted areas of an image. To explore these capabilities, you will edit a different digital image now: a portrait of a girl on the beach.

Adjusting shadows and highlights

To bring out the detail in dark or light areas of an image, you can use the Shadows/Highlights command. Shadows/Highlights adjustments work best when the subject of the image is silhouetted against strong back-lighting or is washed out because the camera flash was too close. You can also use the adjustments to pull details from the shadows in an image that is otherwise well-lit.

1 Click the Launch Bridge button (Br).
In the Favorites panel in Bridge, click the Lessons folder. In the Content panel, double-click the Lesson05 folder. Double-click the 05C_Start.psd image to open it in Photoshop.

2 Choose File > Save As. Name the file **05C_Working.psd**, and click Save.

3 Choose Image > Adjustments > Shadows/Highlights. Photoshop automatically applies default settings to the image, lightening the background. You'll customize the settings to bring out more detail in both the shadows and the highlights, and to enhance the sunset.

4 In the Shadows/Highlights dialog box, select Show More Options to expand the dialog box. Then do the following:

- In the Shadows area, set Amount to **50**%, Tonal Width to **50**%, and Radius to **38** px.

- In the Highlights area, set Amount to **14**%, Tonal Width to **46**%, and Radius to **43** px.

- In the Adjustments area, drag the Color Correction slider to **+5**, set the Midtone Contrast slider to **22**, and leave the Black Clip and White Clip settings at their defaults.

5 Click OK to accept your changes.

6 Choose File > Save to save your work so far.

Correcting red eye

Red eye occurs when the retina of a subject's eye is reflected by the camera flash. It commonly occurs in photographs of a subject in a darkened room, because the subject's irises are wide open. Red eye is easy to fix in Photoshop. In this exercise, you will remove the red eye from the girl's eyes in the portrait.

1 Select the Zoom tool ( ), and then drag a marquee around the girl's eyes to zoom in to them. You may need to deselect Scrubby Zoom to drag a marquee.

2 Select the Red Eye tool ( ), hidden under the Healing Brush tool.

3 In the options bar, leave Pupil Size set to 50%, but change Darken Amount to **74%**. The Darken Amount specifies how dark the pupil should be.

4 Click on the red area in the girl's left eye. The red reflection disappears.

5 Click on the red area in the girl's right eye to remove that reflection, as well.

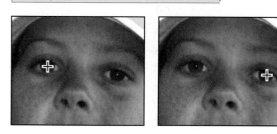

6 Double-click the Zoom tool to zoom out to 100%.

7 Choose File > Save to save your work so far.

Reducing noise

Random, extraneous pixels that aren't part of the image detail are called *noise*. Noise can result from using a high ISO setting on a digital camera, from underexposure, or from shooting in darkness with a long shutter speed. Scanned images may contain noise that results from the scanning sensor, or from a grain pattern from the scanned film.

There are two types of image noise: *luminance noise*, which is grayscale data that makes an image look grainy or patchy; and *color noise*, which appears as colored artifacts in the image. The Reduce Noise filter can address both types of noise in individual color channels while preserving edge detail, and can also correct JPEG compression artifacts.

First, zoom in to the girl's face to get a good look at the noise in this image.

1   Using the Zoom tool (🔍), click in the center of the face and zoom in to about 300%.

The noise in this image is speckled and rough, with uneven graininess in the skin. Using the Reduce Noise filter, you can smooth out this area.

2   Choose Filter > Noise > Reduce Noise.

3   In the Reduce Noise dialog box, do the following:

   • Increase Strength to **8**. (Strength controls the amount of luminance noise.)

   • Decrease Preserve Details to **30**%.

   • Increase Reduce Color Noise to **80**%.

   • Move Sharpen Details to **30**%.

● **Note:** To correct noise in individual channels of the image, select Advanced and click the Per Channel tab to adjust the settings in each channel.

You don't need to select Remove JPEG Artifact, because this image is not a JPEG and has no JPEG artifacts.

4   Click the plus button at the bottom of the dialog box twice to zoom in to about 300%, and then drag to position the face in the preview area. Click and hold the mouse button down in the preview area to see the "before" image, and release the mouse button to see the corrected result.

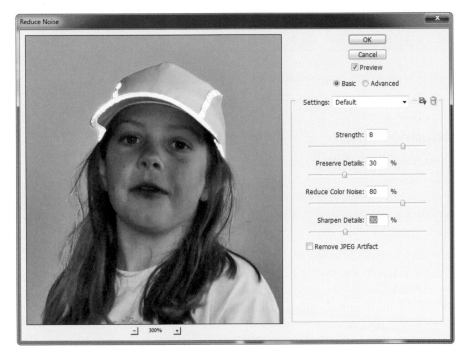

5 Click OK to apply your changes and to close the Reduce Noise dialog box, and then double-click the Zoom tool to return to 100%.

6 Choose File > Save to save your work, and then close the file.

Correcting image distortion

The Lens Correction filter fixes common camera lens flaws, such as barrel and pincushion distortion, chromatic aberration, and vignetting. *Barrel distortion* is a lens defect that causes straight lines to bow out toward the edges of the image. *Pincushion distortion* is the opposite effect, causing straight lines to bend inward. *Chromatic aberration* appears as a color fringe along the edges of image objects. *Vignetting* occurs when the edges of an image, especially the corners, are darker than the center.

Some lenses exhibit these defects depending on the focal length or the f-stop used. The Lens Correction filter can apply settings based on the camera, lens, and focal length that were used to make the image. The filter can also rotate an image or fix image perspective caused by tilting a camera vertically or horizontally. The filter's image grid makes it easier and more accurate to make these adjustments than using the Transform command.

In this exercise, you will adjust the lens distortion in an image of a Greek temple.

1 Click the Launch Bridge button (![Br]). In Bridge, navigate to the Lesson05 folder. Double-click the 05D_Start.psd image to open it in Photoshop.

The columns in this image bend toward the camera and appear to be warped. This photo was shot at a range that was too close with a wide-angle lens.

2 Choose Filter > Lens Correction. The Lens Correction dialog box opens.

3 Select Show Grid at the bottom of the dialog box, if it's not already selected. An alignment grid overlays the image, next to options for removing distortion, correcting chromatic aberration, removing vignettes, and transforming perspective.

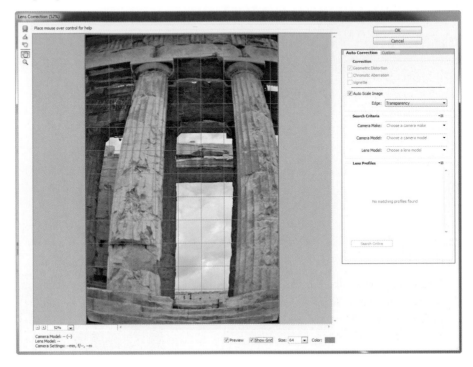

The Lens Correction dialog box includes auto-correction options. You'll adjust one setting in the Auto Corrections pane and then customize the settings.

4 In the Correction area of the Auto Corrections pane, make sure Auto Scale Image is selected, and that Transparency is selected from the Edge menu.

5 Select the Custom tab.

6 In the Custom pane, drag the Remove Distortion slider to about **+52.00** to remove the barrel distortion in the image. Alternatively, you could select the Remove Distortion tool (▣) and drag in the image preview area until the columns are straight.

The adjustment causes the image borders to bow inward. However, because you selected Auto Scale Image, the Lens Correction filter automatically scales the image to adjust the borders.

▶ **Tip:** Watch the alignment grid as you make these changes so that you can see when the vertical columns are straightened in the image.

7 Click OK to apply your changes and close the Lens Correction dialog box.

The curving distortion caused by the wide-angle lens and low shooting angle are eliminated.

8 (Optional) To see the effect of your change in the main image window, press Ctrl+Z (Windows) or Command+Z (Mac OS) twice to undo and redo the filter.

9 Choose File > Save As. In the Save As dialog box, name the file **Columns_Final.psd**, and save it in the Lesson05 folder. Click OK if a compatibility warning appears. Then, close the image.

Adding depth of field

When you're shooting a photo, you often have to choose to focus either the background or the foreground. If you want the entire image to be in focus, take two photos—one with the background in focus and one with the foreground in focus—and then merge the two in Photoshop.

Because you'll need to align the images exactly, it's helpful to use a tripod to keep the camera steady. Even with a handheld camera, though, you can get some amazing results. You'll add depth of field to an image of a wine glass in front of a beach.

1 In Photoshop, choose File > Open. Navigate to the Lessons/Lesson05 folder, and double-click the 05E_Start.psd file to open it.

2 In the Layers panel, hide the Beach layer, so that only the Glass layer is visible. The glass is in focus, but the background is blurred. Then, show the Beach layer and hide the Glass layer. Now the beach is in focus, but the glass is blurred.

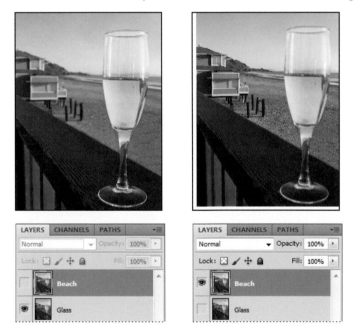

You'll merge the layers, using the part of each layer that is in focus. First, you need to align the layers.

3 Show both layers again, and then Shift-click to select both of them.

4 Choose Edit > Auto-Align Layers.

Because these images were shot from the same angle, Auto will work just fine.

5 Select Auto, if it isn't already selected. Then click OK to align the layers.

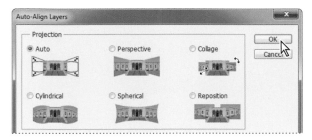

Now that the layers are perfectly aligned, you're ready to blend them.

6 Make sure both layers are still selected in the Layers panel. Then choose Edit > Auto-Blend Layers.

7 Select Stack Images, and make sure Seamless Tones And Colors is selected. Then click OK.

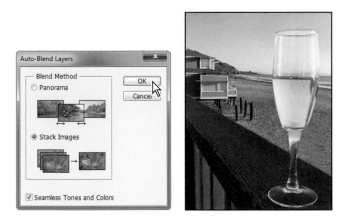

Both the wine glass and the beach behind it are in focus. Now, you'll add a Vibrance adjustment layer to give the image a little extra punch.

8 Click the Vibrance button in the Adjustments panel.

9 Move the Vibrance slider to **+33**, and then move the Saturation slider to **-5**.

The Vibrance adjustment layer affects all the layers beneath it.

10 Choose File > Save As. Name the file **Glass_Final.psd**, and save it in the Lesson05 folder. Click OK if a compatibility warning appears. Then close the file.

You've enhanced five images, using different techniques to adjust lighting and tone, merge multiple exposures, remove red eye, correct lens distortion, add depth of field, and more. You can use these techniques separately or together on your own images.

Review questions

1 What happens to camera raw images when you edit them in Camera Raw?

2 What is the advantage of the Adobe Digital Negative (DNG) file format?

3 How do you correct red eye in Photoshop?

4 Describe how to fix common camera lens flaws in Photoshop. What causes these defects?

Review answers

1 A camera raw file contains unprocessed picture data from a digital camera's image sensor. Camera raw files give photographers control over interpreting the image data, rather than letting the camera make the adjustments and conversions. When you edit the image in Camera Raw, it preserves the original raw file data. This way, you can edit the image as you desire, export it, and keep the original intact for future use or other adjustments.

2 The Adobe Digital Negative (DNG) file format contains the raw image data from a digital camera as well as metadata that defines what the image data means. DNG is an industry-wide standard for camera raw image data that helps photographers manage proprietary camera raw file formats and provides a compatible archival format.

3 Red eye occurs when the retinas of a subject's eyes are reflected by the camera flash. To correct red eye in Adobe Photoshop, zoom in to the subject's eyes, select the Red Eye tool, and then click the red eyes.

4 The Lens Correction filter fixes common camera lens flaws, such as barrel and pincushion distortion, in which straight lines bow out towards the edges of the image (barrel) or bend inward (pincushion); chromatic aberration, where a color fringe appears along the edges of image objects; and vignetting at the edges of an image, especially corners, that are darker than the center. Defects can occur from incorrectly setting the lens's focal length or f-stop, or by tilting the camera vertically or horizontally.

6 MASKS AND CHANNELS

Lesson overview

In this lesson, you'll learn how to do the following:

- Create a mask to remove a subject from a background.

- Refine a mask to include complex edges.

- Create a quick mask to make changes to a selected area.

- Edit a mask using the Masks panel.

- Manipulate an image using Puppet Warp.

- Save a selection as an alpha channel.

- View a mask using the Channels panel.

- Load a channel as a selection.

- Isolate a channel to make specific image changes.

 This lesson will take about an hour to complete. Copy the Lesson06 folder onto your hard drive if you haven't already done so. As you work on this lesson, you'll preserve the start files. If you need to restore the start files, copy them from the *Adobe Photoshop CS5 Classroom in a Book* DVD.

Use masks to isolate and manipulate specific parts of an image. The cutout portion of a mask can be altered, but the area surrounding the cutout is protected from change. You can create a temporary mask to use once, or you can save masks for repeated use.

Working with masks and channels

Photoshop masks isolate and protect parts of an image, just as masking tape protects window panes or trim from paint when a house is painted. When you create a mask based on a selection, the area you haven't selected is *masked,* or protected from editing. With masks, you can create and save time-consuming selections and then use them again. In addition, you can use masks for other complex editing tasks—for example, to apply color changes or filter effects to an image.

In Photoshop, you can make temporary masks, called *quick masks*, or you can create permanent masks and store them as special grayscale channels called *alpha channels*. Photoshop also uses channels to store an image's color information. Unlike layers, channels do not print. You use the Channels panel to view and work with alpha channels.

A key concept in masking is that black hides and white reveals. As in life, rarely is anything black and white. Shades of gray partially hide, depending on the gray levels (255 is the value for black, hiding artwork completely; 0 is the value for white, revealing artwork completely).

Getting started

First, you'll view the image that you'll create using masks and channels.

1 Start Photoshop, and then immediately hold down Ctrl+Alt+Shift (Windows) or Command+Option+Shift (Mac OS) to restore the default preferences. (See "Restoring default preferences" on page 5.)

2 When prompted, click Yes to delete the Adobe Photoshop Settings file.

3 Click the Launch Bridge button (Br) in the Application bar to open Adobe Bridge.

4 Click the Favorites tab on the left side of the Bridge window. Select the Lessons folder, and then double-click the Lesson06 folder in the Content panel.

5 Study the 06End.psd file. To enlarge the thumbnail so that you can see it more clearly, move the thumbnail slider at the bottom of the Bridge window to the right.

In this lesson, you'll create a magazine cover. The model for the cover was photographed in front of a different background. You'll use masking and the Refine Mask feature to place the model on the appropriate background.

6 Double-click the 06Start.psd file's thumbnail to open it in Photoshop. Click OK if you see an Embedded Profile Mismatch dialog box.

Creating a mask

You'll use the Quick Selection tool to create the initial mask in order to separate the model from the background.

1 Choose File > Save As, rename the file **06Working.psd**, and click Save. Click OK if a compatibility warning appears.

Saving a working version of the file lets you return to the original if you need it.

2 Select the Quick Selection tool (✐). In the options bar, set up a brush with a size of **15** px and Hardness of **100**%.

3 Select the man. It's fairly easy to select his shirt and face, but the hair is trickier. Don't worry if the selection isn't perfect. You'll refine the mask in the next exercise.

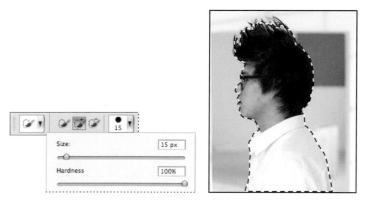

4 Select the Masks tab to make the Masks panel active. (It's grouped with the Adjustments panel by default. Choose Window > Masks if the Masks panel isn't open.)

5 In the Masks panel, click the Add A Pixel Mask button.

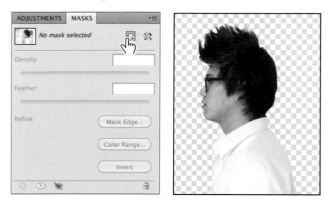

The selection becomes a pixel mask, and a new layer appears in the Layers panel. Everything outside the selection is transparent, represented by a checkerboard pattern.

Julieanne Kost is an official Adobe Photoshop evangelist.

Tool tips from the Photoshop evangelist

Zoom tool shortcuts

Often when you are editing an image, you'll need to zoom in to work on a detail and then zoom out again to see the changes in context. Here are several keyboard shortcuts that make the zooming even faster and easier.

- Press Ctrl+spacebar (Windows) or Command+spacebar (Mac OS) to temporarily select the Zoom In tool. When you finish zooming, release the keys to return to the tool you were previously using.

- Press Alt+spacebar (Windows) or Option+spacebar (Mac OS) to temporarily select the Zoom Out tool. When you finish zooming, release the keys to return to the tool you were using.

- Double-click the Zoom tool in the Tools panel to return the image to 100% view.

- When Scrubby Zoom is selected in the options bar, just drag the Zoom tool to the left to zoom in and drag it to the right to zoom out.

- Press Alt (Windows) or Option (Mac OS) to change the Zoom In tool to the Zoom Out tool, and click the area of the image you want to reduce. Each Alt/Option-click reduces the image by the next preset increment.

- With any tool selected, press Ctrl (Windows) or Command (Mac OS) with the plus sign (+) to zoom in, or with the minus sign (-) to zoom out.

Refining a mask

The mask is pretty good, but the Quick Selection tool couldn't quite capture all of the model's hair. The mask is also a little choppy around the contours of the shirt and face. You'll smooth the mask, and then fine-tune the mask around the hair.

1 In the Masks panel, click Mask Edge. The Refine Mask dialog box opens.

2 In the View Mode area of the dialog box, click the arrow next to the preview window. Choose On Black from the pop-up menu.

The mask appears against a black background, which makes it easier to see the edge of the white shirt and the face.

3 In the Adjust Edge area of the dialog box, move the sliders to create a smooth, unfeathered edge along the shirt and face. The optimal settings depend on the selection you created, but they'll probably be similar to ours. We moved the Smooth slider to 15, Contrast to 40%, and Shift Edge to -8%.

4 In the Output area of the dialog box, select Decontaminate Colors. Choose New Layer With Layer Mask from the Output To menu.

5 Select the Zoom tool in the Refine Mask dialog box, and then click it to zoom in to the face.

6 Select the Refine Radius tool (✎) in the Refine Mask dialog box. Use it to paint out any white background that remains around the lips and the nose. Press [to decrease the brush size and] to increase it.

7 When you're satisfied with the mask around the face, click OK.

A new layer, named Layer 0 copy, appears in the Layers panel. You'll use this layer to add the spikes to the mask of the hair.

8 With Layer 0 copy active, click Mask Edge in the Masks panel to open the Refine Mask dialog box again.

9 From the View pop-up menu, choose On White. The black hair shows up well against the white matte. If necessary, zoom out or use the Hand tool to reposition the image so that you can see all of the hair.

10 Select the Refine Radius tool in the Refine Mask dialog box. Press the] key to increase the size of the brush. (The options bar displays the brush size; we used 300 px at first.) Then, begin brushing along the top of the hair, high enough to include the spikes. Press the [key to decrease the brush size by about half. Then, paint along the right side of the head, where the hair is a solid color, to pick up any small, fine hairs that protrude.

As you paint, Photoshop refines the mask edge, including the hair, but eliminating most of the background. If you were painting on a layer mask, the background would be included. The Refine Mask feature is good, but it's not perfect. You'll clean up any areas of background that are included with the hair.

11 Select the Erase Refinements tool (🖌), hidden behind the Refine Radius tool in the Refine Mask dialog box. Click once or twice in each area where background color shows. When you erase an area, the Refine Mask feature erases similar colors, cleaning up more of the mask for you. Be careful not to erase the refinements you made to the hair edge. You can undo a step or use the Refine Radius tool to restore the edge if necessary.

12 Select Decontaminate Colors, and move the Amount slider to 85%. Choose New Layer With Layer Mask from the Output menu. Then click OK.

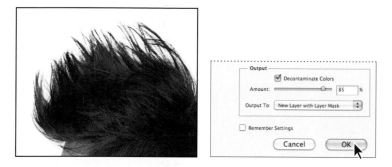

13 In the Layers panel, make the Magazine Background layer visible. The model appears in front of an orange patterned background.

Masking tips and shortcuts

Mastering masks can help you work more efficiently in Photoshop. These tips will help get you started.

- Masks are nondestructive, which means that you can edit the masks later without losing the pixels that they hide.

- When editing a mask, be aware of the color selected in the Tools panel. Black hides, white reveals, and shades of gray partially hide or reveal. The darker the gray, the more is hidden in the mask.

- To reveal a layer's content without masking effects, turn off the mask by Shift-clicking the layer mask thumbnail, or choose Layer > Layer Mask > Disable. A red X appears over the mask thumbnail in the Layers panel when the mask is disabled.

- To turn a layer mask back on, Shift-click the layer mask thumbnail with the red X in the Layers panel, or choose Layer > Layer Mask > Enable. If the mask doesn't show up in the Layers panel, choose Layer > Layer Mask > Reveal All to display it.

- Unlink a layer from its mask to move the two independently and shift the mask's boundaries separately from the layer. To unlink a layer or group from its layer mask or vector mask, click the link icon between the thumbnails in the Layers panel. To relink them, click the blank space between the two thumbnails.

- To convert a vector mask to a layer mask, select the layer containing the vector mask you want to convert, and choose Layer > Rasterize > Vector Mask. Note, however, that once you rasterize a vector mask, you can't change it back into a vector object.

- To modify a mask, use the Density and Feather sliders in the Masks panel. The Density slider determines the opacity of the mask: At 100%, the mask is fully in effect; at lower opacities, the contrast lessens; and at 0%, the mask has no effect. The Feather slider softens the edge of the mask.

Creating a quick mask

You'll create a quick mask to change the color of the glasses frames. First, you'll clean up the Layers panel.

1   Hide the Magazine Background layer so you can focus on the model. Then delete the Layer 0 and Layer 0 copy layers. Click Yes or Delete to confirm deletion of the layers or their masks, if prompted; you do not need to apply the mask to the current layer because Layer 0 copy 2 already has the mask applied.

2 Double-click the Layer 0 copy 2 layer name, and rename it **Model**.

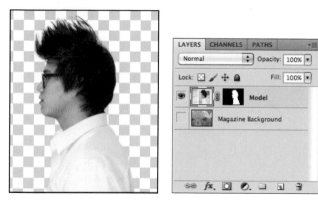

3 Click the Edit In Quick Mask Mode button (⬚) in the Tools panel. (By default, you have been working in Standard mode.)

In Quick Mask mode, a red overlay appears as you make a selection, masking the area outside the selection the way a rubylith, or red acetate, was used to mask images in traditional print shops. You can apply changes only to the unprotected area that is visible and selected. Notice that the highlight for the selected layer in the Layers panel appears gray instead of blue, indicating you're in Quick Mask mode.

4 In the Tools panel, select the Brush tool (✏).

5 In the options bar, make sure that the mode is Normal. Open the Brush pop-up panel, and select a small brush with a diameter of **13** px. Click outside the panel to close it.

6 Paint the earpiece of the glasses frames. The area you paint will appear red, creating a mask.

7 Continue painting with the Brush tool to mask the earpiece of the frames and the frame around the lenses. Reduce the brush size to paint around the lenses. Don't worry about the part of the earpiece that is overlapped by hair; the color change won't affect that area.

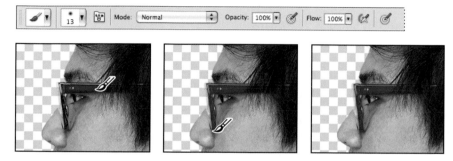

In Quick Mask mode, Photoshop automatically defaults to Grayscale mode, with a foreground color of black, and a background color of white. When using a painting or editing tool in Quick Mask mode, keep these principles in mind:

- Painting with black adds to the mask (the red overlay) and decreases the selected area.

- Painting with white erases the mask (the red overlay) and increases the selected area.

- Painting with gray partially adds to the mask.

8 Click the Edit In Standard Mode button to exit Quick Mask Mode.

The unmasked area is selected. Unless you save a quick mask as a more permanent alpha-channel mask, Photoshop discards the temporary mask once it is converted to a selection.

9 Choose Select > Inverse to select the area you originally masked.

10 Choose Image > Adjustments > Hue/Saturation.

11 In the Hue/Saturation dialog box, change the Hue to **70**, a green color that fills the glasses frame. Click OK.

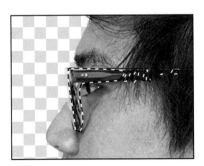

12 Choose Select > Deselect.

13 Save your work so far.

Manipulating an image with Puppet Warp

The new Puppet Warp feature in Photoshop CS5 gives you greater flexibility in manipulating an image. You can reposition areas, such as hair or an arm, just as you might pull the strings on a puppet. You place pins where you want to control movement. You'll use Puppet Warp to tilt the model's head back, so he appears to be looking up.

1 With the Model layer selected in the Layers panel, choose Edit > Puppet Warp.

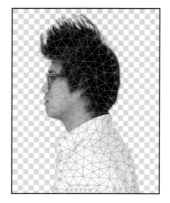

A mesh appears over the visible areas in the layer—in this case, the mesh appears over the model. You'll use the mesh to place pins where you want to control movement (or to ensure there is no movement).

2 Click around the edges of the shirt. Each time you click, Puppet Warp adds a pin. Approximately 10 pins should do the trick.

The pins you've added around the shirt will keep it in place as you tilt the head.

3 Select the pin at the nape of the neck. A black dot appears in the center of the pin to indicate that it's selected.

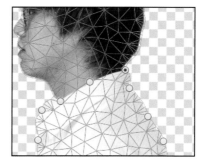

4 Press Alt (Windows) or Option (Mac OS). A larger circle appears around the pin and a curved double arrow appears next to it. Continue pressing Alt or Option as you drag the pointer to rotate the head backwards. You can see the angle of rotation in the options bar; you can enter **135** there to rotate the head back.

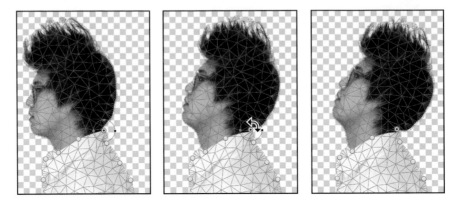

5 When you're satisfied with the rotation, click the Commit Puppet Warp button (✔) in the options bar, or press Enter or Return.

6 Save your work so far.

Working with channels

Just as different information in an image is stored on different layers, channels also let you access specific kinds of information. Alpha channels store selections as gray-scale images. Color information channels store information about each color in an image; for example, an RGB image automatically has red, green, blue, and composite channels.

To avoid confusing channels and layers, think of channels as containing an image's color and selection information; think of layers as containing painting and effects.

You'll use an alpha channel to create a shadow for the model. Then, you'll convert the image to CMYK mode and use the Black channel to add color highlights to the hair.

Using an alpha channel to create a shadow

You've already created a mask of the model. To create a shadow, you want to essentially duplicate that mask and then shift it. You'll use an alpha channel to make that possible.

1 In the Layers panel, Ctrl-click (Windows) or Command-click (Mac OS) the layer icon in the Model layer. The masked area is selected.

2 Choose Select > Save Selection. In the Save Selection dialog box, make sure New is chosen in the Channel menu. Then name the channel **Model Outline,** and click OK.

Nothing changes in the Layers panel or in the image window. However, a new channel named Model Outline has been added to the Channels panel.

3 Click the Create A New Layer icon at the bottom of the Layers panel. Drag the new layer below the Model layer. Then double-click its name, and rename it **Shadow**.

4 With the Shadow layer selected, choose Select > Refine Edge. In the Refine Edge dialog box, move the Shift Edge slider to **+36**%. Then click OK.

5 Choose Edit > Fill. In the Fill dialog box, choose Black from the Use menu, and then click OK.

The Shadow layer displays a filled-in black outline of the model. Shadows aren't usually as dark as the person that casts them. You'll reduce the layer opacity.

6 In the Layers panel, change the layer opacity to **30**%.

The shadow is in exactly the same position as the model, where it can't be seen. You'll shift it.

7 Choose Select > Deselect to remove the selection.

8 Choose Edit > Transform > Skew. Rotate the shadow by hand, or enter **-15°** in the Rotate field in the options bar. Then drag the shadow to the left, or enter **845** in the X field in the options bar. Click the Commit Transform button in the options bar, or press Enter or Return, to accept the transformation.

9 Choose File > Save to save your work so far.

About alpha channels

If you work in Photoshop very long, you're bound to work with alpha channels. It's a good idea to know a few things about them:

- An image can contain up to 56 channels, including all color and alpha channels.

- All channels are 8-bit grayscale images, capable of displaying 256 levels of gray.

- You can specify a name, color, mask option, and opacity for each channel. (The opacity affects the preview of the channel, not the image.)

- All new channels have the same dimensions and number of pixels as the original image.

- You can edit the mask in an alpha channel using the painting tools, editing tools, and filters.

- You can convert alpha channels to spot-color channels.

Adjusting an individual channel

You're almost done with the magazine cover image. All that remains is to add color highlights to the model's hair. You'll convert the image to CMYK mode so you can take advantage of the Black channel to do just that.

1 Select the Model layer in the Layers panel.

2 Choose Image > Mode > CMYK Color. Click Don't Merge in the dialog box that appears, because you want to keep your layers intact. Click OK if you're prompted about color profiles.

3 Alt-click (Windows) or Option-click (Mac OS) the visibility icon for the Model layer to hide the other layers.

4 Select the Channels tab. In the Channels panel, select the Black channel. Then choose Duplicate Channel from the Channels panel menu. Name the channel **Hair**, and click OK.

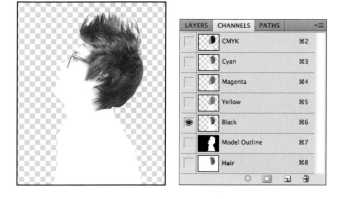

Individual channels appear in grayscale. If more than one channel is visible in the Channels panel, the channels appear in color.

5 Make the Hair channel visible, and hide the Black channel. Then select the Hair channel, and choose Image > Adjustments > Levels.

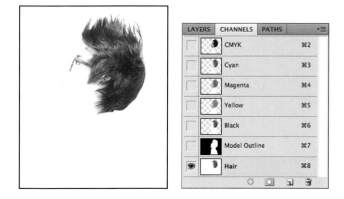

6 In the Levels dialog box, adjust the levels to move Black to **85**, Midtones to **1**, and White to **165**. Click OK.

7 With the Hair channel still selected, choose Image > Adjustments > Invert. The channel appears white against a black background.

8 Select the Brush tool, and click the Switch Foreground And Background Colors icon in the Tools panel to make the Foreground color black. Then paint over the glasses, eyes, and anything in the channel that isn't hair.

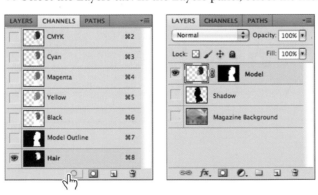

9 Click the Load Channel As Selection icon at the bottom of the Channels panel.

10 Select the Layers tab. In the Layers panel, select the Model layer.

11 Choose Select > Refine Edge. In the Refine Edge dialog box, move the Feather slider to **1.2** px, and then click OK.

12 Choose Image > Adjustments > Hue/Saturation. Select Colorize, and then move the sliders as follows, and click OK:

- Hue: **230**

- Saturation: **56**

- Lightness: **11**

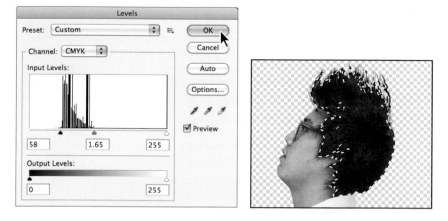

13 Choose Image > Adjustments > Levels. In the Levels dialog box, move the sliders so that the Black slider is positioned where the blacks peak, the White slider where the whites peak, and the Midtones in between. Then click OK. We used the values 58, 1.65, 255, but your values may vary.

14 In the Layers panel, make the Shadow and Magazine Background layers visible.

15 Choose Select > Deselect.

Your magazine cover is ready to go!

About masks and masking

Alpha channels, channel masks, clipping masks, layer masks, vector masks—what's the difference? In some cases, they're interchangeable: A channel mask can be converted to a layer mask, a layer mask can be converted to a vector mask, and vice versa.

Here's a brief description to help you keep them all straight. What they have in common is that they all store selections, and they all let you edit an image nondestructively, so you can return at any time to your original.

- An **alpha channel**—also called a *mask* or *selection*—is an extra channel added to an image; it stores selections as grayscale images. You can add alpha channels to create and store masks.

- A **layer mask** is like an alpha channel, but it's attached to a specific layer. A layer mask controls which part of a layer is revealed or hidden. It appears as a blank thumbnail next to the layer thumbnail in the Layers panel until you add content to it; a black outline indicates that it's selected.

- A **vector mask** is essentially a layer mask made up of vectors, not pixels. Resolution-independent, vector masks have crisp edges and are created with the pen or shape tools. They don't support transparency, so their edges can't be feathered. Their thumbnails appear the same as layer mask thumbnails.

- A **clipping mask** applies to a layer. It confines the influence of an effect to specific layers, rather than to everything below the layer in the layer stack. Using a clipping mask clips layers to a base layer; only that base layer is affected. Thumbnails of a clipped layer are indented with a right-angle arrow pointing to the layer below. The name of the clipped base layer is underlined.

- A **channel mask** restricts editing to a specific channel (for example, a Cyan channel in a CMYK image). Channel masks are useful for making intricate, fringed, or wispy-edged selections. You can create a channel mask based on a dominant color in an image or a pronounced contrast in an isolated channel, for example, between the subject and the background.

Review questions

1   What is the benefit of using a quick mask?

2   What happens to a quick mask when you deselect it?

3   When you save a selection as a mask, where is the mask stored?

4   How can you edit a mask in a channel once you've saved it?

5   How do channels differ from layers?

Review answers

1   Quick masks are helpful for creating quick, one-time selections. In addition, using a quick mask is an easy way to edit a selection using the painting tools.

2   The quick mask disappears when you deselect it.

3   Masks are saved in channels, which can be thought of as storage areas for color and selection information in an image.

4   You can paint on a mask in a channel using black, white, and shades of gray.

5   Channels are used as storage areas for saved selections. Unless you explicitly display a channel, it does not appear in the image or print. Layers can be used to isolate various parts of an image so that they can be edited as discrete objects with the painting or editing tools or other effects.

7 TYPOGRAPHIC DESIGN

Lesson overview

In this lesson, you'll learn how to do the following:

- Use guides to position text in a composition.

- Make a clipping mask from type.

- Merge type with other layers.

- Format text.

- Distribute text along a path.

- Control type and positioning using advanced features.

 This lesson will take less than an hour to complete. Copy the Lesson07 folder onto your hard drive if you haven't already done so. As you work on this lesson, you'll preserve the start files. If you need to restore the start files, copy them from the *Adobe Photoshop CS5 Classroom in a Book* DVD.

Photoshop provides powerful, flexible text tools so you can add type to your images with great control and creativity.

About type

Type in Photoshop consists of mathematically defined shapes that describe the letters, numbers, and symbols of a typeface. Many typefaces are available in more than one format, the most common formats being Type 1 or PostScript fonts, TrueType, and OpenType (see "OpenType in Photoshop" later in this lesson).

When you add type to an image in Photoshop, the characters are composed of pixels and have the same resolution as the image file—zooming in on characters shows jagged edges. However, Photoshop preserves the vector-based type outlines and uses them when you scale or resize type, save a PDF or EPS file, or print the image to a PostScript printer. As a result, you can produce type with crisp, resolution-independent edges, apply effects and styles to type, and transform its shape and size.

Getting started

In this lesson, you'll work on the layout for the cover of a technology magazine. You'll start with the artwork you created in Lesson 6: The cover has a model, his shadow, and the orange background. You'll add and stylize type for the cover, including warping the text.

You'll start the lesson by viewing an image of the final composition.

1 Start Photoshop, and then immediately hold down Ctrl+Alt+Shift (Windows) or Command+Option+Shift (Mac OS) to restore the default preferences. (See "Restoring default preferences" on page 5.)

2 When prompted, click Yes to delete the Adobe Photoshop Settings file.

3 Click the Launch Bridge button (Br) in the Application bar to open Adobe Bridge.

4 In the Favorites panel on the left side of Bridge, click the Lessons folder, and then double-click the Lesson07 folder in the Content panel.

Note: Though this lesson starts where Lesson 6 left off, use the 07Start.psd file. We've included a path and a sticky note in the start file that won't be in the 06Working.psd file you saved.

5 Select the 07End.psd file. Increase the thumbnail size to see the image clearly by dragging the thumbnail slider to the right.

You'll apply the type treatment in Photoshop to finish the magazine cover. All of the type controls you need are available in Photoshop, so you don't have to switch to another application to complete the project.

6 Double-click the 07Start.psd file to open it in Photoshop.

7 Choose File > Save As, rename the file **07Working.psd**, and click Save.

8 Click OK if the Photoshop Format Options dialog box appears.

Creating a clipping mask from type

A *clipping mask* is an object or a group of objects whose shape masks other artwork so that only areas that lie within the clipping mask are visible. In effect, you are clipping the artwork to conform to the shape of the object (or mask). In Photoshop, you can create a clipping mask from shapes or letters. In this exercise, you'll use letters as a clipping mask to allow an image in another layer to show through the letters.

Adding guides to position type

The 07Working.psd file includes a background layer, which will be the foundation for your typography. You'll start by zooming in on the work area and using ruler guides to help position the type.

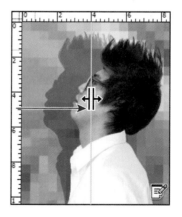

1 Choose View > Fit On Screen to see the whole cover clearly.

2 Choose View > Rulers to display rulers along the left and top borders of the image window.

3 Drag a vertical guide from the left ruler to the center of the cover (4 ¼").

Adding point type

Now you're ready to add type to the composition. Photoshop lets you create horizontal or vertical type anywhere in an image. You can enter *point type* (a single letter, word, or line) or *paragraph type*. You will do both in this lesson. First, you'll create point type.

1   In the Layers panel, select the Background layer.

2   Select the Horizontal Type tool (T), and, in the options bar, do the following:

  • Choose a sans serif typeface, such as Myriad Pro, from the Font Family pop-up menu, and choose Semibold from the Font Style pop-up menu.

  • Type **144 pt** for the Size, and press Enter or Return.

  • Click the Center Text button.

● **Note:** After you type, you must commit your editing in the layer by clicking the Commit Any Current Edits button or switching to another tool or layer. You cannot commit to current edits by pressing Enter or Return; doing so merely creates a new line of type.

3   Click on the center guide you added to set an insertion point, and type **DIGITAL** in all capital letters. Then click the Commit Any Current Edits button (✔) in the options bar.

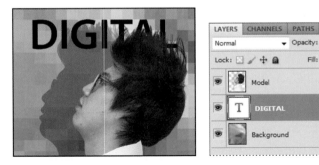

The word "DIGITAL" is added to the label, and it appears in the Layers panel as a new type layer, DIGITAL. You can edit and manage the type layer as you would any other layer. You can add or change the text, change the orientation of the type, apply anti-aliasing, apply layer styles and transformations, and create masks. You can move, restack, and copy a type layer, or edit its layer options, just as you would for any other layer.

4   Press Ctrl (Windows) or Command (Mac OS), and drag the DIGITAL text to move it to the top of the cover, if it's not there already.

5   Choose File > Save to save your work so far.

Making a clipping mask and applying a drop shadow

You added the letters in black, the default text color. However, you want the letters to appear to be filled with an image of a circuit board, so you'll use the letters to make a clipping mask that will allow another image layer to show through.

1 Open the circuit_board.tif file, which is in the Lesson07 folder. You can open it using Bridge or by choosing File > Open.

2 In Photoshop, click the Arrange Documents button (▦) in the Application bar, and then select a 2 Up layout option. The circuit_board.tif and 07Working.psd files appear onscreen together. Click the circuit_board.tif file to ensure that it's the active window.

3 Hold down the Shift key as you drag the Background layer from the Layers panel in the circuit_board.tif file onto the center of the 07Working.psd file. Pressing Shift as you drag centers the circuit_board.tif image in the composition.

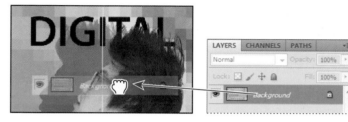

A new layer appears in the Layers panel for the 07Working.psd file: Layer 1. This new layer contains the image of the circuit board, which will show through the type. But before you make the clipping mask, you'll resize the circuit board image, as it's currently too large for the composition.

4 Close the circuit_board.tif file without saving any changes to it.

5 In the 07Working.psd file, select Layer 1, and then choose Edit > Transform > Scale.

6 Grab a corner handle on the bounding box for the circuit board. Press Shift as you resize it to approximately the same width as the area of text. Pressing Shift retains the image proportions. Reposition the circuit board so that the image covers the text.

7 Press Enter or Return to apply the transformation.

8 Double-click the Layer 1 name, and change it to **Circuit Board**. Then press Enter or Return, or click away from the name in the Layers panel, to apply the change.

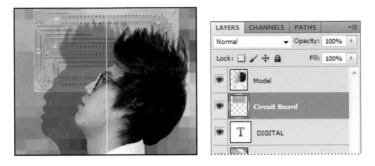

▶ **Tip:** You can also make a clipping mask by holding down the Alt (Windows) or Option (Mac OS) key and clicking between the Circuit Board and DIGITAL type layers.

9 Select the Circuit Board layer, if it isn't already selected, and choose Create Clipping Mask from the Layers panel menu.

The circuit board now shows through the DIGITAL letters. A small arrow in the Circuit Board layer and the underlined type layer name indicate the clipping mask is applied. Next, you'll add an inner shadow to give the letters depth.

10 Select the DIGITAL layer to make it active, click the Add A Layer Style button (*fx*) at the bottom of the Layers panel, and then choose Inner Shadow from the pop-up menu.

11 In the Layer Style dialog box, change the Blending Mode to Multiply, Opacity to **48**%, Distance to **18**, Choke to **0**, and Size to **16**. Then click OK.

12 Choose File > Save to save your work so far.

Julieanne Kost is an official Adobe Photoshop evangelist.

Tool tips from the Photoshop evangelist

Type tool tricks

- Shift-click in the image window with the Type tool (T) to create a new type layer—in case you're close to another block of type and Photoshop tries to autoselect it.

- Double-click the thumbnail icon on any type layer in the Layers panel to select all of the type on that layer.

- With any text selected, right-click (Windows) or Control-click (Mac OS) on the text to access the context menu. Choose Check Spelling to run a spell check.

Creating type on a path

In Photoshop, you can create type that follows along a path you create with a pen or shape tool. The direction the type flows depends on the order in which anchor points were added to the path. When you use the Horizontal Type tool to add text to a path, the letters are perpendicular to the baseline of the path. If you change the location or shape of the path, the type moves with it.

You'll create type on a path to make it look as if questions are coming from the model's mouth. We've already created the path for you.

1   In the Layers panel, select the Background layer.

2   Select the Paths tab in the Layers panel group.

3   In the Paths panel, select the path named Speech Path. The path appears to be coming out of the model's mouth.

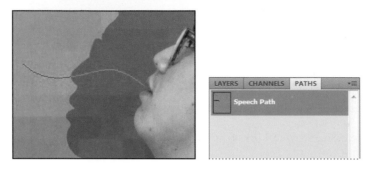

4   Select the Horizontal Type tool. Then, choose Window > Character to display the Character panel.

5   In the Character panel, select the following settings:

    •   Font Family: Myriad Pro

    •   Font Style: Regular

    •   Font Size (⬛T): **16** pt

    •   Tracking (⬛): **-10**

    •   Color: White

    •   All Caps (**TT**)

6   Move the Type tool over the path. When a small slanted line appears across the I-bar, click the beginning of the path, and type **WHAT'S NEW WITH GAMES?**

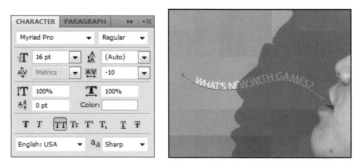

7 Select the word "GAMES," and change its font style to Bold. Click the Commit Edits button (✔) in the options bar.

8 In the Layers panel, select the What's New with Games layer, and then choose Duplicate Layer from the Layers panel menu. Name the new layer **What's new with MP3s?**

9 With the Type tool, select "GAMES," and replace it with **MP3s**. Click the Commit Edits button in the options bar.

10 Choose Edit > Free Transform Path. Rotate the left side of the path approximately 30 degrees, and then shift the path up above the first path. Click the Commit Transform button in the options bar.

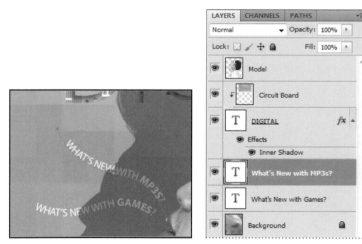

11 Repeat steps 8-10, replacing the word "GAMES" with **PHONES**. Rotate the left side of the path approximately -30 degrees, and move it below the original path.

12 Choose File > Save to save your work so far.

Warping point type

The text on a path is more interesting than straight lines would be, but you'll warp the text to make it more playful. *Warping* lets you distort type to conform to a variety of shapes, such as an arc or a wave. The warp style you select is an attribute of the type layer—you can change a layer's warp style at any time to change the overall shape of the warp. Warping options give you precise control over the orientation and perspective of the warp effect.

1 Scroll or use the Hand tool (🖐) to move the visible area of the image window so that the sentences to the left of the model are in the center of the screen.

2 Right-click (Windows) or Control-click (Mac OS) the What's New with Games? layer in the Layers panel, and choose Warp Text from the context menu.

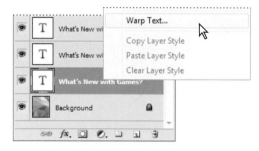

3 In the Warp Text dialog box, choose Wave from the Style menu, and click the Horizontal option. Specify the following values: Bend, +**33**%; Horizontal Distortion, -**23**%; and Vertical Distortion, +**5**%. Then click OK.

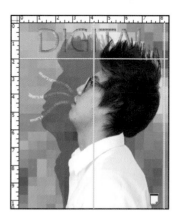

The words "What's new with games?" appear to float like a wave on the cover. Repeat steps 2 and 3 to warp the other two text layers you typed on a path.

4 Save your work.

Designing paragraphs of type

All of the text you've written on this label so far has been a few discrete words or lines—point type. However, many designs call for full paragraphs of text. You can design complete paragraphs of type in Photoshop; you don't have to switch to a dedicated page layout program for sophisticated paragraph type controls.

Using guides for positioning

You will add paragraphs to the cover in Photoshop. First, you'll add some guides to the work area to help you position the paragraph, and create a new paragraph style.

1 Drag a guide from the left vertical ruler, placing it approximately ¼" from the right side of the cover.

2 Drag a guide down from the top horizontal ruler, placing it approximately 2" from the top of the cover.

Adding paragraph type from a sticky note

You're ready to add the text. In a real design environment, the text might be provided to you in a word-processing document or the body of an email message, which you could copy and paste into Photoshop. Or you might have to type it in. Another easy way to add a bit of text is for the copywriter to attach it to the image file in a sticky note, as we've done for you here.

1   Double-click the yellow sticky note in the lower-right corner of the image window to open the Notes panel. Expand the Notes panel, if necessary, to see all the text.

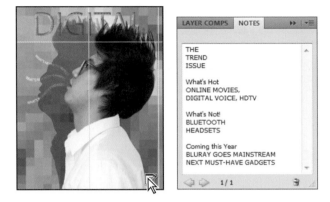

2   In the Notes panel, select all the text. Press Ctrl+C (Windows) or Command+C (Mac OS) to copy the text to the clipboard. Close the Notes panel.

3   Select the Model layer. Then, with the Horizontal Type tool, drag a text box on the right side of the magazine cover. The text box should be about 4 inches by 8 inches, about ¼ inch from the right edge of the cover. Align the top and right edges using the guides you just added.

4   Press Ctrl+V (Windows) or Command+V (Mac OS) to paste the text. The new text layer is at the top of the Layers panel, so the text appears in front of the model.

5   Select the first three lines ("The Trend Issue"), and then apply the following settings in the Character panel:

   • Font Family: Myriad Pro (or another sans serif font)

   • Font Style: Regular

   • Font Size (🇹): **70** pt

   • Leading (🅰): **55** pt

   • Color: White

6 Click the Paragraph tab in the Character panel group to make the Paragraph panel active.

7 With "The Trend Issue" still selected, click the Right Align Text option.

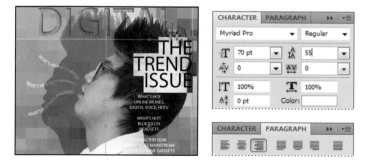

You've formatted the title. Now you'll format the rest of the text.

8 Select the rest of the text you pasted. In the Character panel, select the following settings:

- Font Family: Myriad Pro

- Font Style: Bold

- Font Size: **28** pt

- Leading: **28** pt

- Color: White

9 In the Paragraph panel, select the Right Align Text option.

Next, you'll make quick adjustments to some of the text you just formatted.

10 Select the text below the "What's Hot" heading ("online movies, digital voice, HDTV").

11 In the Character panel, change the font size to **22** pt and the leading to **28** pt.

12 Repeat steps 11 and 12 for the text beneath "What's Not" and "Coming This Year."

Now there are just two more changes to make to the text.

13 Select "Coming this year" and all the text that follows it. Then, in the Character panel, change the text color to Black.

14 Finally, select the word "Trend," and change the font style to Bold. Then, click the Commit button to accept the type changes.

OpenType in Photoshop

OpenType is a cross-platform font file format developed jointly by Adobe and Microsoft. The format uses a single font file for both Mac OS and Windows, so you can move files from one platform to another without font substitution or reflowed text. OpenType offers widely expanded character sets and layout features, such as swashes and discretionary ligatures, that aren't available in traditional PostScript and TrueType fonts. This, in turn, provides richer linguistic support and advanced typography control. Here are some highlights of OpenType.

The OpenType menu The Character panel menu includes an OpenType submenu that displays all available features for a selected OpenType font, including ligatures, alternates, and fractions. Dimmed features are unavailable for that typeface; a check mark appears next to features that have been applied.

Discretionary ligatures To add a discretionary ligature to two OpenType letters, such as to "th" in the Bickham Script Standard typeface, select them in the image, and choose OpenType > Discretionary Ligatures from the Character panel menu.

Swashes Adding swashes or alternate characters works the same way. Select the letter, such as a capital "T" in Bickham Script, and choose OpenType > Swash to change the ordinary capital into a dramatically ornate swash T.

Creating true fractions Type fractions as usual—for example, 1/2—and then select the characters, and from the Character panel menu, choose OpenType > Fractions. Photoshop applies the true fraction (½).

▶ **Tip:** Use the Adobe Illustrator CS5 Glyphs panel to preview OpenType options: Copy your text in Photoshop and paste it into an Illustrator document. Then, choose Window > Type > Glyphs. Select the text you want to change, and choose Show > Alternates For Current Selection. Double-click a glyph to apply it, and when you've finished, copy and paste the new type into your Photoshop file.

Adding vertical type

You're almost done with the text for the magazine cover. All that remains to do is add the volume number in the upper-right corner. You'll use vertical type to add it.

1   Choose Select > Deselect Layers. Then select the Vertical Type tool (↓T), which is hidden under the Horizontal Type tool.

2   Press the Shift key, and begin dragging in the upper-right corner of the cover, near the letter "L." Release the Shift key, and drag a vertical rectangle.

Pressing the Shift key as you begin dragging ensures that you create a new text box instead of selecting the title.

3   Type **VOL 9**.

4 Select the letters either by dragging or triple-clicking them, and then, in the Character panel, select the following:

- Font Family: a serif typeface, such as Myriad Pro.

- Font size: **15** pt

- Tracking: **150**

- Color: Black

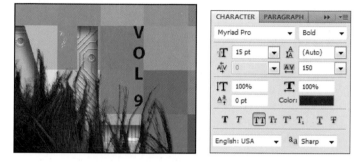

5 Click the Commit Any Current Edits button (✔) in the options bar. Your vertical text now appears as the layer named VOL 9. Use the Move tool (▶╬) to drag it to the right, if necessary.

Now, you'll clean up a bit.

6 Click the note to select it. Then right-click (Windows) or Control-click (Mac OS) and choose Delete Note from the context menu; click Yes to confirm that you want to delete the note.

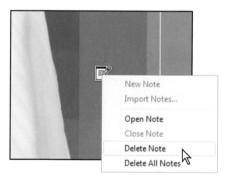

7 Hide the guides: choose the Hand tool (), and then press Ctrl+; (Windows) or Command+; (Mac OS). Then zoom out to get a nice look at your work.

8 Choose File > Save to save your work.

Congratulations! You've added and stylized all of the type on the Digital magazine cover. Now that the magazine cover is ready to go, you'll flatten it and prepare it for printing.

9 Choose File > Save As, and rename the file **07Working_flattened**. Click OK if you see the Maximize Compatibility dialog box.

Keeping a layered version lets you return to the 07Working.psd file in the future to edit it.

10 Choose Layer > Flatten Image.

11 Choose File > Save, and then close the image window.

Review questions

1 How does Photoshop treat type?

2 How is a text layer the same as or different from other layers in Photoshop?

3 What is a clipping mask, and how do you make one from type?

Review answers

1 Type in Photoshop consists of mathematically defined shapes that describe the letters, numbers, and symbols of a typeface. When you add type to an image in Photoshop, the characters are composed of pixels and have the same resolution as the image file. However, Photoshop preserves the vector-based type outlines and uses them when you scale or resize type, save a PDF or EPS file, or print the image to a PostScript printer.

2 Type that is added to an image appears in the Layers panel as a text layer that can be edited and managed in the same way as any other kind of layer. You can add and edit the text, change the orientation of the type, and apply anti-aliasing as well as move, restack, copy, and change the options for layers.

3 A clipping mask is an object or group whose shape masks other artwork so that only areas that lie within the shape are visible. To convert the letters on any text layer to a clipping mask, select both the text layer and the layer you want to show through the letters, and then choose Create Clipping Mask from the Layers panel menu.

8 VECTOR DRAWING TECHNIQUES

Lesson overview

In this lesson, you'll learn how to do the following:

- Differentiate between bitmap and vector graphics.

- Draw straight and curved paths using the Pen tool.

- Convert a path to a selection, and convert a selection to a path.

- Save paths.

- Draw and edit shape layers.

- Draw custom shapes.

- Import and edit a Smart Object from Adobe Illustrator.

This lesson will take about 90 minutes to complete. Copy the Lesson08 folder onto your hard drive if you haven't already done so. As you work on this lesson, you'll preserve the start files. If you need to restore the start files, copy them from the *Adobe Photoshop CS5 Classroom in a Book* DVD.

Copyright Jeff Brown Productions

Unlike bitmap images, vector images retain their crisp edges when you enlarge them to any size. You can draw vector shapes and paths in your Photoshop images and add vector masks to control what is shown in an image.

About bitmap images and vector graphics

Before working with vector shapes and vector paths, it's important to understand the basic differences between the two main categories of computer graphics: *bitmap images* and *vector graphics*. You can use Photoshop to work with either type of graphic; in fact, you can combine both bitmap and vector data in an individual Photoshop image file.

Bitmap images, technically called *raster images*, are based on a grid of dots known as *pixels*. Each pixel is assigned a specific location and color value. In working with bitmap images, you edit groups of pixels rather than objects or shapes. Because bitmap graphics can represent subtle gradations of shade and color, they are appropriate for continuous-tone images such as photographs or artwork created in painting programs. A disadvantage of bitmap graphics is that they contain a fixed number of pixels. As a result, they can lose detail and appear jagged when scaled up onscreen or printed at a lower resolution than they were created for.

Vector graphics are made up of lines and curves defined by mathematical objects called *vectors*. These graphics retain their crispness whether they are moved, resized, or have their color changed. Vector graphics are appropriate for illustrations, type, and graphics such as logos that may be scaled to different sizes.

Logo drawn as vector art

Logo rasterized as bitmap art

About paths and the Pen tool

In Photoshop, the outline of a vector shape is a *path*. A path is a curved or straight line segment you draw using the Pen tool or Freeform Pen tool. The Pen tool draws paths with the greatest precision; the Freeform Pen tool draws paths as if you were drawing with a pencil on paper.

Paths can be open or closed. Open paths (such as a wavy line) have two distinct endpoints. Closed paths (such as a circle) are continuous. The type of path you draw affects how it can be selected and adjusted.

Paths that have no fill or stroke do not print when you print your artwork. This is because paths are vector objects that contain no pixels, unlike the bitmap shapes drawn by the Pencil tool and other painting tools.

Getting started

Before you begin, you'll view the image you'll be creating—a poster for a fictitious toy company.

1 Start Adobe Photoshop, holding down Ctrl+Alt+Shift (Windows) or Command+Option+Shift (Mac OS) to restore the default preferences. (See "Restoring default preferences" on page 5.)

2 When prompted, click Yes to delete the Adobe Photoshop Settings file.

3 Click the Launch Mini Bridge button (Mb) in the Application bar to open the Mini Bridge panel.

4 In the Mini Bridge panel, click Browse Files to see the Navigation pane. Select the Favorites folder, and then the Lessons folder. Then, double-click the Lesson08 folder in the Content pane.

5 Select the 08End.psd file, and press the spacebar to see it in full-screen view.

● **Note:** If you open the 08End.psd file in Photoshop, you might be prompted to update type layers. If so, click Update. You may need to update type layers when files are transferred between computers, especially between operating systems.

To create this poster, you'll work with an image of a toy spaceship, and practice making paths and selections using the Pen tool. As you create the background shapes and type, you'll learn advanced methods of using path and vector masks, as well as ways to use Smart Objects.

6 When you've finished looking at 08End.psd, press the spacebar again. Then double-click the Spaceship.psd file to open it in Photoshop.

7 Choose File > Save As, rename the file **08Working.psd**, and click Save. Click OK in the Photoshop Format Options dialog box.

Using paths with artwork

You'll use the Pen tool to select the toy spaceship. The spaceship has long, smooth, curved edges that would be difficult to select using other methods.

You'll draw a path around the spaceship, and create another path inside it. You'll convert the paths to selections, and then subtract one selection from the other so that only the spaceship and none of the background is selected. Finally, you'll make a new layer from the spaceship image, and change the image that appears behind it.

When drawing a freehand path using the Pen tool, use as few points as possible to create the shape you want. The fewer points you use, the smoother the curves are—and the more efficient your file is.

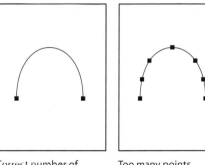

Correct number of points   Too many points

Creating paths with the Pen tool

You can use the Pen tool to create paths that are straight or curved, open or closed. If you're unfamiliar with the Pen tool, it can be confusing to use at first. Understanding the elements of a path and how to create them with the Pen tool makes paths much easier to draw.

To create a straight path, click the mouse button. The first time you click, you set the starting point. Each time that you click thereafter, a straight line is drawn between the previous point and the current point. To draw complex straight-segment paths with the Pen tool, simply continue to add points.

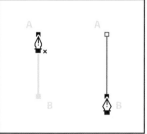

To create a curved path, click to place an anchor point, drag to create a direction line for that point, and then click to place the next anchor point. Each direction line ends in two direction points; the positions of direction lines and points determine the size and shape of the curved segment. Moving the direction lines and points reshapes the curves in a path.

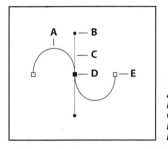

A. Curved line segment
B. Direction point
C. Direction line
D. Selected anchor point
E. Unselected anchor point

Continues on next page

Continued from previous page

Smooth curves are connected by anchor points called *smooth points*. Sharply curved paths are connected by *corner points*. When you move a direction line on a smooth point, the curved segments on both sides of the point adjust simultaneously, but when you move a direction line on a corner point, only the curve on the same side of the point as the direction line is adjusted.

Path segments and anchor points can be moved after they're drawn, either individually or as a group. When a path contains more than one segment, you can drag individual anchor points to adjust individual segments of the path, or select all of the anchor points in a path to edit the entire path. Use the Direct Selection tool to select and adjust an anchor point, a path segment, or an entire path.

Creating a closed path differs from creating an open path in the way that you end it. To end an open path, click the Pen tool in the Tools panel. To create a closed path, position the Pen tool pointer over the starting point, and click. Closing a path automatically ends the path. After the path closes, the Pen tool pointer appears with a small x, indicating that your next click will start a new path.

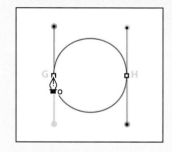

As you draw paths, a temporary storage area named Work Path appears in the Paths panel. It's a good idea to save work paths, and it's essential if you use multiple discrete paths in the same image file. If you deselect an existing Work Path in the Paths panel and then start drawing again, a new work path will replace the original one, which will be lost. To save a work path, double-click it in the Paths panel, type a name in the Save Path dialog box, and click OK to rename and save the path. The path remains selected in the Paths panel.

Drawing the outline of a shape

You'll use the Pen tool to connect the dots from point A to point S, and then back to point A. You'll set straight segments, smooth curve points, and corner points.

The first step is to configure the Pen tool options and the work area. Then you'll trace the outline of a spaceship using a template.

1   In the Workspace Switcher in the Application bar, click Design. Photoshop reconfigures panels for the Design workspace.

2   In the Tools panel, select the Pen tool ( ).

3 In the options bar, select or verify the following settings:

- Select the Paths (◰) option.

- In the Pen Options pop-up menu, make sure that Rubber Band is not selected.

- Make sure that the Auto Add/Delete option is selected.

- Select the Add To Path Area option (◱).

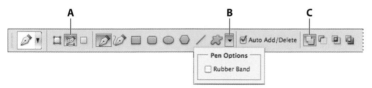

A. Paths option **B.** Pen Options menu **C.** Add To Path Area option

4 Click the Paths tab to bring that panel to the front of the Layers panel group.

The Paths panel displays thumbnail previews of the paths you draw. Currently, the panel is empty, because you haven't started drawing.

5 If necessary, zoom in so that you can easily see the lettered points and red dots on the shape template. Make sure you can see the whole template in the image window, and be sure to reselect the Pen tool after you zoom.

6 Click point A (the blue dot at the top of the spaceship), and release the mouse. You've set the first anchor point.

7 Click point B, and drag the cursor to the red dot labeled b. Release the mouse. You've set the direction of the curve.

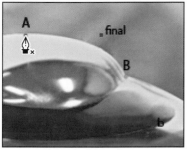
Creating the first anchor point at A

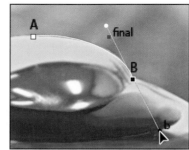
Setting a smooth point at B

At the corner of the cockpit (point B), you'll need to convert the smooth point to a corner point to create a sharp transition between the curved segment and the straight one.

8 Alt-click (Windows) or Option-click (Mac OS) point B to convert the smooth point into a corner point and remove one of the direction lines.

9 Click point C, and drag to the red dot labeled c. Do the same for points D and E.

  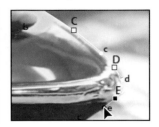

Converting the smooth point   Adding a segment   Rounding the corner
to a corner point

If you make a mistake while you're drawing, choose Edit > Undo to undo the step. Then resume drawing.

10 Click point F, and release the mouse without dragging a handle. Click point G, and drag up from point G to its red dot. Do the same for point H. Alt-click or Option-click to create another corner point at point H.

11 Continue around the spaceship through point N, setting corner points at I, J, L, and M.

12 Click points O and P, leaving straight lines. Click Point Q, and drag the handle to the corresponding red dot to create the curve around the tail of the fin.

13 Click at points R and S without dragging to create straight lines.

14 Move the pointer over point A so that a small circle appears in the pointer icon, indicating that you are about to close the path. (The small circle may be difficult to see.) Drag from point A to the red dot labeled "final," and then release the mouse button to draw the last curved line.

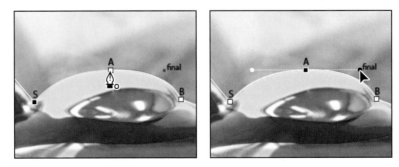

15 In the Paths panel, double-click Work Path, type **Spaceship** in the Save Path dialog box, and click OK to save it.

16 Choose File > Save to save your work.

Converting selections to paths

Now, you'll create a second path using a different method. First you'll use a selection tool to select a similarly colored area, and then you'll convert the selection to a path. (You can convert any selection made with a selection tool into a path.)

1 Click the Layers tab to display the Layers panel, and then drag the Template layer to the Delete button at the bottom of the panel. You no longer need this layer.

2 Select the Magic Wand tool (✹) in the Tools panel, hidden under the Quick Selection tool.

3 In the options bar, make sure the Tolerance value is **32**.

4 Carefully click the green area inside the spaceship's vertical fin.

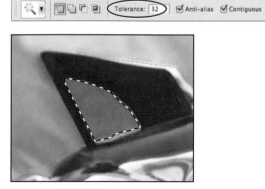

5 Click the Paths tab to bring the Paths panel forward. Then, click the Make Work Path From Selection button (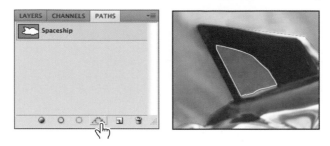) at the bottom of the panel.

The selection is converted to a path, and a new work path is created.

6 Double-click the path named Work Path, name it **Fin**, and then click OK to save the path.

7 Choose File > Save to save your work.

Converting paths to selections

Just as you can convert selection borders to paths, you can convert paths to selections. With their smooth outlines, paths let you make precise selections. Now that you've drawn paths for the spaceship and its fin, you'll convert those paths to a selection and apply a filter to the selection.

1 In the Paths panel, click the Spaceship path to make it active.

2 Choose Make Selection from the Paths panel menu, and then click OK to convert the Spaceship path to a selection.

▶ **Tip:** You can also click the Load Path As Selection button at the bottom of the Paths panel to convert the active path to a selection.

Next, you'll subtract the Fin selection from the Spaceship selection so that you can see the background through the vacant areas in the fin.

3 In the Paths panel, click the Fin path to make it active. Then, from the Paths panel menu, choose Make Selection.

4 In the Operation area of the Make Selection dialog box, select Subtract From Selection, and click OK.

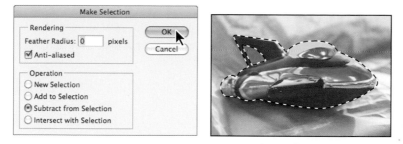

The Fin path is simultaneously converted to a selection and subtracted from the Spaceship selection.

Leave the paths selected, because you'll use them in the next exercise.

Converting the selection to a layer

Now you'll see how creating the selection with the Pen tool can help you achieve interesting effects. Because you've isolated the spaceship, you can create a duplicate of it on a new layer. Then, you can copy it to another image file—specifically, to the image that's the background for the toy-store poster.

1 Make sure that you can still see the selection outline in the image window. If you can't, repeat the previous exercise, "Converting paths to selections."

2 Choose Layer > New > Layer Via Copy.

3 Click the Layers tab to bring the Layers panel to the front. A new layer appears in the Layers panel, called Layer 2. The Layer 2 thumbnail shows that the layer contains only the image of the spaceship, not the background of the original layer.

4 In the Layers panel, rename Layer 2 **Spaceship**, and press Enter or Return.

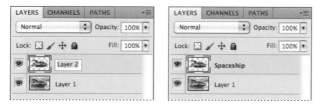

5 Choose File > Open, and double-click the 08Start.psd file in the Lessons/ Lesson08 folder.

The 08Start.psd file is the landscape that you'll use as the background for the spaceship.

6 Click the Arrange Documents button in the Application bar, and select a 2 Up layout so that you can see both the 08Working.psd and 08Start.psd files. Click the 08Working.psd image to make it active.

7 Select the Move tool (⊹), and drag the spaceship from the 08Working.psd image window to the 08Start.psd image window so that the spaceship appears to be hovering over the planet.

8 Close the 08Working.psd image without saving changes, leaving the 08Start.psd file open and active.

Now you'll position the spaceship more precisely over the poster background.

9 Select the Spaceship layer in the Layers panel, and choose Edit > Free Transform.

A bounding box appears around the spaceship.

● **Note:** If you accidentally distort the spaceship instead of rotating it, press Esc and start over.

10 Position the pointer near any corner handle until it turns into the rotate cursor (↻), and then drag to rotate the spaceship until its angle is about -12 degrees. For precise rotation, you can enter the value in the Rotate box in the options bar. When you're satisfied, press Enter or Return.

11 Make sure the Spaceship layer is still selected, and then use the Move tool to drag the saucer so that it grazes the top of the planet, as in the following image.

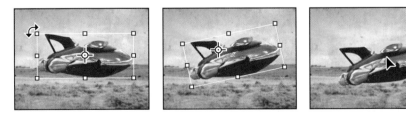

12 Choose File > Save As, rename the file **08B_Working.psd**, and click Save. Click OK in the Photoshop Format Options dialog box.

Creating vector objects for the background

Many posters are designed to be scalable, either up or down, while retaining a crisp appearance. This is a good use for vector shapes. Next, you'll create vector shapes with paths, and use masks to control what appears in the poster. Because they're vectors, the shapes can be scaled in future design revisions without a loss of quality or detail.

Drawing a scalable shape

You'll begin by creating a white kidney-shaped object for the backdrop of the poster.

1 Choose View > Rulers to display the horizontal and vertical rulers.

2 Drag the tab for the Paths panel out of the Layers panel group so that it floats independently. Since you'll be using the Layers and Paths panels frequently in this exercise, it's convenient to have them separated.

3 Hide all of the layers except Retro Shape Guide Layer and Background by clicking the appropriate eye icons in the Layers panel. Select the Background layer to make it active.

The guide layer will serve as a template as you draw the kidney shape.

A. Default Foreground And Background Colors button
B. Foreground Color button
C. Switch Foreground And Background Colors button
D. Background Color button

🔘 **Note:** If you have trouble, open the spaceship image again and practice drawing the path around the spaceship shape until you get more comfortable with drawing curved path segments. Also, be sure to read the sidebar, "Creating paths with the Pen tool."

4   Set the foreground and background colors to their defaults (black and white, respectively) by clicking the Default Foreground And Background Colors button (▪) in the Tools panel (or type the keyboard shortcut D), and then swap the foreground and background colors by clicking the Switch Foreground And Background Colors button (↪) (or type X). Now the foreground color is white.

5   In the Tools panel, select the Pen tool (✐). Then, in the options bar, select the Shape Layers option (▱).

6   Create the shape by clicking and dragging as follows:

*   Click point A, drag a direction line up and to the left of point B, and then release.

*   Click point C, drag a direction line toward and above point D, and then release.

*   Continue to draw curved segments in this way around the shape until you return to point A, and then click on A to close the path. Don't worry if the shape flips in on itself; it will right itself as you continue.

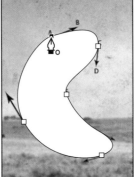

Notice that as you drew, Photoshop automatically created a new layer, Shape 1, just above the active layer (the Background layer) in the Layers panel.

7 Double-click the Shape 1 layer name, rename the layer **Retro Shape**, and press Enter or Return.

8 Hide Retro Shape Guide Layer in the Layers panel.

9 Choose File > Save to save your work.

Deselecting paths

You may need to deselect paths to see the appropriate options in the options bar when you select a vector tool. Deselecting paths can also help you view certain effects that might be obscured if a path is highlighted.

Notice that the border between the white kidney shape and the background has a grainy quality. What you see is actually the path itself, which is a nonprinting item. This is a visual clue that the Retro Shape layer is still selected. Before proceeding to the next exercise, you'll make sure that all paths are deselected.

1 Select the Path Selection tool (↖), which may be hidden under the Direct Selection tool (↘).

2 In the options bar, click the Dismiss Target Path button (✔).

● **Note:** You can also deselect paths by clicking in the blank area below the paths in the Paths panel.

About shape layers

A shape layer has two components: a fill and a shape. The fill properties determine the color (or colors), pattern, and transparency of the layer. The shape is a layer mask that defines the areas in which the fill can be seen and those areas in which the fill is hidden.

In the layer you've just created, the fill is white. The fill color is visible within the shape you drew and not in the rest of the image, so the background sky can be seen around it.

In the Layers panel, the Retro Shape layer sits above the Background layer, because the background was selected when you started to draw. The shape layer has three items along with the layer name: two thumbnail images and a link icon between them.

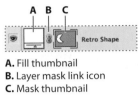

A. Fill thumbnail
B. Layer mask link icon
C. Mask thumbnail

The Fill thumbnail on the left shows that the entire layer is filled with the white foreground color. The nonfunctioning small slider underneath the thumbnail symbolizes that the layer is editable.

The Mask thumbnail on the right shows the vector mask for the layer. In this thumbnail, white indicates the area where the image is exposed, and gray indicates the areas where the image is blocked.

The icon between the two thumbnails shows that the layer and the vector mask are linked.

Subtracting shapes from a shape layer

After you create a shape layer (vector graphic), you can set options to subtract new shapes from the vector graphic. You can also use the Path Selection tool and the Direct Selection tool to move, resize, and edit shapes. You'll add some interest to the retro shape by subtracting a star shape from it, allowing the outer-space background to show through. To help you position the star, you'll refer to the Star Guide layer, which has been created for you. Currently, that layer is hidden.

1   In the Layers panel, show the Star Guide layer, but leave the Retro Shape layer selected. The Star Guide layer is now visible in the image window.

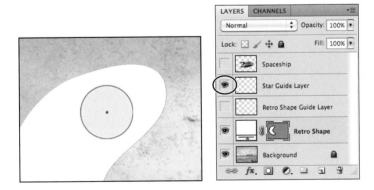

2 In the Paths panel, select the Retro Shape vector mask.

3 In the Tools panel, select the Polygon tool (⬡), hidden under the Rectangle tool (▢).

4 On the options bar, do the following:

- For Sides, type **11**.

- Click the arrow immediately to the left of the Sides option to display the Polygon Options window. Select Star, and type **50%** in the Indent Sides By box. Then click anywhere outside the Polygon Options window to close it.

- Select the Subtract From Shape Area option (⬚), or press either the hyphen or minus key to select it with a keyboard shortcut. The pointer now appears as cross-hairs with a small minus sign (+₋).

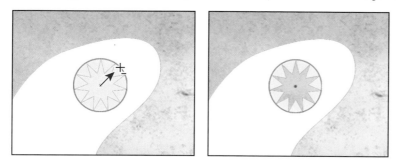

5 Click on the orange dot in the center of the orange circle in the image window, and drag outward until the tips of the star rays touch the circle's perimeter.

● **Note:** As you drag, you can rotate the star by dragging the pointer to the side.

When you release the mouse button, the star shape becomes a cutout, allowing the sky to show through.

Notice that the star has a grainy outline, reminding you that the shape is selected. Another indication that the shape is selected is that the Retro Shape vector mask thumbnail is highlighted (outlined in white) in the Layers panel.

6 In the Layers panel, hide the Star Guide layer.

Notice how the thumbnails have changed in the panels. In the Layers panel, the left thumbnail for the Retro Shape layer is unchanged, but the mask thumbnails in both the Layers panel and Paths panel show the retro shape with the star-shaped cutout.

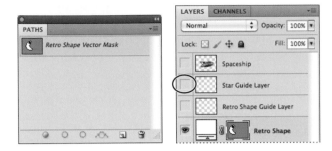

7 Select the Path Selection tool (➤), and click the Dismiss Target Path button (✔) in the options bar to deselect the star and retro shape paths.

The paths are now deselected, and the grainy path lines have disappeared, leaving a sharp edge between the blue and white areas. Also, the Retro Shape Vector Mask path is no longer highlighted in the Paths panel. That shape is pretty bright, though, and may overpower the spaceship. You'll make the shape semitransparent.

8 In the Layers panel, reduce the opacity of the Retro Shape layer to **40%**.

9 Choose File > Save to save your work.

Working with defined custom shapes

Another way to use shapes in your artwork is to draw a custom or preset shape. Doing so is as easy as selecting the Custom Shape tool, picking a shape from the Custom Shape picker, and drawing in the image window. You'll do just that to add checkerboard patterns to the background of your poster for the toy store.

1 Make sure the Retro Shape layer is selected in the Layers panel. Then click the New Layer button (⬚) to add a layer above it. Rename the new layer **Pattern**, and then press Enter or Return.

2 In the Tools panel, select the Custom Shape tool (⬘), which is hidden under the Polygon tool (⬡).

3 In the options bar, select the Fill Pixels option.

4 In the options bar, click the arrow next to the Shape option to open the Custom Shape picker.

5 Double-click the checkerboard preset on the right side of the Custom Shape picker (you may need to scroll or drag the corner of the picker to see it) to select it.

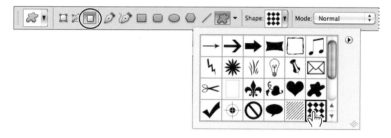

6 Make sure that the foreground color is white. Then press Shift and drag diagonally in the image window to draw and size the shape so that it's about 2 inches square. Pressing Shift constrains the shape to its original proportions.

7 Add five more checkerboards of various sizes until your poster resembles the following figure.

8 In the Layers panel, reduce the opacity of the Pattern layer to **75%**.

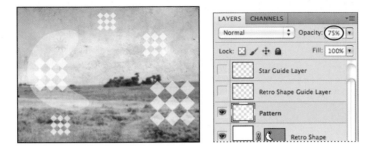

Your poster background is now complete.

9 In the Layers panel, show the Spaceship layer so you can see the whole composition.

10 Choose File > Save to save your work.

Importing a Smart Object

Smart Objects are layers that you can edit in Photoshop nondestructively; that is, changes you make to the image remain editable and don't affect the actual image pixels, which are preserved. Regardless of how often you scale, rotate, skew, or otherwise transform a Smart Object, it retains its sharp, precise edges.

You can import vector objects from Adobe Illustrator as Smart Objects. If you edit the original object in Illustrator, the changes will be reflected in the placed Smart Object in your Photoshop image file. You'll work with a Smart Object now by placing text created in Illustrator into the toy store poster.

Adding the title

The toy-store name was created in Illustrator. You'll add it to the poster now.

1 Select the Spaceship layer, and choose File > Place. Navigate to the Lessons/ Lesson08 folder, select the Title.ai file, and click Place. Click OK in the Place PDF dialog box that appears.

The Retro Toyz text is added to the middle of the composition, inside a bounding box with adjustable handles. A new layer, title, appears in the Layers panel.

2 Drag the Retro Toyz object to the upper-left corner of the poster, and then press Shift and drag a corner to make the text object proportionally larger— so that it fills the top portion of the poster, as in the following figure. When you've finished, either press Enter or Return, or click the Commit Transform button (✔) in the options bar.

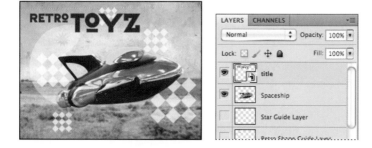

When you commit to the transformation, the layer thumbnail icon changes to reflect that the title layer is a Smart Object.

Because the Retro Toyz title is a Smart Object, you can continue to edit its size and shape, if you'd like. Simply select the layer, choose Edit > Free Transform to access the control handles, and drag to adjust them. Or, select the Move tool (▸₊), and select Show Transform Controls in the options bar. Then adjust the handles.

Adding a vector mask to a Smart Object

For a fun effect, you'll turn the center of each letter "O" in the title into a star that matches the cutout you created earlier. You'll use a vector mask, which you can link to a Smart Object in Photoshop.

1 Select the title layer, and then click the Add Layer Mask button at the bottom of the Layers panel.

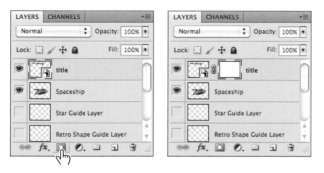

2 Select the Polygon tool (⬡), hidden beneath the Custom Shape tool (🔷). The options you used earlier to create the star should still be in effect. The Polygon tool holds your settings until you change them again. If you need to reset the options, refer to "Subtracting shapes from a shape layer."

3 Click the Switch Foreground And Background Colors button in the Tools panel, so that black is the foreground color.

4 Click in the center of the "O" in "Toyz," and drag the cursor outward until the star covers the center of the "O."

5 Repeat step 4 to add a star in the small "O" in Retro.

Rotating the canvas (OpenGL only)

You've been working with the image with "Retro Toyz" at the top of the work area and the ground at the bottom. But if your video card supports OpenGL, you can rotate the work area to draw, type, or position objects from a different perspective. You'll rotate the view as you add a copyright statement along the side of the image. (If your video card doesn't support OpenGL, skip this section.)

First, you'll type the text.

1 In the Character panel, select a serif font such as Myriad Pro with a small text size such as 10 pt, and set the color to white.

2 Select the Horizontal Type tool, and then click in the lower-left corner of the image. Type **Copyright YOUR NAME Productions**, substituting your own name.

You want the copyright to run along the left side of the image. You'll rotate the canvas to make it easier to place.

3 Select the Rotate View tool (🖐), hidden beneath the Hand tool (🖐).

4 Press the Shift key as you drag the tool in an arc to rotate the canvas 90 degrees clockwise. Pressing the Shift key restrains the rotation to 45-degree increments.

▶ **Tip:** You can also enter a value in the Rotation Angle box in the options bar.

5 Select the Copyright text layer, and then choose Edit > Transform > Rotate 90° CCW.

6 Use the Move tool to align the text along the top edge of the image, which will be the left edge when it is in its usual position.

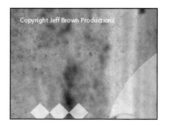

7 Select the Rotate View tool again, and then click Reset View in the options bar.

8 Choose File > Save to save your work.

Finishing up

As a final step, clean up the Layers panel by deleting your guide template layers.

1 Make sure that the Copyright, title, Spaceship, Pattern, Retro Shape, and Background layers are the only visible layers in the Layers panel.

2 Choose Delete Hidden Layers from the Layers panel menu, and then click Yes to confirm the deletion.

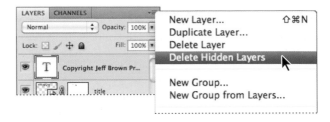

3 Choose File > Save to save your work.

Congratulations! You've finished the poster.It should look similar to the following image.

Extra Credit

If you have Adobe Illustrator CS or later, you can go even further with the Retro Toyz text Smart Object—you can edit it in Illustrator, and it will update automatically in Photoshop. Try this:

1 Double-click the Smart Object thumbnail in the title layer. If an alert dialog box appears, click OK. Illustrator opens and displays the Retro Toyz Smart Object in a document window.

2 Using the Direct Selection tool, drag a marquee around the type to select all of the letters.

3 In Illustrator CS3 or later, in the options bar, choose 2 pt from the Stroke menu. If you're using an earlier version of Illustrator, open the Stroke panel, and specify a 2-pt stroke.

A 2-point black stroke appears around the Retro Toyz type.

4 Close the Vector Smart Object document, and click Save when prompted. Click OK if an alert box appears.

5 Switch back to Photoshop. The Retro Toyz poster image window updates to reflect the stroked type.

Review questions

1 How can the Pen tool be useful as a selection tool?

2 What is the difference between a bitmap image and a vector graphic?

3 What does a shape layer do?

4 What tools can you use to move and resize paths and shapes?

5 What are Smart Objects, and what is the benefit of using them?

Review answers

1 If you need to create an intricate selection, it can be easier to draw the path with the Pen tool and then convert the path to a selection.

2 Bitmap, or raster, images are based on a grid of pixels and are appropriate for continuous-tone images such as photographs or artwork created in painting programs. Vector graphics are made up of shapes based on mathematical expressions and are appropriate for illustrations, type, and drawings that require clear, smooth lines.

3 A shape layer stores the outline of a shape in the Paths panel. You can change the outline of a shape by editing its path.

4 You use the Path Selection tool and the Direct Selection tool to move, resize, and edit shapes. You can also modify and scale a shape or path by choosing Edit > Free Transform Path.

5 Smart Objects are vector objects that you can place and edit in Photoshop without a loss of quality. Regardless of how often you scale, rotate, skew, or otherwise transform a Smart Object, it retains sharp, precise edges. A great benefit of using Smart Objects is that you can edit the original object in the authoring application, such as Illustrator, and the changes will be reflected in the placed Smart Object in your Photoshop image file.

9 ADVANCED LAYERING

Lesson overview

In this lesson, you'll learn how to do the following:

- Import a layer from another file.

- Clip a layer.

- Create and edit an adjustment layer.

- Use Vanishing Point 3D effects with layers.

- Create layer comps to showcase your work.

- Manage layers.

- Flatten a layered image.

- Merge and stamp layers.

 This lesson will take less than an hour to complete. Copy the Lesson09 folder onto your hard drive if you haven't already done so. As you work on this lesson, you'll preserve the start files. If you need to restore the start files, copy them from the *Adobe Photoshop CS5 Classroom in a Book* DVD.

Once you've learned basic layer techniques, you can create more complex effects in your artwork using layer masks, adjustment layers, filters, and more layer styles. You can also add layers from other documents.

Getting started

In this lesson, you'll combine several images to create a cell phone package. You'll create three different, multilayered designs, which you can display selectively using layer comps. You'll gain more experience with adjustment layers, layer effects, layer masks, and layer filters. Beyond this lesson, the best way to learn how to work with layers is by experimenting with combinations of filters, effects, layer masks, and layer properties in new ways.

1   Start Photoshop, and then immediately hold down Ctrl+Alt+Shift (Windows) or Command+Option+Shift (Mac OS) to restore the default preferences. (See "Restoring default preferences" on page 5.)

2   When prompted, click Yes to delete the Adobe Photoshop Settings file.

3   Click the Launch Bridge button (⊞) in the Application bar to open Adobe Bridge.

4   In the Favorites panel in the upper-left corner of Bridge, click the Lessons folder, and then double-click the Lesson09 folder in the Content panel.

5   Study the 09End.psd file in the Content panel. If necessary, drag the thumbnail slider at the bottom of the window to enlarge the thumbnail.

Your goal in this lesson is to create a package prototype by assembling artwork from various files, layering the artwork, adding perspective, and then refining the design. You'll create several layer comps to show the design to your client.

6   Double-click the 09Start.psd file to open it in Photoshop. Choose File > Save As, rename the file **09Working.psd**, and click Save. Click OK in the Photoshop Format Options dialog box.

7   Drag the Layers panel by its tab to the top of the work area. Drag its corner to expand the panel so that you'll be able to see about 10 layers without scrolling.

The panel lists three layers, two of which are visible—the gray three-dimensional box displayed in the image window and the background stacked underneath it. The Full Art layer is hidden.

8 In the Layers panel, select the Full Art layer. Notice that even though the layer is selected, it remains hidden.

Clipping a layer to a shape

To start building a composite image, you'll add more artwork and clip it to a shape.

1 Click the Mini Bridge button (![Mb]) in the Application bar.

2 In the Mini Bridge panel, click Favorites, and then double-click the Lessons folder and the the Lesson09 folder in the Content pane. Finally, double-click the Phone_Art.psd file to open it.

This file has two layers: Phone Art and Mask. You will clip the phone art image so that it fits within the freeform shape in the Mask layer below it.

3 In the Layers panel, make sure that the Mask layer is below the Phone Art layer. A clipping shape must be below the image that you're clipping.

4 Select the Phone Art layer. Then press Alt (Windows) or Option (Mac OS) as you position the pointer between the Phone Art layer and the Mask layer until it becomes a double-circle icon (![icon]), and click.

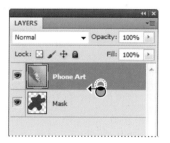

The thumbnail of the clipped layer, Phone Art, is indented in the Layers panel, and an arrow points to the layer beneath it, which is now underlined.

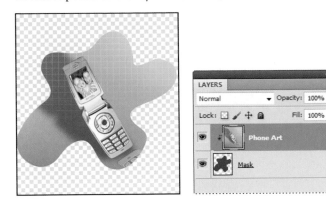

You will import this new image into the Start file. But first, you need to flatten the image to one layer.

5 Choose Merge Visible from the Layers panel menu.

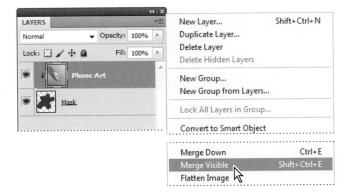

You can merge the layers in other ways. But don't choose Flatten Image, because it would remove the transparency already set up in the file.

Now you'll add artwork from another file, simply by dragging and dropping.

6 Click the Arrange Documents button in the Application bar, and select a 2 Up layout so you can see both images.

7 With the Move tool, drag the merged Phone Art layer from the Layers panel into the 09Working.psd image window. The layer appears above the active layer (Full Art) and at the top of the 09Working.psd Layers panel. The artwork covers the box.

8 In the 09Working.psd Layers panel, double-click the Phone Art layer name, and type **Shape Art** to rename it. Press Enter or Return.

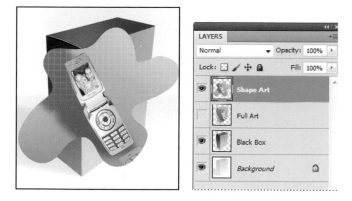

9 Choose File > Save to save your work so far.

10 Close the Phone_Art.psd file without saving your changes.

Setting up a Vanishing Point grid

The artwork you've added sits on top of the box—not exactly the effect you want. You'll fix that by making the artwork appear in perspective, wrapped around the box.

1 With the Shape Art layer selected in the Layers panel, press Ctrl+A (Windows) or Command+A (Mac OS) to select all of the layer's contents.

2 Press Ctrl+X (Windows) or Command+X (Mac OS) to cut the contents to the clipboard. Now only the box is visible, not the artwork.

3 Choose Filter > Vanishing Point. You'll use the Vanishing Point filter to draw a perspective plane that matches the dimensions of the box.

4 With the Create Plane tool (⊞), which is selected by default, click the upper-left corner of the front of the box to begin defining the plane. It's easiest to define planes when you can use a rectangular object in the image as a guide.

5 Continue drawing the plane by clicking each corner of the box side. Click the last corner to complete the plane. When you complete the plane, a grid appears on the front of the box, and the Edit Plane tool (🖈) is automatically selected. You can adjust the size of this grid at the top of the dialog box using the Edit Plane tool.

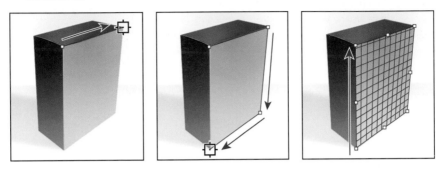

6 Use the Edit Plane pointer to adjust corner points to refine your plane, as needed.

Now you'll extend the grid to the side and top of the box to complete the perspective.

7 With the Edit Plane tool selected, press Ctrl (Windows) or Command (Mac OS), and drag the center point of the left side of the plane, extending the plane along the side of the box. As the grid appears on the side of the box, the grid on the front face disappears, but its blue border remains.

8 Use the Edit Plane pointer to adjust any corner points along the side plane, so that it more closely matches the shape of the box.

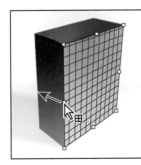

9 When you're satisfied with the grid's placement, repeat steps 7 and 8 to extend the grid across the top of the box.

● **Note:** The final grid doesn't have to match the box dimensions exactly.

If you were applying perspective to many planes, you might want to create a separate layer for each plane. Putting the Vanishing Point results in a separate layer preserves your original image and lets you use the layer opacity control, styles, and blending modes.

You're ready to add the artwork and give it perspective.

10 Press Ctrl+V (Windows) or Command+V (Mac OS) to paste the contents of the clipboard onto the grid. This action automatically selects the Marquee tool in the Vanishing Point dialog box.

11 Using the Marquee tool (⬚), select the contents, and drag it to the center of the front perspective plane so that most of the artwork appears on the front panel, but wraps around the side and top. It's important to place the artwork on the front panel so that it wraps correctly.

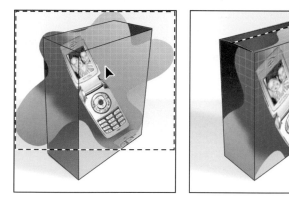

12 When you're satisfied with the positioning, click OK.

13 Choose File > Save to save your work so far.

Creating your own keyboard shortcuts

Photoshop comes with keyboard shortcuts for most common tools and commands. But you can customize shortcuts to fit your workflow. As you build the composite image, you'll place several images created in Adobe Illustrator. To make your work more efficient, create a keyboard shortcut for the Place command.

1 Choose Edit > Keyboard Shortcuts. The Keyboard Shortcuts And Menus dialog box appears.

2 Under Application Menu Command, click the triangle to the left of File to expand its contents. Scroll down to Place, and select it.

3 Press the F7 key on the keyboard to assign that key as a new shortcut. An alert appears, warning you that the F7 key is already in use. It's the keyboard shortcut for the File > Layers command, which opens the Layers panel.

4 Click Accept, and then click OK.

Placing imported artwork

Now you'll take advantage of your new keyboard shortcut as you add more artwork to the package. The imported artwork contains the words *ZX-Tel cellular,* originally created with the Type tool in Illustrator, but then converted to a graphic. You can no longer edit the text with the Type tool. However, because of this conversion, you don't have to worry about whether others working on the file can see the type correctly if they don't have the same font installed.

1 Press F7 to open the Place dialog box.

2 Select the ZX-Tel logo.ai file in the Lesson09 folder. Click Place. The Place PDF dialog box appears.

3 Leave the settings at their defaults, and click OK to place the file. The logo image opens in Free Transform mode, so you can modify it.

The Place command adds a photo, art, or any file Photoshop supports as a Smart Object to your document. You may remember from earlier lessons that Smart Objects preserve an image's source content with all its original characteristics, enabling you to edit the Smart Object layer nondestructively. However, when you're using a Smart Object, some filters and effects are not available.

4 Drag the logo over the front panel, and then drag the corner points to resize the logo to roughly the width of the box front. Don't worry about being exact; you'll use the Vanishing Point filter to position the logo in perspective soon.

5 When you are satisfied with the positioning, press Enter or Return to place the file.

The placed image appears as the ZX-Tel logo layer at the top of the Layers panel. The icon in the lower-right corner of the layer thumbnail indicates that it is a Smart Object.

6 Choose File > Save to save your work so far.

Adding artwork in perspective

You'll apply the text you just placed to the three-dimensional box. Then, you'll transform and stylize it so that it looks realistic and in perspective. Because Smart Objects don't support the Vanishing Point filter, you'll start by converting the vector data in the Smart Object layer to pixels.

1   In the Layers panel, right-click (Windows) or Control-click (Mac OS) the ZX-Tel layer name, and choose Rasterize Layer from the context menu. This converts the Smart Object to a flat, raster layer.

2   Choose Image > Adjustments > Invert to invert the color from black to gray. This will make it easier to read the text when it's added to the box.

3   With the ZX-Tel logo layer selected in the Layers panel, choose Select > All. The entire ZX-Tel logo layer is selected.

4   Choose Edit > Cut.

5   Choose Filter > Vanishing Point to return to the perspective plane. The 3D box with the cell phone artwork is already there.

6 Press Ctrl+V (Windows) or Command+V (Mac OS) to paste the logo onto the perspective plane, and drag it into position on the front of the box.

7 Press Ctrl+T (Windows) or Command+T (Mac OS) to access the free transform handles. Drag the handles to adjust the logo so that it matches the perspective of the box. You may need to rotate the logo.

8 Press the Alt (Windows) or Option (Mac OS) key, and drag a cloned copy of the logo directly upwards and onto the top of the box. When you're satisfied with the positioning, click OK.

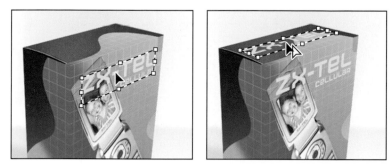

9 Choose File > Save to save your work.

Adding a layer style

Now you'll add a layer style to give the logo some depth. Layer styles are automated effects that you can apply to a layer.

1 In the Layers panel, select the ZX-Tel logo layer.

2 Choose Layer > Layer Style > Bevel And Emboss. Leave the settings at their defaults, and click OK.

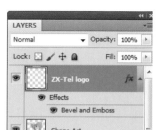

Now the logo has sharp, deep edges, to give the box the appearance of more depth.

Placing the side panel artwork

To complete the package, you'll add product copy to the side panel of the box.

1   Press F7, and select the Side Box Copy.ai file. Click Place. In the Place PDF dialog box, leave the settings at their defaults, and click OK.

2   Press the Shift key, and drag a corner to resize the placed image down to roughly the size of the side panel. Then press Enter or Return to place the artwork.

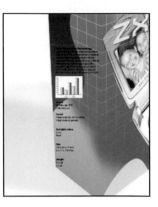

3   In the Layers panel, right-click (Windows) or Control-click (Mac OS) the side box copy layer name, and choose Rasterize Layer from the context menu.

You will select the type and change its color to make it more legible.

4   Select the Polygonal Lasso tool (⊬) in the Tools panel, hidden under the Lasso tool (⦾).

5   Using the Polygonal Lasso tool, click at each corner to draw a box around the top block of text. Then hold down the Shift key, and draw another box around the bottom block of text to add to the selection. You don't want to include the graph.

You used the Polygonal Lasso tool because the lines of text form a slightly irregular shape. You could also use the Rectangular Marquee tool.

6   Press Ctrl+I (Windows) or Command+I (Mac OS) to invert the color from black to white. Then choose Select > Deselect.

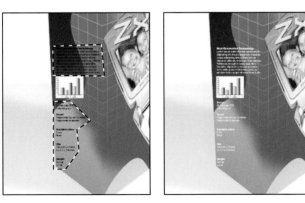

Adding more artwork in perspective

Now you'll add the copy from the side panel to your 3D box.

1 Select the side box copy layer, and choose Select > All.

2 Press Ctrl+X (Windows) or Command+X (Mac OS) to cut the contents to the clipboard.

3 Choose Filter > Vanishing Point.

4 Press Ctrl+V (Windows) or Command+V (Mac OS) to paste the side copy artwork onto the perspective plane.

5 Position the artwork so that it fits along the side panel. If necessary, press Ctrl+T (Windows) or Command+T (Mac OS), and use the free transform handles to adjust the artwork so that it fits properly.

6 When you're satisfied with how the side copy artwork looks, click OK.

Now you'll repeat this procedure one more time to place the last piece of artwork and add it to the box in perspective.

7 Press F7, and double-click the Special Offer.ai file. Click OK to close the Place PDF dialog box. Resize the artwork to fit in the lower-left corner of the box front, and then press Enter or Return to place the file.

8 In the Layers panel, right-click (Windows) or Control-click (Mac OS) the special offer layer name, and choose Rasterize Layer from the context menu. The layer is no longer a Smart Object.

9 Place the special offer layer on the box in perspective, following the same procedure you used to add the box artwork, text, and side copy:

- With the special offer layer active, choose Select > All.

- Press Ctrl+X (Windows) or Command+X (Mac OS) to cut the contents to the clipboard.

- Choose Filter > Vanishing Point.

- Press Ctrl+V (Windows) or Command+V (Mac OS) to paste the contents from the clipboard.

- Position the artwork in the lower-left corner of the front panel, and then click OK.

10 Choose File > Save to save your work.

Adding an adjustment layer

To enhance the realism of the package, you'll add an adjustment layer that creates a shadow over the side panel.

Adjustment layers can be added to an image to apply color and tonal adjustments without permanently changing the pixel values in the image. For example, if you add a Color Balance adjustment layer to an image, you can experiment with different colors repeatedly, because the change occurs only on the adjustment layer. If you decide to return to the original pixel values, you can hide or delete the adjustment layer.

You've used adjustment layers in other lessons. Here, you'll add a Levels adjustment layer to increase the tonal range of the selection, in effect increasing the overall contrast. An adjustment layer affects all layers below it in the image's stacking order, unless a selection is active when you create it.

1 In the Layers panel, select the side box copy layer.

2 Select the Polygonal Lasso tool (⊬) in the Tools panel, and click at each corner to draw a rectangular shape around the side panel.

3 Click the Levels button in the Adjustments panel to create an adjustment layer. (If the Adjustments panel isn't open, choose Window > Adjustments.)

4 In the Layers panel, double-click the name Levels 1, and rename it **Shadow**. Press Enter or Return.

5 In the Adjustments panel, drag the right (white) triangle in the Output Levels slider to about **210** to decrease the brightness. Then click the Return To Adjustment List button (◀) at the bottom of the Adjustments panel.

6 Choose File > Save to save your work.

7 Experiment by clicking the Show/Hide Visibility button (👁) for the Shadow adjustment layer to see its effect. Because you made a selection before you created the adjustment layer, it affects only the selected area.When you finish, make sure that all layers but Full Art are visible.

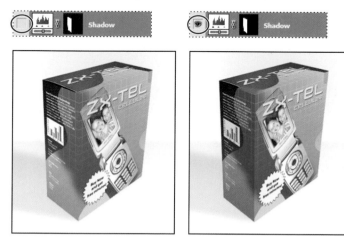

Working with layer comps

Next, you'll save this configuration as a layer comp. Layer comps let you easily switch between various combinations of layers and effects within the same Photoshop file. A layer comp is a snapshot of a state of the Layers panel.

1 Choose Window > Layer Comps.

2 At the bottom of the Layer Comps panel, click the New Layer Comp button. Name the new layer comp **Black Box**, and type a description of its appearance in the Comment box: **3D box, black top and side shape with full-color art**. Click OK.

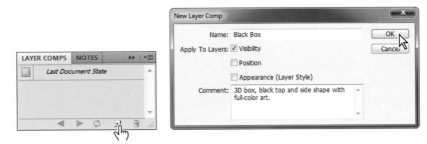

Now you'll make some changes and save the new look as a different layer comp.

3 In the Layers panel, hide the Black Box and Shape Art layers, and show the Full Art layer.

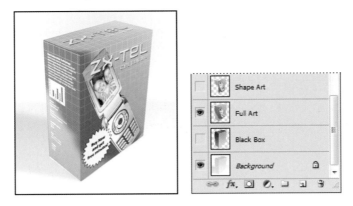

You'll save this version as a new layer comp.

4 In the Layer Comps panel, click the New Layer Comp button. Type **Full Image**, and enter a description: **3D box, blue top with full-color art**. Click OK.

5 In the Layer Comps panel, toggle the visibility icons to show and hide your two layer comps and view the differences.

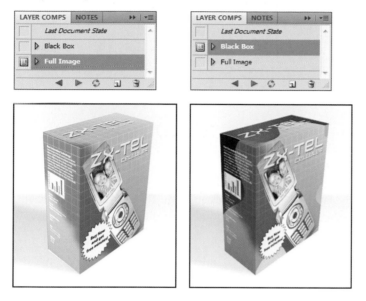

You can also use layer comps to record the layer position in the document or the layer appearance, including layer styles and blending modes.

6 Choose File > Save to save your work.

Managing layers

With layer comps, you learned a great way to present different design options for a package. It's also helpful to be able to group your layers by content. You'll organize your type and art elements by creating a separate group for each.

1 In the Layers panel, Control-click (Windows) or Command-click (Mac OS) to select the special offer, side box copy, and ZX-Tel logo layers.

2 From the Layers panel menu, choose New Group From Layers. Type **Box Type** for the name, and click OK.

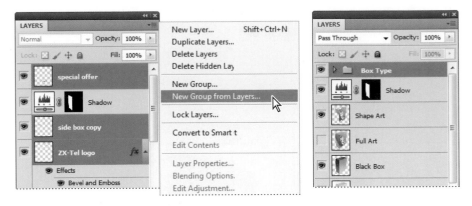

3 Select the Shadow adjustment layer, and then Shift-click the Full Art layer to select them and the layer (Shape Art) between them. Then, choose New Group From Layers from the Layers panel menu, and name this group **Box Artwork**. Then click OK.

Layer groups help you organize and manage individual layers. You can expand a layer group to view its layers, or collapse the group to simplify your view. You can change the stacking order of layers within a layer group.

4 Hide each layer group to see how the layers are grouped together. Then show the layer groups again.

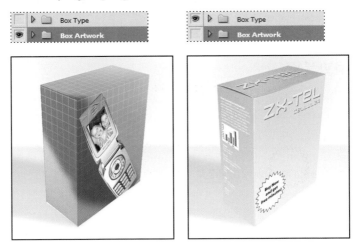

Layer groups can function like layers in a number of ways. You can select, duplicate, and move entire groups, as well as apply attributes and masks to the entire layer group. Any changes you make at the group level apply to all the layers within the group.

Flattening a layered image

As you've done in previous lessons of this book, you'll now flatten the layered image. When you flatten a file, all layers are merged into a single background, greatly reducing the size of the file. If you plan to send a file out for proofs, it's a good idea to save two versions of the file—one containing all the layers so that you can edit the file if necessary, and one flattened version to send to the print shop.

1 Note the values in the lower-left corner of the image or application window. If the display does not show the file size (such as "Doc: 5.01M/43M"), click the arrow, and choose Show > Document Sizes.

| 25% | Doc: 5.01M/31.4M | ▶ ◀ |

The first number is the printing size of the image, which is about the size that the saved, flattened file would be in Adobe Photoshop format. The number on the right indicates the approximate document size of the file as it is now, including layers and channels.

2 Choose Image > Duplicate, name the duplicate file **09Final.psd**, and click OK.

3 From the Layers panel menu, choose Flatten Image. Click OK when prompted to discard hidden layers.

The layers for the 09Final.psd file are combined onto a single background layer. Now the file sizes in the lower-left area of the work area are similar to the smaller number that you saw earlier. Note that flattening fills transparent areas with white.

| 25% | Doc: 5.01M/5.01M | ▶ ◀ |

4 Choose Edit > Undo Flatten Image.

You'll try another way to merge layers and reduce the file size.

Merging layers and layer groups

Unlike flattening a layered image, merging layers allows you to select which layers to flatten or leave unflattened.

You'll merge all the elements of the box, while keeping the Box Type layer group and Background layer untouched. This way, you could return to the file and reuse the Background and Box Type layers at any time.

1 In the Layers panel, hide the Box Type layer group to hide all of its layers.

2 Select the Box Artwork layer group in the Layers panel.

3 Choose Layer > Merge Visible. Any layers that aren't visible in the layer group will remain, unmerged, in the Layers panel.

4 Choose Edit > Undo Merge Visible.

You'll try another way to merge layers and reduce the file size.

Stamping layers

You can combine the benefits of flattening an image while keeping some layers intact by *stamping* the layers. Stamping flattens two or more layers and places the flattened image into a new layer, while leaving other layers intact. This is useful if you need to use a flattened image but also need to keep some layers intact for your work.

1 In the Layers panel, select the Box Artwork group.

2 Press Alt (Windows) or Option (Mac OS) while you choose Layer > Merge Group. The Layers panel displays a new layer that includes your merged image. To reduce the file size, you could delete the original layers from the file.

3 Choose File > Save. In the Save As dialog box that appears, click Save to save the file in Photoshop format. Click OK if the Photoshop Format Options dialog box appears.

You've created a three-dimensional composite image and explored multiple ways to save final artwork.

Review questions

1 Why would you use layer groups?

2 How can you clip a layer to a shape?

3 How do adjustment layers work, and what is the benefit of using them?

4 What are layer styles, and why would you use them?

5 What is the difference between flattening, merging, and stamping layers?

Review answers

1 Layer groups let you organize and manage layers. For example, you can move all the layers in a layer group, and then apply attributes or a mask to the entire group.

2 Position the layer you want to clip above the layer you want to use as a clipping path. Select the first layer, and then press Alt or Option as you position the pointer between the layers, and click. The clipped layer is indented, with an arrow pointing down to the clipping path layer.

3 An adjustment layer applies color and tonal adjustments without changing the underlying pixels. You can show or hide, edit, delete, or mask adjustment layers without permanently affecting the image.

4 Layer styles are customizable effects that you can apply to layers. You can use them to apply changes to a layer, and you can modify or remove them at any time.

5 Flattening an image merges all layers into a single background, greatly reducing the size of the file. Merging layers lets you choose which layers to flatten; this technique combines all selected or visible layers in one layer. Stamping combines the benefits of flattening an image with the benefits of keeping some layers intact; it flattens two or more layers and places the flattened image into a new layer, while leaving other layers intact.

10 ADVANCED COMPOSITING

Lesson overview

In this lesson, you'll learn how to do the following:

- Add guides to help you place and align images precisely.

- Save selections and load them as masks.

- Apply color effects only to unmasked areas of an image.

- Apply filters to selections to create various effects.

- Add layer styles to create editable special effects.

- Record and play back an action to automate a series of steps.

- Blend images to create a panorama.

 This lesson will take about 90 minutes to complete. Copy the Lesson10 folder onto your hard drive if you haven't already done so. As you work on this lesson, you'll preserve the start files. If you need to restore the start files, copy them from the *Adobe Photoshop CS5 Classroom in a Book* DVD.

Filters can transform ordinary images into extraordinary digital artwork. Choose from filters that blur, bend, sharpen, or fragment images, or that simulate a traditional artistic medium, such as watercolor. You can also use adjustment layers and painting modes to vary the look of your artwork.

Getting started

In this lesson, you'll create souvenirs from a vacation to Washington, D.C. You'll assemble a montage of images for a postcard, and then stitch together a panorama to create a poster. First, look at the final projects to see what you'll be creating.

1   Start Photoshop, and then immediately hold down Ctrl+Alt+Shift (Windows) or Command+Option+Shift (Mac OS) to restore the default preferences. (See "Restoring default preferences" on page 5.)

2   When prompted, click Yes to delete the Adobe Photoshop Settings file.

3   Click the Mini Bridge button (Mb) in the Application bar to open the Mini Bridge panel.

4   In the Mini Bridge panel, click Browse Files, and then click Favorites. Then, double-click the Lessons folder. In the Content pane, double-click the Lesson10 folder.

5   View the 10A_End.psd thumbnail, and press the spacebar for a full-screen view.

This file is a postcard that comprises four photos. Each image has had a specific filter or effect applied to it.

6   Press the spacebar to return to Photoshop. Then, select the 10B_End.psd thumbnail, and press the spacebar to see a full-screen view of it.

This file is a poster with a panoramic image and text. You'll create the postcard with multiple images first.

7   Press the spacebar to return to Photoshop. Then, double-click the 10A_Start.jpg thumbnail to open the file in Photoshop.

Assembling a montage of images

The postcard is a montage of four different images. You'll crop each image, and add them as separate layers to a composite image. Using guides, you'll align the images precisely without much effort. Before you make additional changes to the images, you'll add the text and apply effects to it.

Opening and cropping the images

The images you'll use in the insets are larger than you need, so you'll crop them before combining them in a composite file. Cropping images involves aesthetic choices about where and how much of the image to crop. The 10A_Start.jpg file is already open, so you'll start with it.

1 Select the Crop tool (⌗). In the options bar, enter **500 px** for the Width and **500 px** for the Height. Enter **300** pixels/inch for the Resolution.

● **Note:** Be sure to enter 500 pixels, not 500 inches!

The crop box will be a fixed size of 500 pixels by 500 pixels.

2 Drag a crop box around the right side of the image, so that the Smithsonian Institution is the focus of the cropped area. You can use the Right Arrow and Left Arrow keys on your keyboard to nudge the crop box into position if necessary.

3 When you're satisfied with the crop area, double-click inside the crop area, or press Enter or Return to apply it.

Because you're working with several files, you'll give the 10A_Start.jpg file a descriptive name, so that it will be easy to identify. You'll also save the file in the Photoshop format, because each time you edit and then resave a JPEG file, its quality degrades.

4 Choose File > Save As, choose Photoshop for the Format, and name the cropped image **Museum.psd**. Make sure it's in the Lesson10 folder, and click Save.

5 In the Mini Bridge panel, double-click the Capitol_Building.jpg and then the Washington_Monument.jpg file to open them.

The image files open in Photoshop, each with its own tab.

6 Select the Washington_Monument.jpg file, and choose File > Save As. Choose Photoshop for the Format, and rename the file **Monument.psd**. Then click Save.

7 Select the Capitol_Building.jpg tab. Choose File > Save As, choose Photoshop for the Format, and rename the file **Capitol.psd**. Then click Save.

8 Follow steps 1–3 to crop the Capitol.psd and Monument.psd files. Then save each file.

Cropped versions of Museum.psd, Capitol.psd, and Monument.psd

9 In Mini Bridge, double-click the Background.jpg file to open it in Photoshop.

10 Choose File > Save As. Choose Photoshop for the Format, and rename the file **10A_Working.psd**. Then click Save. Leave all four files open for the next exercise.

Positioning images using guides

Guides are nonprinting lines that help you align elements in your document, either horizontally or vertically. If you choose a Snap To command, the guides behave like magnets: When you drag an object close to a guide and then release the mouse button, the object snaps into place along the guide. You'll add guides to the background image that you'll use as the basis for the composite.

1 Click the View Extras button (▦) in the Application bar, and choose Show Rulers. Rulers appear along the top and left edges of the window.

2 Choose Window > Info to open the Info panel.

3 From the horizontal ruler, drag a guide to the middle of the image, and release the mouse when the Y coordinate value in the Info panel is 3.000 inches. A blue guide line appears across the image.

 **Note:** If the ruler units are marked in a unit other than inches, right-click or Control-click a ruler, and choose Inches from the context menu.

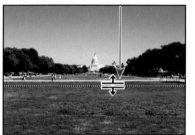
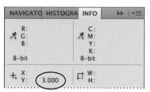

4 Drag another guide, this time from the vertical ruler, and release the mouse when X = 3.000 inches.

5 Choose View > Snap To, and make sure Guides is selected.

6 Drag another guide from the vertical ruler to the middle of the image. Though you could move it further, it snaps into place at the exact midpoint of the image.

▶ **Tip:** If you need to adjust a ruler guide, use the Move tool.

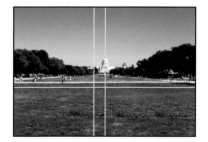

7 Click the Arrange Documents button (▦) on the Application bar, and select the Tile All In Grid option. All four images are visible, each in its own window.

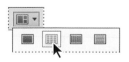

8 Select the Move tool (⊹), and then drag the Museum.psd image onto the 10A_Working.psd image. Photoshop places the Museum.psd image on its own layer in the 10A_Working.psd file.

9 Drag the Monument.psd and Capitol.psd images onto the 10A_Working.psd file.

10 Close the Monument.psd, Capitol.psd, and Museum.psd files without saving them.

11 Rename the layers in the Layers panel to correspond with the appropriate images: **Musuem**, **Monument**, and **Capitol**. If you dragged them in the order listed above, rename Layer 1 **Museum**, Layer 2 **Monument**, and Layer 3 **Capitol**.

12 Select the Monument layer, and then select the Move tool (⊹) in the Tools panel. Move the Monument layer to the center of the canvas, with its top edge aligned to the horizontal guide.

13 Select the Capitol layer, and then drag it to the left of the monument so that the top of the image snaps onto the horizontal guide. Space it evenly between the image of the monument and the left edge of the postcard. Do the same for the Museum layer, placing it to the right of the monument image.

14 Choose View > Show > Guides to hide the guides. Then choose View > Rulers to hide them.

15 Choose File > Save to save your work so far. Click OK if the Photoshop Format Options dialog box appears.

Extra Credit

It was easy to align the images using centered guides, but for greater precision, Smart Guides are an excellent way to align photos and objects. Using your working file as it is after the "Positioning images using guides" exercise, you can try another way to align these photos; or continue with the lesson and try this technique some other time.

1 Select the Museum layer in the Layers panel. In the image window, use the Move tool to move the image out of alignment.

2 Choose View > Show > Smart Guides.

3 Using the Move tool, drag the Museum image in the image window to align its top edge with the top edge of the monument

4 Choose View > Show > Smart Guides to hide the Smart Guides.

Adding text to a montage

You'll add text to the postcard, and then apply some effects to it.

1 Select the Text tool (T). Then click in the sky area and type **Greetings From**. Click the Commit Edits button in the options bar to accept the text. Photoshop creates a new text layer.

2 With the Greetings From text layer selected, choose Window > Character, and then enter the following settings in the Character panel:

- Font: Chapparal Pro, Regular
- Font size: **36** pt
- Tracking: **220**
- Color: Red
- All Caps (TT)
- Anti-Aliasing (ᵃa): smooth

3 Select the Move tool (►₊), and then move the text across the center of the top of the canvas. It snaps into place when it's centered even though the guides are hidden, because Snap To Guides is still selected.

4 Select the Text tool again, click on the canvas, and type **Washington, D.C.** Then click the Commit Edits button.

Photoshop used the current settings in the Character panel for the new text.

5 Enter the following settings in the Character panel:

- Font: Myriad Pro, Bold
- Font Size: **48** pt
- Tracking: **0**
- Color: White

(Leave All Caps selected, and Anti-Aliasing set to smooth.)

6 Use the Move tool to drag the Washington, D.C. text to the center of the canvas, just below the other text.

7 Select the Greetings From text layer in the Layers panel. Click the Add A Layer Style button (*fx*) at the bottom of the Layers panel, and choose Outer Glow.

8 Apply these settings in the Outer Glow area of the Layer Style dialog box:

- Blend Mode: Screen

- Opacity: **40**%

- Color: White

- Spread: **14**%

- Size: **40** px

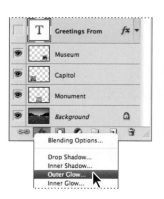

9 Click OK to accept the layer style.

10 In the Tools panel, click the Foreground Color swatch, and then select red from the Color Picker dialog box. Click OK.

You'll use the foreground color to create stripes in the lower text.

11 Select the Washington, D.C. text layer, click the Add A Layer Style button (*fx*), and choose Gradient Overlay.

12 In the Gradient Overlay area of the Layer Style dialog box, click the arrow next to the Gradient swatch to open the Gradient pop-up menu. Select the gradient that looks like red and transparent stripes (the next-to-last one in the menu). You'll use the defaults for the other settings.

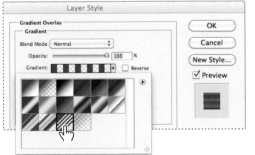

13 Click Drop Shadow in the list on the left to add another effect to the same text. In the Drop Shadow area of the dialog box, change the Opacity to **45**% and the Distance to **9** px. Leave the other settings unchanged.

14 Click OK to apply the effects and close the Layer Style dialog box. Then choose File > Save to save your work so far.

Applying filters

Photoshop includes many filters for creating special effects. The best way to learn about them is to test different filters with various options on your files. You can use the Filter Gallery to preview a filter's effect on your image without committing to it.

You've used filters in some earlier lessons. In this lesson, you'll apply the Graphic Pen filter to the museum image for a hand-sketched effect.

Improving performance with filters

Some filter effects can be memory-intensive, especially when applied to a high-resolution image. You can use these techniques to improve performance:

- Test filters and settings on a small portion of an image.

- Apply the effect to individual channels—for example, to each RGB channel—if the image is large and you're having problems with insufficient memory. (Note, however, that some filters may produce different results when you apply them to individual channels rather than the composite image, especially if the filter randomly modifies pixels.)

- Free up memory before running the filter by using the Purge commands in the Edit menu.

- Close other open applications to free more memory for Photoshop. If you're using Mac OS, allocate more RAM to Photoshop.

- Try changing settings to improve the speed of memory-intensive filters such as Lighting Effects, Cutout, Stained Glass, Chrome, Ripple, Spatter, Sprayed Strokes, and Glass filters. For example, with the Stained Glass filter, you might increase cell size. With the Cutout filter, try increasing Edge Simplicity, decreasing Edge Fidelity, or both.

- If you plan to print to a grayscale printer, convert a copy of the image to grayscale before applying filters. However, applying a filter to a color image and then converting to grayscale may not have the same effect as applying the filter to a grayscale version of the image.

1 Select the Museum layer in the Layers panel.

2 In the Tools panel, click the Default Foreground And Background Colors button (⬛) to return the foreground color to black.

The Graphic Pen filter uses the foreground color.

3 Choose Filter > Filter Gallery.

The Filter Gallery includes a preview window, lists of available filters, and the settings for the selected filter. This is a great place to test filter settings on your image before you decide which settings to apply.

4 Click the triangle next to Sketch to expand the section. Then, select Graphic Pen. The image preview immediately changes to reflect the default values for that filter.

5 In the rightmost pane, set the Light/Dark Balance to **25**. Leave the other options at their default settings. (Stroke Length should be 15, and the Stroke Direction should be Right Diagonal.) The preview updates.

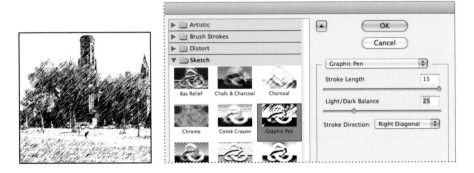

6 Click OK to apply the filter and close the Filter Gallery.

7 Choose File > Save to save your work so far.

Using filters

As you consider which filter to use and the effect it might have, keep in mind the following:

- The last filter chosen appears at the top of the Filter menu.
- Filters are applied to the active, visible layer.
- Filters cannot be applied to bitmap-mode or indexed-color images.
- Some filters work only on RGB images.
- Some filters are processed entirely in RAM.
- To apply more than one filter in the Filter Gallery, click the New Filter button at the bottom of the filters list, and then select a filter.
- See "Using filters" in Photoshop Help for a list of filters that can be used with 16- and 32-bit-per-channel images.
- Photoshop Help provides specific information on individual filters.

Julieanne Kost is an official Adobe Photoshop evangelist.

Tool tips from the Photoshop evangelist

Using filter shortcuts

These powerful shortcuts can save time when working with filters:

- To reapply the most recently used filter with its last values, press Ctrl+F (Windows) or Command+F (Mac OS).
- To display the dialog box for the last filter you applied, press Ctrl+Alt+F (Windows) or Command+Option+F (Mac OS).
- To reduce the effect of the last filter you applied, press Ctrl+Shift+F (Windows) or Command+Shift+F (Mac OS).

Hand-coloring selections on a layer

Before the days of color photography, artists painted color onto black-and-white images. You can create the same effect by hand-coloring selections on a layer. In this exercise, you'll hand-color the museum image, and then add stars to the sky in the background image.

Applying painting effects

You'll use different brushes, with varying opacities and blending modes, to add color to the sky, grass, and building in the museum image.

1   In the Layers panel, Ctrl-click (Windows) or Command-click (Mac OS) the image thumbnail on the Museum layer. The contents of the layer are selected.

You can paint only within the selection, so you don't need to worry about painting the background image or the other images. Just make sure you see the selection border around the image before you start painting.

2   Zoom in to the museum image so that you can see it clearly.

▶ **Tip:** You can change the brush opacity by pressing a number on the keypad from 0 to 9 (where 1 is 10%, 9 is 90%, and 0 is 100%).

3   Select the Brush tool (✍). In the options bar, select a **90**-pixel brush with a Hardness of **0**. Choose Darken from the Mode menu. Set the brush opacity to **20**%.

4   Click the Foreground Color swatch in the Tools panel, and select a color of bright blue (not too light). You'll use this color to paint the sky.

▶ **Tip:** To change the brush size as you paint, press the bracket keys on your keyboard. The Left Bracket key ([) decreases the brush size; the Right Bracket (]) increases it.

5   Paint the sky in the museum image. Because the opacity is set to 20%, you can paint over the same area again to darken it. Don't be afraid to paint near the borders; nothing outside the image border is affected by the paintbrush. You can change the brush size and opacity as you paint; for example, you may need a smaller brush to paint the areas between tree tops. If you make a mistake, press Ctrl+Z (Windows) or Command+Z (Mac OS) to undo it. But remember that you're going for a handpainted look; it doesn't need to be perfect.

6 Paint the trees and grass the same way. Change the foreground color to green, and then set up a **70**-pixel soft brush, using the Darken blending mode, and **80%** opacity. It's fine to paint over the black sketched areas; only the white areas show much color.

▶ **Tip:** When hand-coloring an image, work from the background forward, so that you can overpaint any stray marks.

7 Next, paint the museum façade a dark red color. Start with a **40**-pixel brush, using the Lighten blending mode, and **80%** opacity.

Using the Lighten blending mode affects the black lines rather than the white areas.

8 When you're satisfied with the painting, choose Select > Deselect to deselect the image. Then choose File > Save to save your work.

Saving selections

In order to fill the background sky with handpainted stars, you need to save a selection of the sky. First, you'll save the background image as a Smart Object so that you can apply Smart Filters to it later.

1   In the Layers panel, right-click (Windows) or Control-click (Mac OS) the Background layer, and choose Convert To Smart Object. (The Background layer is at the bottom of the layer stack.)

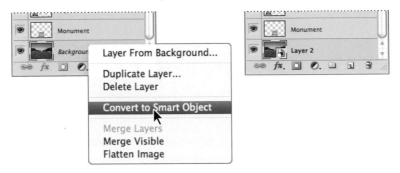

The layer name changes to Layer 2. An icon appears in the layer thumbnail, indicating that the layer is now a Smart Object. Filters, called *Smart Filters*, are applied to Smart Objects nondestructively, so that you can continue to edit them later.

2   Rename Layer 2 **Capitol and Mall**.

3   Double-click the image thumbnail on the Capitol and Mall layer; click OK in the informational message.

The Smart Object opens in its own image window. You can edit it without affecting any other objects.

4   Select the Quick Selection tool (⟋), and use it to select the sky. If you need to remove an area of the selection, click the Subtract From Selection button in the options bar, and then click the area you need to deselect. Don't worry about making the selection perfect.

For help using the Quick Selection tool and other selection tools, see Lesson 3, "Working with Selections."

5 With the sky selected, click Refine Edge in the options bar. Change the following settings, and click OK:

- Smooth: **25**
- Feather: **30**
- Shift Edge: **-20**

These settings will feather the edge of the skyline so that the selection will not have a hard edge.

6 Choose Select > Save Selection. In the Save Selection dialog box, name the selection **Sky**, and click OK.

7 Choose Select > Deselect.

Painting with a special effects brush

You'll add stars to the sky you just selected, using a star-shaped brush.

1 Press D to restore the default foreground and background colors to the Tools panel. Then press X to switch them, so that white is the foreground color.

You'll paint white stars on the sky, so the foreground color needs to be white.

2 Select the Brush tool (✐). In the options bar, open the Brush Preset picker.

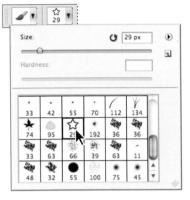

3 Scroll down in the Brush Preset picker, and select the Star brush. Increase its size to **300** pixels, choose Normal from the Mode menu, and select **100%** opacity.

Now that you have your brush set up, you need to load the selection you saved.

4 Choose Select > Load Selection. In the Load Selection dialog box, choose Sky from the Channel menu, and click OK.

5 In the Layers panel, click the New Layer button. Rename the layer **Paint**.

6 Paint stars in the sky. You can paint near the edges, because only the selection will be affected. Just make sure the selection remains active.

● **Note:** If you want to start over, just delete the Paint layer and create a new layer. To delete a layer, drag it to the Delete Layer button in the Layers panel.

7 When you're satisfied with the arrangement of the stars, change the Opacity of the Paint layer to **50**% in the Layers panel. Then, in the Layers panel, choose Overlay from the Blending Mode menu.

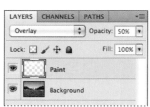

8 Choose File > Save, and then close the Smart Object. When Photoshop returns you to the 10A_Working.psd image, choose View > Fit On Screen so you can see the entire postcard.

The stars have been added to your postcard. You can edit the stars at any time by double-clicking the image thumbnail in the Layers panel to open the Smart Object.

9 Choose File > Save to save your work.

Applying Smart Filters

Unlike regular filters, which permanently change an image, Smart Filters are non-destructive: They can be adjusted, turned off and on, and deleted. However, you can apply Smart Filters only to a Smart Object.

You already converted the Capitol and Mall layer to a Smart Object. You'll apply several Smart Filters to the layer, and then add some layer styles.

1   Select the Capitol and Mall layer in the Layers panel. Then choose Filter > Artistic > Cutout.

Photoshop opens the Filter Gallery, with the Cutout filter selected and applied to the preview. The Cutout filter makes an image appear as if it were constructed from roughly cut pieces of colored paper.

2   On the right side of the dialog box, change the Number of Levels to **8**, leave Edge Simplicity at **4**, and move the Edge Fidelity slider to **3**. Then click OK.

Smart Filters appear with the Smart Object in the Layers panel. An icon appears to the right of a layer name if filter effects are applied to a layer.

3 Double-click the Cutout filter in the Layers panel to open the Filter Gallery again. Click the New Effect Layer button (⬛) at the bottom of the applied filters list, and then select any filter. Experiment with the settings until you're satisfied, but don't click OK yet.

We chose Film Grain from the Artistic folder, and used the following settings: Grain 2, Highlight Area 6, and Intensity 1.

You can mix and match Smart Filters and turn them off and on.

4 In the applied filters list in the Filter Gallery, drag the Cutout filter above the second filter you applied to see how the effect changes. Click OK to close the Filter Gallery.

The order in which you apply filters can change the effect. You can also hide an effect by clicking the eye icon (👁) next to its name in the filter list.

You'll use filters to give the other inset images a handpainted look without going to all the trouble of painting them manually. First, you'll convert them to Smart Objects.

5 Select the Capitol layer, and then choose Filter > Convert For Smart Filters. Click OK in the informational dialog box. The Capitol layer is now a Smart Object.

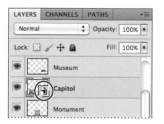

6 Select the Monument layer, and choose Filter > Convert For Smart Filters to convert it to a Smart Object, too.

7 Select the Capitol layer, and then choose Filter > Filter Gallery, and select a filter you like. Experiment with the settings until you find an effect you like. Then click OK to apply the filter.

We chose the Crosshatch filter (in the Brush Strokes folder), with a Stroke Length of 12, Sharpness of 9, and Strength of 1.

8 Select the Monument layer, and choose Filter > Filter Gallery. Select a filter you like, and then click OK to apply it.

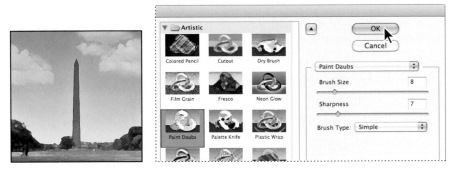

You can apply almost any filter, including third-party filters, as a Smart Filter. The only exceptions are the Extract, Liquify, Pattern Maker, and Vanishing Point filters, because those require access to the original image pixels. In addition to filters, you can apply the Shadows/Highlights and Variations adjustments to Smart Objects.

9 Choose File > Save to save your work.

Adding drop shadows and a border

You're almost done with the postcard. To make the inset images stand out a little more, you'll add drop shadows to them. Then, you'll add a border around the entire postcard.

1 Select the Capitol layer, and click the Add A Layer Style button (*fx*) at the bottom of the Layers panel. Choose Drop Shadow.

2 In the Layer Style dialog box, change the Opacity to **40**%, Distance to **15** px, Spread to **9**%, and the Size to **9** px. Then click OK.

3 In the Layers panel, press Alt (Windows) or Option (Mac OS) as you drag the Drop Shadow effect from the Capitol layer onto the Monument layer.

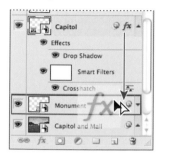

4 Alt-drag or Option-drag the same Drop Shadow effect onto the Museum layer.

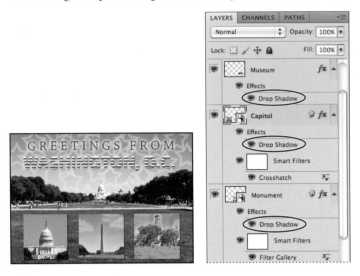

Now you'll expand the canvas so that you can add a border without covering any of your image.

5 Choose Image > Canvas Size, and enter **7** inches for the Width and **5** inches for the Height. Click OK.

A transparent border appears around the image. You'll make that border appear white.

6 Press D to return the foreground and background colors to the defaults in the Tools panel, so that the background layer is white.

7 In the Layers panel, click the Create A New Layer button (⬛), and then drag the new layer to the bottom of the layer stack. Name it **Border**.

8 With the Border layer selected, choose Select > All.

9 Choose Edit > Fill. In the Fill dialog box, choose Background Color from the Use menu, and click OK.

10 Choose File > Save to save the postcard.

The postcard is ready to print and mail. It's a standard U.S. Postal Service postcard size.

11 Close the 10A_Working.psd file. You'll use different files to create the panorama.

Matching color schemes across images

You'll be combining four images into a panorama for the poster. To provide continuity in the panorama, you'll harmonize the color schemes in the images by matching the target image to the dominant colors in a source. First, you'll open the document that you'll use as the source for the color matching.

1 In the Mini Bridge panel, double-click the IMG_1441.psd file to open it. (Click the Mini Bridge button (🔲) in the Application bar if the panel isn't open.)

There are four sequentially numbered images in the same folder. You'll match the colors for these files.

2 In the Mini Bridge panel, double-click the IMG_1442.psd file to open it.

The IMG_1442.psd file is overexposed in some areas, and a little washed out. You'll use the Match Color feature to match its colors to those in the source file.

3 With the IMG_1442.psd file active, choose Image > Adjustments > Match Color. In the Match Color dialog box, do the following:

- Select the Preview option, if it's not already selected.

- Choose IMG_1441.psd from the Source menu.

- Choose the Background layer from the Layer menu. You can select any layer in the source image, but this image has only one layer.

- Experiment with the Luminance, Color Intensity, and Fade settings.

- When the color scheme unifies the colors in the images, click OK.

4 Choose File > Save to save the IMG_1442.psd file with the new colors.

You can use Match Color with any source file to create interesting and unusual effects. The Match Color feature is also useful for certain color corrections (such as skin tones) in some photographs. The feature can also match the color between different layers in the same image. See Photoshop Help for more information.

Automating a multistep task

An *action* is a set of one or more commands that you record and then play back to apply to a single file or a batch of files. In this exercise, you'll use actions to color match, sharpen, and save the images you'll combine in a panorama.

Using actions is one of several ways that you can automate tasks in Adobe Photoshop. To learn more about recording actions, see Photoshop Help.

You've already matched the color for one of the images. Now, you'll sharpen one image using the Unsharp Mask filter, and save it to a new Ready For Panorama folder.

1 With the IMG_1442.psd file active, choose Filter > Sharpen > Unsharp Mask.

2 In the Unsharp Mask dialog box, change the Radius to **1.2**, leave the other settings unchanged, and click OK.

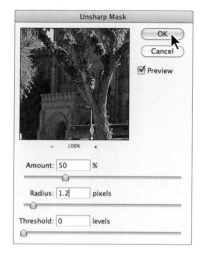

3 Choose File > Save As. Choose TIFF for the Format, use the same name (IMG_1442), and save it to a new folder called **Ready For Panorama**. Then click Save.

4 In the Image Compression area of the TIFF Options dialog box, select LZW, and click OK.

5 Close the IMG_1442.tif file.

Preparing to record an action

You use the Actions panel to record, play, edit, and delete individual actions. You also use the Actions panel to save and load action files. First, you'll open the Actions panel and open the additional files you'll be using.

1 Choose Window > Actions to open the Actions panel.

2 In the Actions panel, click the Create New Set button (□). Name the new set **My Actions**, and click OK.

3 Choose File > Open. In the Open dialog box, navigate to the Lesson10 folder. Shift-select the IMG_1443.psd, IMG_1444.psd, IMG_1445.psd, and IMG_1446.psd files. Then click Open.

Now there are five tabs, representing five open files in Photoshop.

Recording actions

● **Note:** You must finish all steps in this procedure without interruption. If you need to start over, skip ahead to step 8 to stop the recording; then drag the action onto the Delete button in the Actions panel. Use the History panel to delete any states after you opened the files. Then start again at step 1.

You'll record the steps for matching colors, sharpening, and saving the images as an action.

1 Select the IMG_1443.psd tab. Then, in the Actions panel, click the New Action button (▣).

2 In the New Action dialog box, name the action **color match and sharpen**, and make sure that My Actions is selected in the Set menu. Then click Record.

Don't let the fact that you're recording rush you. Take all the time you need to do this procedure accurately. The speed at which you work has no influence on the amount of time required to play a recorded action.

3 Choose Image > Adjustments > Match Color.

4 In the Match Color dialog box, select IMG_1441.psd from the Source menu, select Background from the Layer menu, and make any other changes that you made when you matched color for IMG_1442.psd. Click OK.

5 Choose Filter > Sharpen > Unsharp Mask. The settings in the Unsharp Mask dialog box should be the settings you used for the IMG_1442.psd file. Click OK.

Photoshop preserves your most recent settings in filter dialog boxes until you change them again.

6 Choose File > Save As. In the Save As dialog box, choose TIFF for the Format, keep the same name (IMG_1443), and save the file to the Ready For Panorama folder. Click Save. In the TIFF Options dialog box, make sure LZW is selected, and click OK.

7 Close the image.

8 Click the Stop button (■) at the bottom of the Actions panel to stop recording.

The action you just recorded is now saved in the Actions panel. Click the arrows to expand different sets of steps. You can examine each recorded step and the specific selections you made.

Playing an action

You'll apply the color match and sharpen action to one of the other three image files that you opened.

1 Click the IMG_1444.psd tab to make that image active.

2 In the Actions panel, select the color match and sharpen action in the My Actions set, and then click the Play button (▶).

The IMG_1444.psd image is automatically color matched, sharpened, and saved as a TIFF, and it now matches the IMG_1443.tif image for these properties. Because you recorded closing the file, the file has also been closed.

Batch-playing an action

Applying actions is a timesaving process for performing routine tasks on files, but you can streamline your work even further by applying actions to all open files. Two more files in this project need to be prepared for the panorama, so you'll apply your automated action to them simultaneously.

1 Make sure that the IMG_1445.psd and IMG_1446.psd files are open. Close the IMG_1441.psd file, and then open it again to ensure that it's the third tab.

2 Choose File > Automate > Batch.

3 In the Play area of the Batch dialog box, choose My Actions from the Set menu, and choose color match and sharpen from the Action menu.

4 Choose Opened Files from the Source menu. Leave Destination set to None, and click OK.

● **Note:** If the IMG_1441.psd file is not the third tab, it will close before the color can be matched for one or both of the other images. Match Color requires that the source file be open. Simply rearranging the tabs doesn't change the order in which Photoshop applies the action.

The action is applied to both IMG_1445.psd and IMG_1446.psd, so the files have the same color matching and sharpening and are saved as TIFF files. The same action was applied to IMG_1441.psd, even though its color was matched with itself.

In this exercise, you batch-processed three files instead of making all the same changes in each of them; this was a mild convenience. But creating and applying actions can save significant amounts of time and tedium when you have dozens or even hundreds of files that require any routine, repetitive work.

Stitching a panorama

The files have been color matched, sharpened, and saved to prevent unsightly inconsistencies in your panorama. Now you're ready to stitch the images together! Then, you'll add a border with lettering to complete the poster.

1 With no files open in Photoshop, choose File > Automate > Photomerge.

2 In the Layout area, select Auto. Then, in the Source Files area, click Browse, and navigate to the Lesson10/Ready For Panorama folder. Select the first image, press Shift, and select the last so that all the images are selected, and click OK or Open.

3 At the bottom of the Photomerge dialog box, select Blend Images Together, Vignette Removal, and Geometric Distortion Correction. Then click OK.

Photoshop creates the panorama image. It's a complex process, so you may have to wait several minutes while Photoshop works. When it's finished, you should see an image that looks similar to the one below, with six layers in the Layers panel—one for each of the images. Photoshop has found the overlapping areas of the images and matched them, correcting any angular discrepancies. In the process, it left some empty areas. You'll make the panorama tidy by adding a little sky to fill in some of the empty area, and by cropping the image.

4 Select all the layers in the Layers panel, and then choose Layer > Merge Layers.

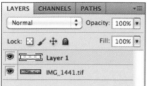

5 Choose File > Save As. Choose Photoshop for the Format, and name the file **10B_Working.psd**. Save the file in the Lesson10 folder. Click Save, and then click OK in the Photoshop Format Options dialog box.

6 Select the Crop tool (⊞). In the options bar, click Clear to remove any values in the Height, Width, and Resolution boxes, so you can crop to any size. Then draw a crop selection from the edge of the grass (where its bottom edge is highest) to the highest point of the image (just above the highest museum tower). Crop out all the transparent areas on the sides. When you are satisfied with your cropped area, press Enter or Return.

7 In the Layers panel, click the Create A New Layer button (⬜).

8 Select the Rectangular Marquee tool (⬚), and then draw a selection across the top of the image, where you want to add sky. It's fine to overlap trees and buildings; just make sure to cover all of the transparent areas (represented by a checkerboard pattern).

9 Select the Eyedropper tool (✐), choose All Layers from the Sample menu in the options bar, and then select a dark blue from the sky for your foreground color. Select a light blue color for the background color.

10 With the selection still active, select the Gradient tool (▦). In the options bar, select the Foreground To Background gradient in the Gradient preset picker. Then, drag the gradient tool vertically from the top to the bottom of the selection.

11 Choose Select > Deselect. Then, select both layers in the Layers panel, and choose Edit > Auto-Blend Layers. In the Blend Method area, select Panorama, and click OK.

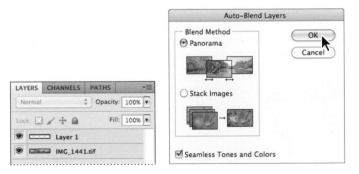

Photoshop blends the layers together based on their content. When it's done, the selected area is filled with sky, and it's no longer blocking the buildings or trees.

12 With both layers selected, choose Layer > Merge Layers.

The poster needs only the lettering on the side to be complete.

13 Choose File > Open, navigate to the Lesson10 folder, and double-click the DC_Letters.psd file to open it.

14 Click the Arrange Documents button in the Application bar, and choose a 2 Up layout option so that you can see both files. Then, use the Move tool (⊹) to drag the DC_Letters.psd image onto the Panorama image. Close the DC_Letters.psd file without saving it.

15 With the Move tool, position the lettering and red background along the left side of the image.

Because you're preparing this poster for printing, you'll convert it to CMYK.

16 Choose Image > Mode > CMYK Color. Click Merge to merge layers. Click OK if you see a color profile informational dialog box.

17 Choose Layer > Flatten Image to reduce the image size.

18 Choose File > Save to save your work.

You've created two photographic souvenirs by combining images. You created a montage of several images, and you blended images into a panorama. You're ready to create montages and panoramas from your own images.

Review questions

1 What is the purpose of saving selections?

2 How can you preview filter effects before you commit to them?

3 What are the differences between using a Smart Filter and a regular filter to apply effects to an image?

4 Describe one use for the Match Color feature.

Review answers

1 By saving a selection, you can create and reuse time-consuming selections and uniformly select artwork in an image. You can also combine selections or create new selections by adding to or subtracting from existing selections.

2 Use the Filter Gallery to test different filters with different settings to see the effect they'll have on your image.

3 Smart Filters are nondestructive: They can be adjusted, turned off and on, and deleted at any time. In contrast, regular filters permanently change an image; once applied, they cannot be removed. Smart Filters can be applied only to a Smart Object layer.

4 You can use the Match Color feature to match color between different images, such as to adjust the facial skin tones in photographs—or to match color between different layers in the same image. You can also use the feature to create unusual color effects.

11 PAINTING WITH THE MIXER BRUSH

Lesson overview

In this lesson, you'll learn how to do the following:

- Customize brush settings.

- Clean the brush.

- Mix colors.

- Create a custom brush preset.

- Use wet and dry brushes to blend color.

 This lesson will take about an hour to complete. Copy the Lesson11 folder onto your hard drive if you have not already done so. As you work on this lesson, you'll preserve the start files. If you need to restore the start files, copy them again from the *Adobe Photoshop CS5 Classroom in a Book* DVD.

The new Mixer Brush tool gives you flexibility, color-mixing abilities, and brush strokes as if you were painting on a physical canvas.

About the Mixer Brush

In previous lessons, you've used brushes in Photoshop to perform various tasks. The Mixer Brush is unlike other brushes, in that it lets you mix colors with each other. You can change the wetness of the brush and how it mixes the brush color with the color already on the canvas.

In Photoshop CS5, brushes have more realistic bristles as well, so you can add textures that resemble those in paintings you might create in the physical world. While this is a great feature in general, it's particularly useful when you're using the Mixer Brush. Combining different bristle settings and brush tips with different wetness, paint-load, and paint-mixing settings gives you opportunities to create exactly the look you want.

Getting started

In this lesson, you'll get acquainted with the Mixer Brush as well as the brush tip and bristle options available in Photoshop CS5. Start by taking a look at the final project you'll create.

1   Start Adobe Photoshop, holding down Ctrl+Alt+Shift (Windows) or Command+Option+Shift (Mac OS) to restore the default preferences. (See "Restoring default preferences" on page 5.)

2   When prompted, click Yes to delete the Adobe Photoshop Settings file.

3   Click the Launch Bridge button (⌷) in the Application bar to open Adobe Bridge.

4   In Bridge, click Lessons in the Favorites panel. Double-click the Lesson11 folder in the Content panel.

5   Preview the Lesson11 end files. You'll use the palette image to explore brush options and learn to mix colors. You'll then apply what you've learned to transform the landscape image into a watercolor.

● **Note:** If you plan to do a lot of painting in Photoshop, consider using a tablet, such as a Wacom tablet, instead of a mouse. Photoshop can sense the way you hold and use the pen to change the brush width, strength, and angle on the fly.

6   Double-click 11Palette_start.psd to open the file in Photoshop.

7   Choose File > Save As, and name the file **11Palette_working.psd**. Click OK if the Photoshop Format Options dialog box appears.

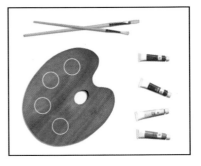

Selecting brush settings

The image includes a palette and four tubes of color, which you'll use to sample the colors you're working with. You'll change settings as you paint different colors, exploring brush tip settings and wetness options.

Note: If you have OpenGL enabled, Photoshop displays a sampling ring so you can preview the color you're picking up.

1 Select the Zoom tool (🔍), and zoom in to see the tubes of paint.

2 Select the Eyedropper tool (🖊), and sample the red color from the red tube. The foreground color changes to red.

3 Select the Mixer Brush tool (🖌), hidden under the Brush tool (🖌).

Note: Depending on the complexity of your project, you may need to be patient. Mixing colors can be a memory-intensive process.

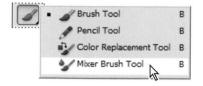

4 Choose Window > Brush to open the Brush panel. Select the first brush.

The Brush panel contains brush presets and several options for customizing brushes.

▶ Tip: Remember that you can Alt-click (Windows) or Option-click (Mac OS) to sample a color instead of using the Eyedropper tool. To sample only solid colors using the keyboard shortcut, choose Load Solid Colors from the Current Brush Load pop-up menu in the options bar.

5   In the options bar, choose Dry from the pop-up menu of blending brush combinations.

The effect of the brush is determined by the Wet, Load, and Mix fields in the options bar. Wet controls how much paint the brush picks up from the canvas. Load controls how much paint the brush holds when you begin painting (as with a physical brush, it runs out of paint as you paint with it). Mix controls the ratio of paint from the canvas and paint from the brush.

You can change these settings separately. However, it's faster to select a standard combination from the pop-up menu. When you select Dry, Wet is set to 0%, Load to 50%, and Mix is not applicable. With the Dry preset, you paint opaque color; you cannot mix colors on a dry canvas.

6   Paint in the area above the red tube. Solid red appears. As you continue painting without releasing the mouse, the paint eventually fades and runs out.

7   Sample the blue color from the blue tube of paint. You can use the Eyedropper tool or Alt-click (Windows) or Option-click (Mac OS) to sample the color. If you use the Eyedropper tool, return to the Mixer Brush tool after you sample the color.

8   In the Brush panel, select the round fan-shaped brush. Choose Wet from the pop-up menu in the options bar.

9 Paint above the blue tube. The paint mixes with the white background.

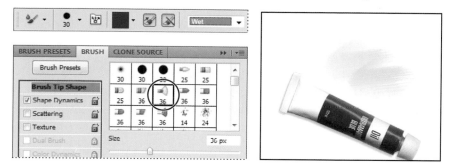

10 Choose Dry from the menu in the options bar, and then paint again above the blue tube. A much darker, more opaque blue appears, and doesn't mix with the white background.

The bristles from the fan brush you selected are much more apparent than the bristles you used originally. Changing bristle qualities makes a big difference in the texture you paint.

11 In the Brush panel, decrease the number of bristles to **40**%. Paint a little more with the blue brush to see the change in texture. The bristles are much more obvious in the stroke.

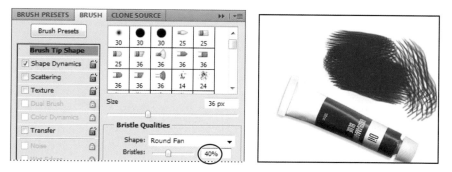

▶ **Tip:** The Bristle Brush Preview, shows you the direction of the bristles as you paint. To show or hide the Bristle Brush Preview, click the Toggle The Bristle Brush Preview button at the bottom of the Brush or Brush Presets panel. The Bristle Brush Preview is available only with Open GL enabled.

12 Sample the yellow color from the yellow paint tube. In the Brush panel, select the flat-point brush with fewer bristles (the one to the right of the fan brush). Choose Dry from the menu in the options bar, and then paint in the area over the yellow paint tube.

● **Note:** When you use the Alt-click or Option-click to load paint from the canvas, the brush picks up any color variation in the sample area. If you want to sample only solid colors, select Load Solid Colors Only in the Current Brush Load menu in the options bar.

▶ **Tip:** For different effects, paint in different directions. With the Mixer Brush tool, you can go wherever your artistic instincts lead you.

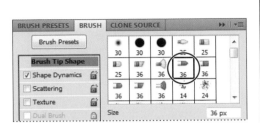

13 Choose Very Wet from the menu in the options bar, and then paint some more. Now the yellow mixes with the white background.

14 Sample the green color from the green paint tube. Select the flat-angled brush (the fourth one after the fan brush). Increase its Thickness value to **80%**. Then choose Moist from the menu in the options bar. Paint in the area above the green paint tube to mix the green with white. You can paint over the paint tube itself to mix the green with those colors.

Mixing colors

You've used wet and dry brushes, changed brush settings, and mixed the paint with the background color. Now, you'll focus more on mixing colors with each other as you add paint to the painter's palette.

1 Zoom out just enough to see the full palette and the paint tubes.

2 Select the Paint mix layer in the Layers panel, so the color you paint won't blend with the brown palette on the Background layer.

The Mixer Brush mixes colors only on the active layer unless you select Sample All Layers in the options bar.

3 Sample the red color from the red paint tube. Select the round blunt brush in the Brush panel (the fifth brush). Then select Wet from the pop-up menu in the options bar, and paint in the top circle on the palette.

4 Click the Clean Brush After Every Stroke icon (✖) in the options bar to deselect it.

5 Sample the blue color from the blue paint tube, and then paint in the same circle, mixing the red with the blue to make purple.

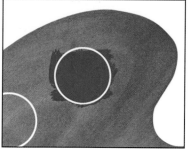 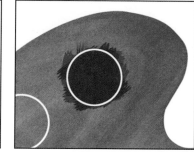

6 Paint in the next circle. You're painting in purple because the paint stays on the brush until you clean it.

7 In the options bar, choose Clean Brush from the Current Brush Load pop-up menu. The preview changes to indicate transparency, meaning the brush has no paint loaded.

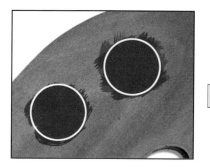 

To remove the paint load from a brush, you can choose Clean Brush in the options bar. To replace the paint load in a brush, sample a different color.

If you want Photoshop to clean the brush after each stroke, select the Clean Brush icon in the options bar. To load the brush with the foreground color after each stroke, select the Load Brush icon in the options bar. By default, both of these options are selected.

8 Choose Load Brush from the Current Brush Load pop-up menu in the options bar to load the brush with blue paint. Paint blue in half of the next circle.

9 Sample the yellow color from the yellow paint tube, and paint over the blue with a wet brush to mix the two colors.

10 Fill the last circle with yellow and red paint, mixing the two with a wet brush to create an orange color.

11 Hide the Circles layer in the Layers panel to remove the outlines on the palette.

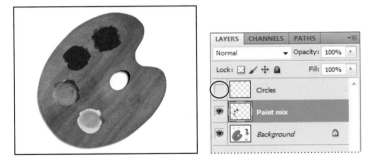

12 Choose File > Save.

Creating a custom brush preset

Photoshop includes numerous brush presets, which are very handy. But if you need to tweak a brush for your project, you might find it easier to create your own preset. You'll create a brush preset to use in the following exercise.

1 In the Brush panel, select the following settings:

- Size: **36** px
- Shape: Round Fan
- Bristles: **25**%
- Length: **25**%
- Thickness: 1%
- Stiffness: **87**%
- Angle: **0**%
- Spacing: **2**%

2 Choose New Brush Preset from the Brush panel menu.

3 Name the brush Landscape, and click OK.

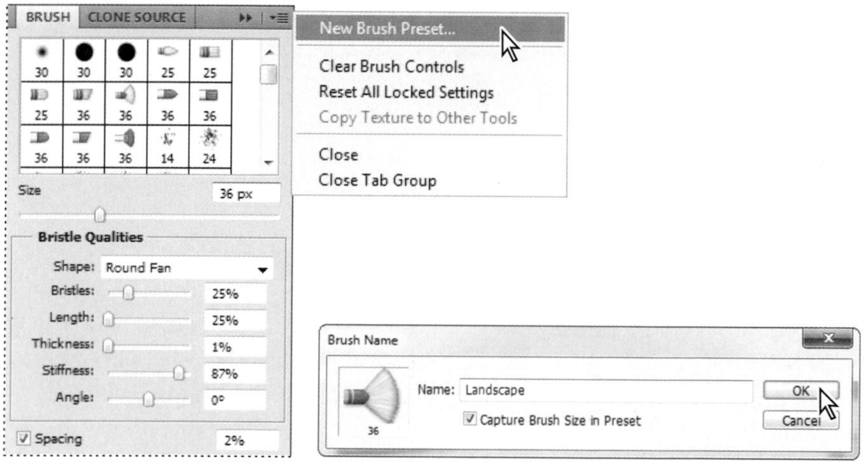

4 Click Brush Presets in the Brush panel to open the Brush Presets panel.

The Brush Presets panel displays samples of the strokes created by different brushes. If you know which brush you want to use, it can be easier to find by name. You'll list them by name now, so you can find your preset for the next exercise.

5 Choose Large List from the Brush Presets panel menu.

6 Scroll to the bottom of the list. The preset you created, named Landscape, is the last preset in the list.

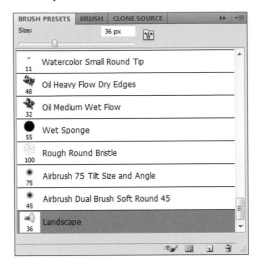

7 Close the 11Palette_working.psd file.

Mixing colors with a photograph

Earlier, you mixed colors with a white background and with each other. Now, you'll use a photograph as your canvas, adding colors and mixing them with each other and with the background colors to transform a photograph of a landscape into a watercolor.

1 Choose File > Open. Double-click the 11Landscape_Start.jpg file in the Lesson11 folder to open it.

2 Choose File > Save As. Rename the file **11Landscape_working.jpg**, and click Save. Click OK in the JPEG Options dialog box.

You'll paint the sky first. Start by setting up the color and selecting the brush.

3 Click the Foreground color swatch in the Tools panel. Select a medium-light blue color (we chose R=185, G=204, B=228), and then click OK.

4 Select the Mixer Brush tool (✐), if it isn't already selected. Choose Dry from the pop-up menu in the options bar. Then select the Landscape brush from the Brush Presets panel.

Presets are saved on your system, so they're available when you work with any image.

5 Paint over the sky, moving in close to the trees. Because you're using a dry brush, the paint isn't mixing with the colors beneath it.

6 Select a darker blue color (we used R=103, G=151, B=212), and add darker color at the top of the sky, still using the dry brush.

7 Select a light blue color again, and choose Very Wet, Heavy Mix from the pop-up menu in the options bar. Use this brush to scrub diagonally across the sky, blending the two colors in with the background color. Paint in close to the trees, and smooth out the entire sky.

Adding darker color with a dry brush   Using a wet brush to blend colors

When you're satisfied with the sky, move on to the grass and trees.

8 Select a light green (we used R=92, G=157, B=13). Choose Dry from the pop-up menu in the options bar. Then, paint along the top section of the grass to highlight it.

9 Sample a darker green from the grass itself. Choose Very Wet, Heavy Mix in the options bar. Then paint using diagonal strokes to blend the colors in the grass.

Adding light green with a dry brush

Blending colors with a wet brush

10 Sample a light green, and then use a dry brush to highlight the lighter areas of the trees and the small tree in the middle of the landscape. Then select a dark green (we used R=26, G=79, B=34), and choose Very Wet, Heavy Mix in the options bar. Paint with the wet brush to mix together the colors in the trees.

Highlighting the trees

Mixing the colors

So far, so good. The background trees and the brown grasses are all that remain to be painted.

11 Select a bluer color for the background trees (we used R=65, G=91, B=116). Paint with a dry brush to add the blue at the top. Then choose Wet in the options bar, and paint to mix the blue into the trees.

12 Sample a brown color from the tall grasses, and then select Very Wet, Heavy Mix in the options bar. Paint along the top of the tall grass with up-and-down strokes for the look of a field. Across the back area, behind the small center tree, paint back and forth to create smooth strokes.

Voilà! You've created a masterpiece with your paints and brushes, and there's no mess to clean up.

Review questions

1 What does the Mixer Brush do that other brushes don't?

2 How do you load a mixer brush?

3 How do you clean a brush?

4 How can you display the names of brush presets?

5 What is the Bristle Brush Preview, and how can you hide it?

Review answers

1 The Mixer Brush mixes the color of the paintbrush with colors on the canvas.

2 You can load a mixer brush by sampling a color, either by using the Eyedropper tool or keyboard shortcuts (Alt-click or Option-click). Or, you can choose Load Brush from the pop-up menu in the options bar to load the brush with the foreground color.

3 To clean a brush, choose Clean Brush from the pop-up menu in the options bar.

4 To display brush presets by name, open the Brush Presets panel, and then choose Large List (or Small List) from the Brush Presets panel menu.

5 The Bristle Brush Preview shows you the direction the brush strokes are moving. It's available if Open GL is enabled. To hide or show the Bristle Brush Preview, click the Toggle The Bristle Brush Preview icon at the bottom of the Brush panel or the Brush Presets panel.

12

WORKING WITH 3D IMAGES

Lesson overview

In this lesson, you'll learn how to do the following:

- Create a 3D shape from a layer.

- Manipulate 3D objects using the Object Rotate tool.

- Adjust the view using the Camera Rotate tool.

- Configure options in the 3D panel.

- Adjust light sources.

- Import 3D objects.

- Manipulate objects using the 3D Axis tool.

- Paint on a 3D object.

- Create 3D text.

- Apply the 3D postcard effect.

- Animate a 3D file.

 This lesson will take about 90 minutes to complete. Copy the Lesson12 folder onto your hard drive if you have not already done so. As you work on this lesson, you'll preserve the start files. If you need to restore the start files, copy them again from the *Adobe Photoshop CS5 Classroom in a Book* DVD.

Traditional 3D artists spend hours, days, and weeks creating photo-realistic images. The 3D capabilities in Photoshop let you create sophisticated, precise 3D images easily—and you can change them easily, too.

Getting started

This lesson explores 3D features, which are available only in Adobe Photoshop CS5 Extended. If you are not using Photoshop CS5 Extended, skip this lesson, and proceed to Lesson 13.

Many of the 3D features in Photoshop CS5 Extended require OpenGL 2.0. If your video card does not support OpenGL 2.0, you won't be able to complete many of the exercises in this lesson. In particular, the Repoussé command and some tools designed to assist you in working with 3D images aren't available if your video card doesn't support OpenGL or if it isn't enabled. If your video card supports OpenGL 2.0, you can enable it in the Photoshop Preferences dialog box.

In this lesson, you'll create and fine-tune the CD cover art for a fictitious band named *Brick Hat*. Then, you'll create a 3D postcard from that cover art for use in an advertisement.

First, you'll view the finished CD cover art.

1 Start Adobe Photoshop, holding down Ctrl+Alt+Shift (Windows) or Command+Option+Shift (Mac OS) to restore the default preferences. (See "Restoring default preferences" on page 5.)

2 When prompted, click Yes to delete the Adobe Photoshop Settings file.

3 Click the Launch Bridge button (▣) in the Application bar to open Adobe Bridge.

4 In Bridge, click Lessons in the Favorites panel. Double-click the Lesson12 folder in the Content panel, and then double-click the 12End folder.

5 View the 12End.psd file and the 12End_Layers.psd file in the Content panel. If your video card supports OpenGL, you should see both images. Both files are CD cover art.

The 12End_Layers.psd file includes all the layers, before the file was flattened. You may find it useful to refer to this file as you work through the lesson.

Creating a 3D shape from a layer

Photoshop includes several 3D shape presets, representing geometric shapes and the shapes of everyday objects, such as a wine bottle or ring. When you create a 3D shape from a layer, Photoshop wraps the layer onto the 3D object preset. You can then rotate, reposition, and resize the 3D object—you can even light it from various angles with a number of colored lights.

You'll start by creating a 3D hat using the layer that contains the image of a brick wall.

1 In Bridge, return to the Lesson12 folder, and then double-click the 12Start.psd thumbnail to open the file in Photoshop. The 12Start.psd file contains several layers with the contents of the final CD cover: music notes, sky, a brick wall texture, and a blank background.

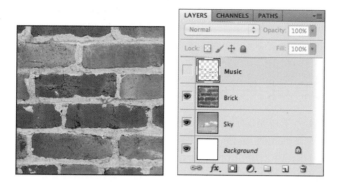

2 Choose Window > Workspace > 3D to display the 3D and Layers panels, which you'll use in this lesson.

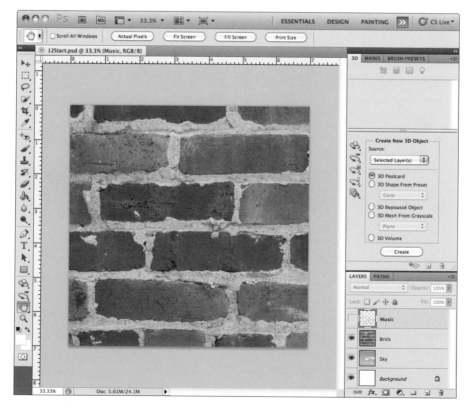

Note: If your video card does not support OpenGL, Photoshop may warn you that the shape will be rendered with software. Click OK to close the warning.

3 Select the Brick layer, and then choose 3D > New Shape From Layer > Hat.

Photoshop creates a 3D object, wrapping the 2D image of bricks around the shape of a hat.

Manipulating 3D objects

The advantage to working with 3D objects is, obviously, that you can work with them in three dimensions. You can also return to a 3D layer at any time to change lighting, color, material, or position without having to re-create a lot of the art. Photoshop CS5 Extended includes several basic tools that make it easy to rotate, resize, and position 3D objects. The 3D Object Rotate tool and the other tools grouped with it in the Tools panel manipulate the object itself. In addition, the 3D Rotate Camera tool and its group change the camera positions and angles, which can have a dramatic effect on your object.

You can use the 3D tools whenever a 3D layer is selected in the Layers panel. A 3D layer behaves like any other layer—you can apply layer styles, mask it, and so on. However, a 3D layer can be quite complex.

Unlike a regular layer, a 3D layer contains one or more *meshes*. A mesh defines the 3D object. In the layer you just created, the mesh is the hat shape. Each mesh, in turn, includes one or more *materials*—the appearance of a part or all of the mesh. Each material includes one or more *maps*, which are the components of the appearance. There are nine typical maps, including the Bump map, and there can be only one of each kind; however, you can also use custom maps. Each map contains one *texture*—the image that defines what the maps and materials look like. The texture may be a simple bitmap graphic or a set of layers. The same texture might be used by many different maps and materials. In the layer you just created, the image of the brick wall composes the texture.

In addition to meshes, a 3D layer also includes one or more *lights*, which affect the appearance of 3D objects and remain in a fixed position as you spin or move the object. A 3D layer also includes *cameras*, which are saved views with the objects in a particular position. The *shader* creates the final appearance based on the materials, object properties, and renderer.

That may all sound complicated, but the most important thing to remember is that some tools move objects in 3D space and some tools move the cameras that view the object.

1 In the Tools panel, select the 3D Rotate Camera tool (⟲). When you select the 3D Rotate Camera tool, several other 3D tools become available in the options bar.

2 In the options bar, choose Top from the View pop-up menu. You're now viewing the top of the hat.

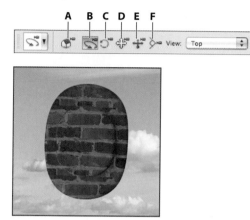

A. Return to initial camera position
B. 3D Rotate Camera tool
C. 3D Roll Camera tool
D. 3D Pan Camera tool
E. 3D Walk Camera tool
F. 3D Zoom Camera tool

● **Note:** If OpenGL is enabled, a 3D widget, called the 3D Axis, appears on the screen, with red, blue, and green representing different axes. You can use the 3D Axis to position and move the object.

Options in the View menu determine the angle from which you see the object.

3 In the Tools panel, select the 3D Object Rotate tool (⟲).

4 Click in the center of the hat and drag outward, in a circle, around the edge of the composition. Drag diagonally, as well, to get a feel for how the 3D Object Rotate tool moves the object on the x and y axes.

5 Select the 3D Object Roll tool (⟳) in the options bar. Drag the hat. Notice that you can flip the hat around, but you're constrained to movement on a single axis.

6 Select the 3D Object Pan tool (⊕) in the options bar. Drag the hat from side to side, up, or down. With the 3D Object Pan tool, you can move the object on the plane, but you can't rotate it.

7 Select the 3D Object Scale tool (🔲) in the options bar. Click just above the hat, and drag toward the center of the hat until the X, Y, and Z values in the options bar are each **0.75**. The hat is 75% of its original size.

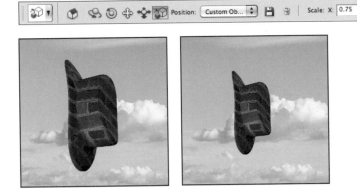

You've used several tools to manipulate the hat. Now, you'll enter values to position the hat precisely.

8 Select the 3D Object Rotate tool (◔) in the options bar. Then, in the Orientation area of the options bar, enter **11** for X, **45** for Y, and **-37** for Z.

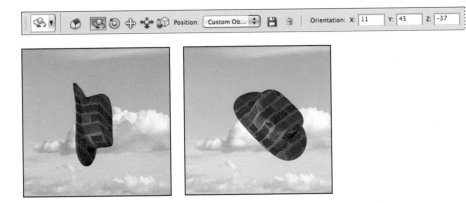

You can use the 3D tools to reposition and rotate a 3D object manually, or, if you know where you want the object to be, select the 3D Object Rotate tool (◔) and type values in the options bar.

9 Choose File > Save As. Navigate to the Lesson12 folder, and save the file as **12Working.psd**. Click OK if the Photoshop Format Options dialog box appears.

Using the 3D panel to adjust lighting and surface texture

One of the benefits of working with a 3D object is that you can adjust the lighting angles and the surface texture on the object. The 3D panel gives you quick access to settings for the scene, mesh, materials, and lighting.

1 In the 3D (Scene) panel, select the Hat Material component. The options in the lower area of the panel change.

2 Enter **80%** for Gloss.

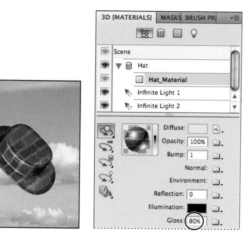

Photoshop adds shine to the hat, as if it's lit from the front.

3 Click the Filter By Lights button (![light icon]) at the top of the 3D panel. The 3D (Lights) panel displays options for lighting.

4 Select the Infinite Light 2 component in the 3D panel.

5 Select the Light Rotate tool (![rotate icon]) in the 3D (Lights) panel.

6 If you're using a video card that supports OpenGL, click the Toggle Misc. 3D Extras button (![extras icon]) at the bottom of the panel, and choose 3D Light to view the light guide.

● **Note:** If your video card does not support OpenGL, the Toggle Misc. 3D Extras button isn't available. However, you can rotate the light without the guide.

7 If light guides are displayed, drag the bulb end of the guide that appears to be entering the top of the hat. As you drag the bulb down, the light shifts over the hat. If guides aren't displayed, move the cursor down on the screen to shift the light.

Because you've selected Infinite Light 2 in the 3D (Lights) panel, only that light changes as you move the cursor across the screen. If you select a different light, the same cursor movement moves the selected light, which creates a different effect.

8 With Infinite Light 2 selected, click the swatch next to Color in the 3D (Lights) panel, and select a pale yellow color. As you select a color for the light, you can preview it in the image window. When you're satisfied with the color, click OK to close the Select Light Color dialog box. Click the Toggle Misc. 3D Extras button, and choose 3D Lights again to hide the light guides.

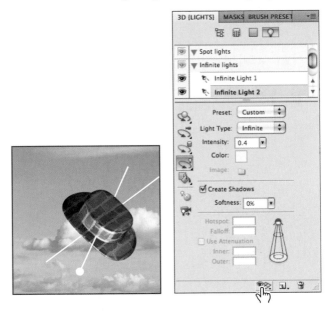

9 Choose File > Save to save your work.

Extra Credit

You can rotate 3D objects, change their lighting, and move the camera positions. But what about seeing what's going on inside? Product designers, medical professionals, and engineers often need to work with 3D objects both outside and in. It's easy to see a cross-section of a 3D object in Photoshop CS5 Extended.

You can take a peek under the hood of this lovely old car to see how cross-sections work.

1   Choose File > Open, and navigate to the Lesson12 folder. Open the Spycar.psd file.

The 3D car was created in a 3D application and imported into Photoshop. You can view a cross-section of any 3D layer in Photoshop Extended, but how much information you see in the cross-section depends on how the object was created and which details the creator included.

2   Choose Window > 3D to open the 3D panel, if it's not already open.

3   Select Cross Section in the 3D panel, and make sure Plane is not selected.

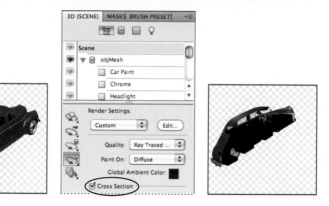

The car is cut in half so that the interior is visible. It's pretty dark, though, and hard to see details. You'll adjust the lighting.

4   Click the Filter By Lights button in the 3D panel.

5   Select the second light in the Infinite Lights category, and then change the Intensity to **4**.

6   Select the Light Rotate tool in the 3D panel, and then drag around the car to rotate the selected light until you can clearly see the interior.

7   Use the 3D tools in the Tools panel to rotate and pan the car so that you can see the cross-section from different angles.

8   To return to viewing the full object, click the Filter By Whole Scene button in the 3D panel, and then deselect Cross Section.

Merging 2D layers onto 3D layers

You created the 3D layer by wrapping a 2D image around a shape. But you can wrap additional 2D layers onto the same shape. Just position them where you want them, and then merge them; they'll follow the shape of the 3D object. You'll merge a layer of musical notes onto the hat.

1 In the Layers panel, select the Music layer, and make it visible. The Music layer is a 2D layer of musical notes. It should be the top layer in the Layers panel, so that it appears in front of the hat and the sky.

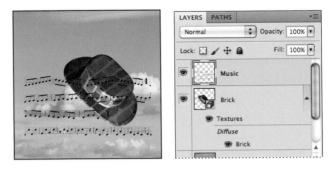

2 Select the Move tool (⊹) in the Tools panel, and then position the Music layer so that the notes are centered over the hat.

3 Choose Layer > Merge Down. The musical notes wrap around the hat, and the Music layer is no longer listed in the Layers panel.

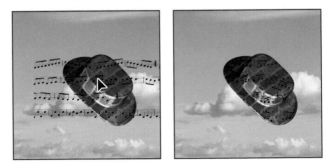

When you use the Merge Down command, Photoshop merges the selected layer with the layer directly beneath it in the Layers panel. The two layers become a single layer, keeping the name of the bottom layer.

Importing 3D files

In Photoshop CS5 Extended, you can open and work with 3D files exported from various applications, such as Collada, 3DS, KMZ (Google Earth) or U3D. You can also work with files saved in Collada format, a file interchange format supported by Autodesk, for example. When you add a 3D file as a 3D layer, it includes the 3D model and a transparent background. The layer uses the dimensions of the existing file, but you can resize it.

You'll create a new 3D layer from the 3D file of a pyramid and scale it down.

1   In the Layers panel, hide the Brick layer, so that only the sky is visible.

2   Select the Sky layer, and choose 3D > New Layer From 3D File. Navigate to the Lesson12 folder, and then double-click the Pyramid.obj file.

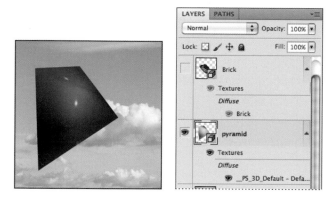

A pyramid appears in the image window, and Photoshop adds a 3D layer named pyramid above the Sky layer in the Layers panel. When you create a 3D layer from an imported file, it's always added above the selected layer.

3 In the Layers panel, make sure the pyramid layer is selected, and then choose Linear Light from the Blending Mode pop-up menu. Lower the Opacity to **85%**.

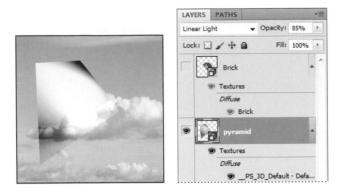

The pyramid looks washed out. You'll change the Diffuse color to give it more body.

4 In the 3D Materials panel, select _PS_3D_Default in the objMesh component.

5 Click the Diffuse color box in the bottom area of the panel, select a gray color (R=145, G=144, B=144) in the Select Diffuse Color dialog box, and click OK.

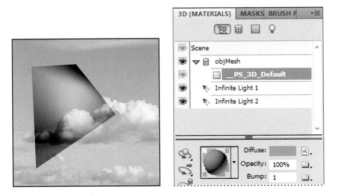

6 Select the 3D Object Scale tool (🔞), hidden under the 3D Object Rotate tool (🔞) in the Tools panel.

7 Click above the pyramid, and drag toward its center until it's half its original size. The X, Y, and Z values in the options bar should each be 0.5.

Merging 3D layers to share the same 3D space

You can include multiple 3D meshes in the same 3D layer. Meshes in the same layer can share lighting effects and be rotated in the same 3D space (also called the *scene*), creating a more realistic 3D effect.

You'll duplicate the pyramid layer, and then merge the two layers into the same 3D layer.

1 In the Layers panel, make sure the pyramid layer is selected, and then choose Duplicate Layer from the Layers panel menu. Click OK in the Duplicate Layer dialog box.

A second pyramid appears directly in front of the first one.

2 Select the pyramid and pyramid copy layers, and then choose 3D > Merge 3D Layers.

The merged layers are in exactly the same position. To position and rotate a mesh individually, you must select the mesh in the 3D (Scene) panel.

Note: To merge 3D layers, their cameras must match. In this case, because the layer was essentially duplicated, the cameras already match.

3 Select the top objMesh component in the 3D (Scene) panel. The panel changes to the 3D (Mesh) panel.

4 Select the 3D Mesh Pan tool (✥), hidden under the 3D Mesh Rotate tool, in the 3D (Mesh) panel.

5 Drag the pyramid to the upper-right corner of the image.

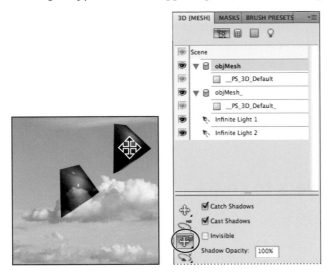

6 Select the objMesh_ component in the 3D (Mesh) panel. The objMesh_ component is the second mesh listed, and it represents the duplicate pyramid.

7 Drag the second pyramid to the lower-left corner of the image window.

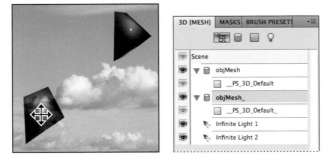

8 With the objMesh_component still selected, select the 3D Mesh Roll tool, hidden beneath the 3D Mesh Pan tool, in the 3D (Mesh) panel. Then click in the bottom center of the image window, and drag to the left to roll the pyramid upright. It doesn't need to be perfect.

You can use the mesh tools to move a selected mesh independently of other meshes in the same layer. However, if you selected the standard 3D Object Roll tool in the Tools panel, all the meshes in the layer would move at the same time.

9 Select the Pan The Mesh tool in the options bar, and drag the upright pyramid back down to the lower-left corner of the image window.

10 Select the objMesh component (the first mesh) in the 3D (Mesh) panel to return to the pyramid in the upper-right corner. Then select the 3D Mesh Scale tool, hidden beneath the 3D Mesh Roll tool in the 3D (Mesh) panel, click in the center of the pyramid, and drag down until the X, Y, and Z values are each **0.6**, so that the pyramid is 60% its original size.

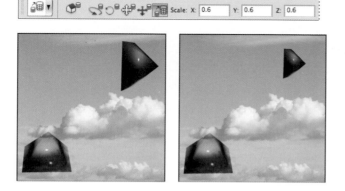

11 Select the 3D Mesh Rotate tool, hidden beneath the 3D Mesh Scale tool, in the 3D (Mesh) panel, and then rotate the pyramid to match the image below. We dragged the right tip of the upper pyramid toward the upper-left corner of the canvas. You may need to use the Drag The Mesh tool to reposition the pyramid after you've rotated it.

12 Click the Filter By Lights button in the 3D (Mesh) panel.

13 Select Infinite Light 1 in the 3D (Lights) panel, and then select the Light Rotate tool (⟲) in the 3D (Lights) panel. Click the Toggle Misc. 3D Extras button, and choose 3D Light. (The Toggle Misc. 3D Extras button is available only if OpenGL is enabled.)

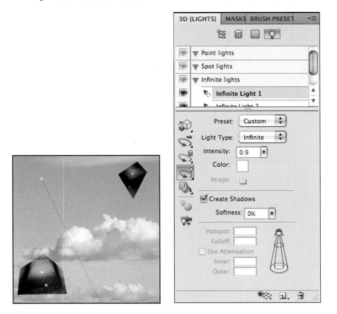

14 Drag the light source (represented by the bulb in the light guide if OpenGL is enabled) to the lower-right corner to change the lighting for both pyramids.

Though the pyramids are different meshes, they can share the same light source because they occupy the same 3D layer.

15 Click the Toggle Misc. 3D Extras button, and choose 3D Light again to hide the light guides. Then choose File > Save.

Adding a spot light

So far, you've manipulated the infinite light sources for 3D objects. You can also intensify the light for a specific area of an object using a spot light. You'll use a spot light to add color to one of the pyramids.

1   Make sure the 3D panel is displaying lighting options; its title should be 3D (Lights). If it isn't, click the Filter By Lights button.

2   Click the Create A New Light button (⊡) at the bottom of the 3D (Lights) panel, and choose New Spot Light.

Spot Light 1 appears in the 3D (Lights) panel in the Spot Lights category.

3   Click the Color swatch in the 3D (Lights) panel, and select a magenta color. (We used R=215, G=101, B=235.) Click OK to close the Select Light Color dialog box.

4   In the 3D (Lights) panel, change the Intensity to 0.7.

5   Select the Light Rotate tool (↻) in the 3D (Lights) panel, and then click on the image and drag down until the top pyramid has a magenta spot light on it. (Or, you can enter values in the options bar. X should be around **98**, Y around **-95**, and Z around **4.5**.)

Tip: If OpenGL is enabled, click the Toggle Misc. 3D Extras button, and choose 3D Light to see the light source shift as you drag.

6 In the Layers panel, make the Brick layer visible so you can see all the elements of your image. Then choose File > Save.

Extra Credit

Manipulating objects in a 3D environment can be tricky and confusing at times. To help you more accurately control the x, y, and z axes, Photoshop provides a 3D Axis widget. If OpenGL is enabled, the 3D Axis widget automatically appears in the upper-left corner of the image when a 3D layer is selected.

The box at the base of the 3D Axis widget scales the 3D object. Each of the colored arrows represents an axis: red for the x axis, green for the y axis, and blue for the z axis. Click the tip of an arrow to move the object on that axis; click the arc to rotate on that axis; click the block to resize on that axis only.

1 In the Layers panel, select the Brick layer.

2 Select the 3D Object Rotate tool in the Tools panel, and then move the cursor over the 3D Axis widget. Notice the black bar that appears above the 3D Axis as the cursor approaches it. This bar makes it possible to resize, reposition, or even hide the 3D Axis widget.

3 Drag the gray bar above the 3D Axis widget to another area on the image. The 3D Axis widget moves with the gray bar.

4 Click the double arrows on the right side of the gray bar to reduce the size of the 3D Axis widget. Click the double arrows again to enlarge the 3D Axis widget.

Moving the 3D Axis widget   *Enlarging the 3D Axis widget*

5 Click the center block at the base of the 3D Axis widget, and then drag it up to enlarge the hat.

6 Click the block on the blue arrow, and drag down to resize the object on the z axis.

Resizing the object on all axes   *Resizing the object on the z axis*

7 Move the cursor over the arc on the blue arrow until you see a yellow circle. Then, drag around that circle to rotate the object on the z axis.

8 Hover over the point of the blue arrow, and drag diagonally to reposition the hat along the z axis.

9 If you're satisfied with the changes you've made, choose File > Save. To return the hat to its previous position, choose File > Revert. Photoshop reverts back to the last version you saved.

Painting on a 3D object

You can paint directly onto 3D objects in Photoshop CS5 Extended using any Photoshop paintbrush, and the paint follows the object's contours.

1 Select the pyramid layer, and then select the Brush tool (✐) in the Tools panel.

2 Click the Foreground Color swatch in the Tools panel, and select a bright green color. (We used R=25, G=207, B=16.)

3 Select a soft, 65-pixel brush, and then paint the tip of the lower pyramid. The green paint follows the edges of the object, and affects nothing else.

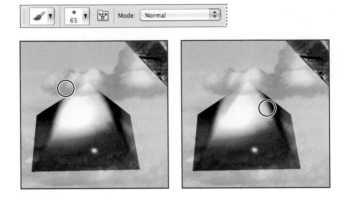

Using Repoussé to create 3D text

The term repoussé refers to a metalworking technique. With repoussé, the faces of objects are shaped by hammering on the opposite side. In Photoshop, you can use the Repoussé command to convert 2D objects into 3D meshes, precisely extruding, inflating, and repositioning them. The Repoussé command requires OpenGL.

You'll use Repoussé to create 3D text, adding dimension to the CD title.

1 Select the Horizontal Type tool, and drag a large text box on the upper-left side of the canvas.

2 Type **BRICK HAT.** Position the type so it's not overlapping with any other objects on the canvas. Select the text, and then, in the options bar, change the font to Myriad Pro, the font style to Bold, the size to **70** pt, and the color to red.

Photoshop adds a new type layer to the Layers panel.

3 With the type layer selected, select the Move tool.

4 In the 3D panel, make sure that Selected Layer(s) is chosen in the Source menu. Then, select 3D Repoussé Object. Click Create.

5 Click Yes when asked whether you want to rasterize the text.

6 In the Repoussé dialog box, select the following settings, and then click OK:

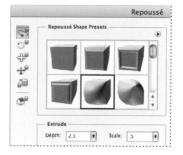

- In the Repoussé Shape Presets area, select Inflate (the middle option in the second row).

- In the Extrude area, enter **2.5** for Depth and **0.5** for Scale.

The extrusion settings make the text appear to recede into space.

7 Use the 3D Object Rotate, 3D Object Scale, and other tools to position the text however you like.

8 Choose File > Save.

Creating a 3D postcard

In Photoshop CS5 Extended, you can transform a 2D object into a 3D postcard that you can manipulate in perspective in a 3D space. It's called a 3D postcard, because it's as if your image became a postcard you could turn over in your hand. To create a 3D postcard, you must flatten all layers in Photoshop.

You'll use a 3D postcard to prepare the CD cover art for use in a larger advertisement.

1 In the Layers panel, choose Flatten Image from the panel menu. Click OK when asked whether you want to flatten layers.

All the layers become a single Background layer.

2 Choose 3D > New 3D Postcard From Layer.

The Background layer becomes a 3D layer. The image doesn't appear to have changed, but when you add a background, it will become more obvious that it's a 3D object. Now, you'll resize it.

3 Select the 3D Object Scale tool (⬡) in the Tools panel. In the options panel, type **.75** for the X and Y values. Press Enter or Return to apply the values.

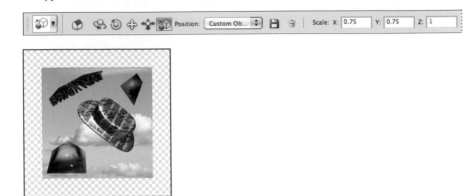

Adding a gradient background

You'll add a gradient in the background to help the postcard stand out.

1 Click the Create A New Layer button in the Layers panel.

2 Rename the new layer **Gradient**, and drag it below the Background layer in the Layers panel.

3 Click the Default Foreground And Background Colors button (◨) in the Tools panel to restore the foreground color to black and the background color to white.

4 Select the Gradient tool (▩) in the Tools panel.

5 Drag the Gradient tool from the top center directly to the bottom of the image.

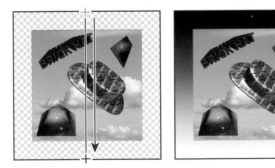

Animating a 3D layer

Now you're ready to have some fun with your 3D postcard. Not only can you swivel it in 3D space, but you can record its movement over time in an animated QuickTime movie. To see the finished animation, play the Lesson12_end.mov file in the Lesson 12 folder. You must have Apple QuickTime installed to view the animation.

1 Rename the Background layer **CD Cover**.

2 Choose Window > Animation to open the Animation panel. The Animation panel lists both layers.

3 In the Animation panel, click the triangle next to the CD Cover layer to display its keyframe attributes. You may need to resize the panel to see the attributes.

4 Click the stopwatch icon (⏱) next to 3D Object Position to create an initial keyframe. The initial keyframe marks the position of the object at 0 seconds.

5 Drag the current-time indicator to 3:00f. This is where you'll set the next keyframe, which will record the object's position at that point in the timeline.

6 Select the 3D Object Rotate tool (◈) in the Tools panel.

7 Hold down the Shift key as you click on the center-left edge of the canvas, and drag the cursor all the way to the right of the canvas. The postcard flips so that you're seeing its back. Photoshop adds a keyframe at 3:00f to mark the new position.

8 Move the current-time indicator back to the beginning of the timeline, and then press Play. Press the spacebar to stop the playback.

It's a catchy little animation, and it's ready to export.

9 Drag the end point of the work area to 3:00f, so the entire work area spans from 0:00 to 3:00f. Photoshop will render the frames included in the work area.

10 In the 3D Panel, choose Ray Traced Final from the Quality panel in the Render Settings area.

11 Choose File > Export > Render Video.

12 In the Render Video dialog box, select QuickTime Export, and choose QuickTime Movie from the pop-up menu. Then click Settings.

13 Click Settings again in the Movie Settings dialog box. From the Compression Type menu, choose H.264. Choose 15 from the Frame Rate menu. Set Quality to Medium, and select Faster Encode for Encoding. Click OK, and click OK again to return to the Render Video dialog box.

14 In the Render Video dialog box, make sure Currently Selected Frames is selected in the Range area. Change the Size to **700** x **700**. Then click Render.

Photoshop renders the movie to your Lesson12 folder.

Extra Credit

3D movies are all the rage again, but now they don't require multi-million-dollar budgets. Photoshop CS5 Extended makes it easy to create images that come to life with traditional red/blue . You can't make the glasses themselves in Photoshop, but if you don't have a pair lying around, you can find them with a quick Internet search or a visit to your local novelty shop.

For extra credit, you can render this CD cover art for a 3D viewing effect.

1   Choose 3D > Render Settings.

2   In the 3D Render Settings dialog box, select the last option. From the Stereo Type menu, choose Red/Blue. For Focal Plane, enter **50**. For Parallax, enter **50**.

3   Click OK, and then render the movie again, using the same settings you used to create the previous QuickTime movie.

When you've created the 3D movie, put on some 3D glasses, and watch the objects on the postcard appear to pop out of the screen!

Review questions

1 How does a 3D layer differ from other layers in Photoshop?

2 What's the difference between the 3D Object Rotate tool and the 3D Camera Rotate tool?

3 What do you use the 3D panel for?

4 Why would you merge two 3D layers?

5 How can you add a spot light to a 3D object?

Review answers

1 A 3D layer behaves like any other layer—you can apply layer styles, mask it, and so on. However, unlike a regular layer, a 3D layer also contains one or more meshes, which define 3D objects. You can work with meshes and the materials, maps, and textures they contain. You can also adjust the lighting for a 3D layer.

2 The 3D Object Rotate tool adjusts the position of the 3D object itself. The 3D Camera Rotate tool changes the camera angle from which the object is viewed.

3 You use the 3D panel to select components in the 3D layer and to set options for modifying meshes, lighting, textures, and other components of the 3D scene.

4 Merging two 3D layers lets you work with the 3D objects in the same 3D space. In a single layer, multiple 3D objects can share lighting sources, for example, but you can continue to manipulate each of the meshes independently.

5 To add a spot light to a 3D object, select its layer in the Layers panel. Then click the Create A New Light button at the bottom of the 3D panel, and choose New Spot Light. Use the options in the 3D (Lights) panel to change the color and intensity of the light. Finally, click on the image and drag the light to position it.

13 PREPARING FILES FOR THE WEB

Lesson overview

In this lesson, you'll learn how to do the following:

- Slice an image in Photoshop.

- Distinguish between user slices and auto slices.

- Link user slices to other HTML pages or locations.

- Optimize images for the web and make good compression choices.

- Export large, high-resolution files that tile for zooming and panning.

- Showcase your images in a media gallery.

 This lesson will take about an hour to complete. Copy the Lesson13 folder onto your hard drive if you have not already done so. As you work on this lesson, you'll preserve the start files. If you need to restore the start files, copy them again from the *Adobe Photoshop CS5 Classroom in a Book* DVD.

Web users expect to click linked graphics to jump to another site or page, and to activate built-in animations. You can prepare a file for the web in Photoshop by adding slices to link to other pages or sites.

Getting started

For this lesson, you will need to use a web browser application such as Firefox, Netscape, Internet Explorer, or Safari. You do not need to connect to the Internet.

In this lesson, you'll fine-tune graphics for the home page of a Spanish art museum's website. You'll add hypertext links to the topics, so that website visitors can jump to other prebuilt pages on the site.

First, you'll explore the final HTML page that you will create from a single Photoshop file.

1   Start Adobe Photoshop, holding down Ctrl+Alt+Shift (Windows) or Command+Option+Shift (Mac OS) to restore the default preferences. (See "Restoring default preferences" on page 5.)

2   When prompted, click Yes to delete the Adobe Photoshop Settings file.

3   Click the Launch Bridge button (⬛) in the Application bar to open Adobe Bridge.

4   In Bridge, click Lessons in the Favorites panel. Double-click the Lesson13 folder in the Content panel, double-click the 13End folder, and finally, double-click the Site folder.

The Site folder contains the contents of the website that you'll be working with.

5   Right-click (Windows) or Control-click (Mac OS) the home.html file, and choose Open With from the context menu. Choose a web browser to open the HTML file.

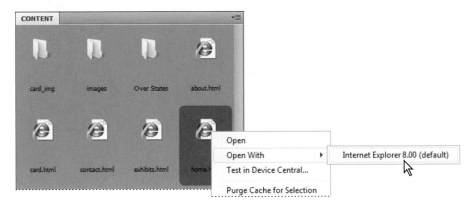

6 Move the pointer over the topics on the left side of the web page and over the images. When the pointer hovers over a link, it changes from an arrow to a pointing hand.

● **Note:** Depending on the settings in your browser, it may display security warnings. You are working with files on your hard disk, not on the Internet, so you can safely display the content.

7 Click the angel in the center of the image. The Zoomify window opens. Click the Zoomify controls to see how they change the magnification and reposition the image.

8 To return to the home page, close the Zoomify tab or window.

9 Click one of the other images to get a closer look at it in its own window. Close its browser window when you have finished.

10 On the home page, click the topics on the left side to jump to their linked pages. To return to the home page, click *Museo Arte* just below the logo in the upper-left corner of the window.

11 When you have finished viewing the web page, quit the web browser, and return to Bridge.

In the preceding steps, you used two different types of links: slices (the topics on the left side of the page) and images (the boy, the New Wing Opening page, and the angel).

Slices are rectangular areas in an image that you define based on layers, guides, or precise selections in the image, or by using the Slice tool. When you define slices in an image, Photoshop creates an HTML table or Cascading Style Sheet (CSS) layers to contain and align the slices. You can generate and preview an HTML file that contains the sliced image along with the table or cascading style sheet.

You can also add hypertext links to images. A website visitor can then click the image to open a linked page. Unlike slices, which are always rectangular, images can be any shape.

Selecting a web design workspace

As the leading application for preparing images for websites, Photoshop has some basic, built-in HTML creation tools. To make it easier to get to these tools for your web design tasks, you can customize the default arrangement of panels, toolbars, and windows, using one of the predefined workspaces in Photoshop.

1 In Bridge, click the Lesson13 folder in the breadcrumbs (the navigation path) at the top of the window to display the Lesson13 folder contents. Double-click the 13Start folder in the Content panel, and then double-click the 13Start.psd thumbnail to open the file in Photoshop.

You'll take advantage of the predefined Design workspace in Photoshop.

2 Choose Design from the Workspace Switcher in the Application bar.

Photoshop displays only the panels you're most likely to need when designing for the web.

3 Choose File > Save As, and rename the file **13Working.psd**. Click OK in the Photoshop Format Options dialog box. Saving a working copy preserves the original start file in case you need to return to it later.

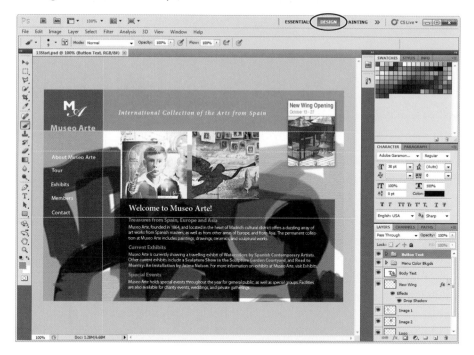

Creating slices

When you define a rectangular area in an image as a *slice*, Photoshop creates an HTML table to contain and align the slice. Once you create slices, you can turn them into buttons, and then program those buttons to make the web page work.

Any new slice you create within an image (a *user slice*) automatically creates other slices (*auto slices*) that cover the entire area of the image outside the user slice.

Selecting slices and setting slice options

You'll start by selecting an existing slice in the start file. We created the first slice for you.

1 In the Tools panel, select the Slice Select tool (⌖) tool, hidden under the Crop tool (🔪).

When you select the Slice or Slice Select tool, Photoshop displays the slices, with their slice numbers, on the image.

The slice numbered 01 includes the upper-left corner of the image; it also has a small icon, or *badge*, that resembles a tiny mountain. The blue color means that the slice is a user slice—a slice we created in the start file.

Also notice the gray slices—02 to the right, and 03 just below slice 01. The gray color indicates that these are auto slices, automatically created by making a user slice. The symbol indicates that the slice contains image content. See "About slice symbols" for a description.

About slice symbols

The blue and gray slice symbols, or *badges*, in the Photoshop image window and Save For Web And Devices dialog box can be useful reminders if you take the time to learn how to read them. Each slice can contain as many badges as are appropriate. These badges indicate the following:

(**01**) The number of the slice. Numbers run sequentially from left to right and top to bottom of the image.

(▨) The slice contains image content.

(▨) The slice contains no image content.

(▣) The slice is layer-based; that is, it was created from a layer.

(▨) The slice is linked to other slices (for optimization purposes).

2 In the upper-left corner of the image, click the slice numbered 01 with the small blue rectangle. A gold bounding box appears, indicating that the slice is selected.

3 Using the Slice Select tool, double-click slice 01. The Slice Options dialog box appears. By default, Photoshop names each slice based on the filename and the slice number—in this case, 13Start_01.

Slices aren't particularly useful until you set options for them. Slice options include the slice name and the URL that opens when the user clicks the slice.

4 In the Slice Options dialog box, name the slice **Logo**. For URL, type #. The pound sign (#) lets you preview a button's functionality without programming an actual link. It's very helpful in the early stages of website design, when you want to see how a button will look and behave.

5 Click OK to apply the changes.

● **Note:** You can set options for an auto slice, but doing so automatically promotes the auto slice to a user slice.

Creating navigation buttons

Now you'll slice the navigation buttons on the left side of the page. You could select one button at a time and add navigation properties to it. But you can do the same thing a faster way.

1 In the Tools panel, select the Slice tool (✐), or press Shift+C. (The Crop tool, Slice tool, and Slice Select tool share the C key as their keyboard shortcut. To change which of the three tools is selected, press Shift+C.)

Notice the guides above and below the words on the left side of the image.

2 Using the guides on the left side of the image, drag the Slice tool diagonally from the upper-left corner above *About Museo Arte*, to the bottom guide below *Contact*, so that all five lines are enclosed.

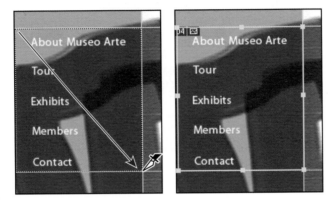

A blue rectangle, similar to the one for slice 01, appears in the upper-left corner of the slice you just created, numbered slice 04. The blue color tells you that this is a user slice, not an auto slice.

The original gray rectangle for auto slice 03 remains unchanged, but the area included in slice 03 is smaller, covering only a small rectangle above the text. Another auto slice, numbered 05, appears below the slice you created.

The gold bounding box indicates the bounds of the slice and that it's selected.

3 With the Slice tool still selected, press Shift+C to toggle to the Slice Select tool (✐). The options bar above the image window changes to include a series of alignment buttons.

Now you'll slice your selection into five separate buttons.

4 Click the Divide button in the options bar.

5 In the Divide Slice dialog box, select Divide Horizontally Into, and type **5** for Slices Down, Evenly Spaced. Click OK.

You'll name each slice and add a corresponding link.

6 Using the Slice Select tool, double-click the top slice, labeled *About Museo Arte*.

7 In the Slice Options dialog box, name the slice **About**; type **about.html** for URL; and type **_self** for Target. (Be sure to include the underscore before the letter *s*.) Click OK.

The Target option controls how a linked file opens when the link is clicked. The _self option displays the linked file in the same frame as the original file.

8 Repeat steps 6 and 7 for the remaining slices in turn, starting from the second slice, as follows:

- Name the second slice **Tour**; type **tour.html** for URL; and type **_self** for Target.

- Name the third slice **Exhibits**; type **exhibits.html** for URL; and type **_self** for Target.

● **Note:** Type the HTML filenames in the URL box exactly as shown, to match the names of the existing pages to which you will link the buttons.

- Name the fourth slice **Members**; type **members.html** for URL; and type **_self** for Target.

- Name the fifth slice **Contact**; type **contact.html** for URL; and type **_self** for Target.

9 Choose File > Save to save your work so far.

Creating slices based on layers

▶ **Tip:** If you find the indicators for the auto slices distracting, select the Slice Select tool and then click the Hide Auto Slices button in the options bar. You can also hide the guides by choosing View > Show > Guides, because you won't need them again in this lesson.

In addition to using the Slice tool, you can create slices based on layers. The advantage of using layers for slices is that Photoshop creates the slice based on the dimensions of the layer and includes all its pixel data. When you edit the layer, move it, or apply a layer effect to it, the layer-based slice adjusts to encompass the new pixels.

1 In the Layers panel, select the Image 1 layer. If you can't see all of the contents of the Layers panel, drag the panel from its dock, and expand it by dragging the lower-right corner.

2 Choose Layer > New Layer Based Slice. In the image window, a slice numbered 04, with a blue badge, appears over the image of the boy. It is numbered according to its position in the slices, starting from the top-left corner of the image.

3 Using the Slice Select tool (✂), double-click the slice, and name it **Image 1**. For URL, type **image1.html**. Type **_blank** for Target. The _blank Target option opens the linked page in a new instance of the web browser. Click OK.

Be sure to enter these options exactly as indicated, to match the pages you'll be linking the slices to.

Now you'll create slices for the New Wing and Image 2 layers.

4 Repeat steps 1–3 for the remaining images, as follows:

- Create a slice from the New Wing layer. Name it **New Wing**; for URL, type **newwing.html**; and type **_blank** for Target. Click OK.

- Create a slice from the Image 2 layer. Name it **Card**; type **card.html** for URL, and type **_blank** for Target. Click OK.

You may have noticed that the dialog box contains more options than the three you specified for these slices. For more information on how to use these options, see Photoshop Help.

5 Choose File > Save to save your work so far.

About creating slices

Here are other methods for creating slices that you can try on your own:

- You can create No Image slices, and then add text or HTML source code to them. No Image slices can have a background color and are saved as part of the HTML file. The primary advantage of using No Image slices for text is that the text can be edited in any HTML editor, saving you the trouble of having to go back to Photoshop to edit it. However, if the text grows too large for the slice, it will break the HTML table and introduce unwanted gaps.

- If you use custom guides in your design work, you can instantly divide up an entire image into slices with the Slices From Guides button on the options bar. Use this technique with caution, however, because it discards any previously created slices and any options associated with those slices. Also, it creates only user slices, and you may not need that many of them.

- When you want to create identically sized, evenly spaced, and aligned slices, try creating a single user slice that precisely encloses the entire area. Then, use the Divide button on the Slice Select options bar to divide the original slice into as many vertical or horizontal rows of slices as you need.

- If you want to unlink a layer-based slice from its layer, you can convert it to a user slice. Select it with the Slice Select tool, and then click Promote in the options bar.

Exporting HTML and images

You're ready to make your final slices, define your links, and export your file so that Photoshop creates an HTML page that will display all of your slices as one unit.

It's important to keep web graphics as small (in file size) as possible, so that web pages open quickly. Photoshop has built-in tools to help you gauge how small you can export each slice without compromising image quality. A good rule of thumb is to use JPEG compression for photographic, continuous-tone images and GIF compression for broad areas of color—in the case of this lesson's site, all of the areas around the three main art images on the page.

You'll use the Save For Web & Devices dialog box to compare settings and compression options for different image formats.

1 Choose File > Save For Web & Devices.

2 Select the 2-Up tab at the top of the Save For Web & Devices dialog box.

3 Choose the Slice Select tool (🔪) in the dialog box, and select slice 07 (the portrait of the boy) from the slices in the top image. Note the file size displayed beneath the image.

4 If necessary, use the Hand tool (✋) in the dialog box to move the image within the window and adjust your view.

5 On the right side of the dialog box, choose JPEG Medium from the Preset pop-up menu. Notice the file size displayed beneath the image; the file size changes dramatically when you choose JPEG Medium.

Now you'll look at a GIF setting for the same slice in the lower image.

6 With the Slice Select tool, select slice 07 in the lower image. On the right side of the dialog box, choose GIF 32 No Dither from the Preset pop-up menu.

Notice that the color area in the portrait in the lower image looks flatter and more posterized, but the image size is roughly the same.

Based on what you've just learned, you will choose which compression to assign to all of the slices on this page.

7 Select the Optimized tab at the top of the dialog box.

8 With the Slice Select tool, Shift-click to select the three main art images in the preview window. From the Preset menu, choose JPEG Medium.

9 Shift-click to select all of the remaining slices in the preview window, and then choose GIF 64 Dithered from the Preset menu.

10 Click Save. In the Save Optimized As dialog box, navigate to the Lesson13/13Start/Museo folder, which contains the rest of the site, including the pages that your slices will link to.

11 For format, choose HTML And Images. Use the default settings, and choose All Slices from the Slices menu. Name the file **home.html**, and click Save. If you're prompted to replace images, click Replace.

12 In Photoshop, click the Launch Bridge button (⎘) to switch to Bridge. Click Lessons in the Favorites panel. Double-click the Lesson13 folder in the Content panel, double-click the 13Start folder, and then double-click the Museo folder.

13 Right-click (Windows) or Control-click (Mac OS) the home.html file, and choose Open With from the context menu. Choose a web browser to open the HTML file.

14 In your web browser, move around the HTML file:

- Position your mouse over some of the slices you created. Notice that the pointer turns into a pointing finger to indicate a button.

- Click the portrait of the boy to open a new window with the full image.

- Click the New Wing Opening link to open its window.

- Click the text links on the left to jump to other pages in the site.

15 When you have finished exploring the file, close your browser.

Optimizing images for the web

Optimizing is the process of selecting format, resolution, and quality settings to make an image efficient, visually appealing, and useful for web browser pages. Simply put, it's balancing file size against good looks. No single collection of settings can maximize the efficiency of every kind of image file; optimizing requires human judgment and a good eye.

Compression options vary according to the file format used to save the image. JPEG and GIF are the two most common formats. The JPEG format is designed to preserve the broad color range and subtle brightness variations of continuous-tone images such as photographs. It can represent images using millions of colors. The GIF format is effective at compressing solid-color images and images with areas of repetitive color, such as line art, logos, and illustrations with type. It uses a panel of 256 colors to represent the image and supports background transparency.

Photoshop offers a range of controls for compressing image file size while optimizing the onscreen quality. Typically, you optimize images before saving them in an HTML file. Use the Save For Web & Devices dialog box to compare the original image to one or more compressed alternatives, adjusting settings as you compare. For more on optimizing GIF and JPEG images, see Photoshop Help.

Using the Zoomify feature

With the Zoomify feature, you can publish high-resolution images on the web that viewers can pan and zoom to see more detail. The basic-size image downloads in the same time as an equivalent-size JPEG file. Photoshop exports the JPEG files and HTML file that you can upload to your website. The Zoomify capabilities work with any web browser.

1 In Bridge, click the 13Start folder in the breadcrumbs at the top of the window. Then, double-click the card.jpg file to open it in Photoshop.

The card is a large bitmap image that you'll export to HTML using the Zoomify feature. You'll convert the angel image into a file that will be linked to one of the links that you've just created in the home page.

2 Choose File > Export > Zoomify.

3 In the Zoomify Export dialog box, click Folder, select the Lesson13/13Start/ Museo folder, and click OK or Choose. For Base Name, type **Card**. Set the quality to **12**; set the Width to **600**, and set the Height to **400** for the base image in the viewer's browser. Make sure that the Open In Web Browser option is selected.

4 Click OK to export the HTML file and images. Zoomify opens them in your web browser.

5 Use the controls in the Zoomify window to zoom in and out of the angel image.

6 When you have finished, close the browser.

Creating a web gallery

Using Bridge, you can easily showcase your images in an online gallery, so that visitors can view individual images or a slide show of your work. You'll create a media gallery linked to the exhibits.html file in the museum website.

1 In Bridge, double-click the Watercolors folder. (The Watercolors folder is in the Lesson13/13Start folder.)

You'll create a slide show from the images in the Watercolors folder.

2 Select the first image, and then Shift-select the last, so that all the images are selected. Remember that you can use the Thumbnails slider at the bottom of the Bridge window to reduce the size of the thumbnails, so that more fit in the Content panel at a time.

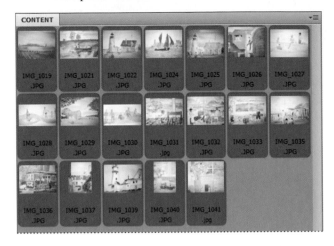

3 Click Output at the top of the Bridge window to display the Output workspace. If there is no Output button, choose Window > Workspace > Output.

4 In the Output panel, click the Web Gallery button.

5 Click the triangle next to Site Info if its contents aren't already displayed. In the Site Info area of the Output panel, enter **Watercolors** for the Gallery Title, **Paintings from the Watercolors exhibit** for the Gallery Caption, and **Now showing at Museo Arte** in the About This Gallery box. You can also add contact name and information if you want to.

6 Click the triangle next to Site Info to collapse its contents. Scroll down to the Create Gallery area. Expand its contents if they aren't already visible.

7 Name the gallery **Watercolors**. Click Browse, and navigate to the Lesson13/13Start/Museo folder. Click OK or Open to close the dialog box, and then click Save at the bottom of the Output panel in Bridge.

▼ Create Gallery

Gallery Name:

Watercolors

Save Location: Browse...

C:\Desktop\Lessons\Lesson13\13Start\Museo

Bridge creates a gallery folder named Watercolors that contains an index.html file and a resources folder containing the watercolor images.

8 Click OK when Bridge reports that the gallery has been created. Then, in Bridge, click the Essentials button at the top of the window to return to the default workspace.

9 Navigate to the Lesson13/13Start/Museo folder. Double-click the Watercolors folder, which is the gallery folder Bridge just created. Right-click or Control-click the index.html file, choose Open With, and select a browser.

10 If you see a security warning, click OK, or follow the instructions to change settings.

The gallery opens. One image is displayed on the right side, and thumbnails of the others are shown on the left.

11 Click the View Slideshow button beneath the larger image to start the slide show. Click the View Gallery button beneath the featured image to return to gallery view.

12 Close the browser application.

The exhibits.html file already contains a link to the folder you created, as long as you named the folder exactly as specified in step 7. Now you'll open your website and use the link to view the gallery.

13 In Bridge, navigate to the Lesson13/13Start/Museo folder. Right-click (Windows) or Control-click (Mac OS) the home.html file, and choose Open With from the context menu. Choose a web browser to open the HTML file.

14 In the website, click the Exhibits link in the navigation area. Then, on the Exhibits page, click the link to the Watercolors gallery. The gallery opens.

15 Explore the gallery and the website further, if you'd like. When you're finished, close the browser application, Bridge, and Photoshop.

You're on your way to building engaging websites from Photoshop images. You've learned how to create slices, optimize images for the web, use Zoomify, and create media slide shows in Bridge.

Review questions

1 What are slices? How do you create them?

2 What is image optimization, and how do you optimize images for the web?

3 How can you create a slide show for the web?

Review answers

1 Slices are rectangular areas of an image that you define for individual web optimization. You can add animated GIFs, URL links, and rollovers to slices. You can create image slices with the Slice tool or by converting layers into slices using the Layer menu.

2 Image optimization is the process of choosing file format, resolution, and quality settings for an image to keep it small, useful, and visually appealing when published to the web. Continuous-tone images are typically optimized in JPEG format; solid-color images or those with repetitive color areas are typically optimized as GIF. To optimize images, choose File > Save For Web & Devices.

3 To create a slide show for use on the web, use Bridge. Select the files you want to include, and then select Web Gallery in the Output panel in Bridge. Set the appropriate settings, and save the gallery. Bridge creates an index.html file with slide show and gallery controls that link to the files you selected.

14 PRODUCING AND PRINTING CONSISTENT COLOR

Lesson overview

In this lesson, you'll learn how to do the following:

- Define RGB, grayscale, and CMYK color spaces for displaying, editing, and printing images.

- Prepare an image for printing on a PostScript CMYK printer.

- Proof an image for printing.

- Save an image as a CMYK EPS file.

- Create and print a four-color separation.

- Understand how images are prepared for printing on presses.

This lesson will take less than an hour to complete. Copy the Lesson14 folder onto your hard drive if you haven't already done so. As you work through this lesson, you'll preserve the start files. If you need to restore the start files, copy them from the *Adobe Photoshop CS5 Classroom in a Book* DVD.

To produce consistent color, you define the color space in which to edit and display RGB images, and the color space in which to edit, display, and print CMYK images. This helps ensure a close match between onscreen and printed colors.

About color management

● **Note:** One exercise in this lesson requires that your computer be connected to a PostScript color printer. If it isn't, you can do most, but not all, of the exercises.

Colors on a monitor are displayed using combinations of red, green, and blue light (called RGB), while printed colors are typically created using a combination of four ink colors—cyan, magenta, yellow, and black (called CMYK). These four inks are called *process colors* because they are the standard inks used in the four-color printing process.

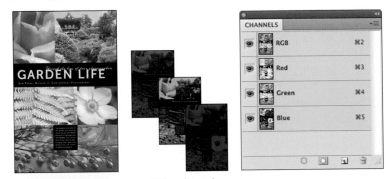

RGB image with red, green, and blue channels

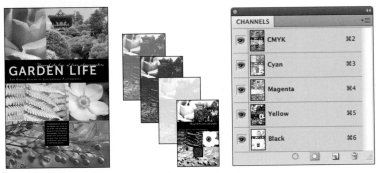

CMYK image with cyan, magenta, yellow, and black channels

Because the RGB and CMYK color models use different methods to display colors, each reproduces a different *gamut*, or range, of colors. For example, RGB uses light to produce color, so its gamut includes neon colors, such as those you'd see in a neon sign. In contrast, printing inks excel at reproducing certain colors that can lie outside the RGB gamut, such as some pastels and pure black.

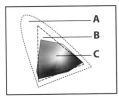
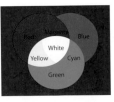
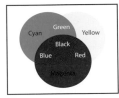

A. Natural color gamut
B. RGB color gamut
C. CMYK color gamut

RGB color model   CMYK color model

But not all RGB and CMYK gamuts are alike. Each monitor and printer model differs, and so each displays a slightly different gamut. For example, one brand of monitor may produce slightly brighter blues than another. The *color space* for a device is defined by the gamut it can reproduce.

RGB model

A large percentage of the visible spectrum can be represented by mixing red, green, and blue (RGB) colored light in various proportions and intensities. Where the colors overlap, they create cyan, magenta, yellow, and white.

Because the RGB colors combine to create white, they are also called *additive* colors. Adding all colors together creates white—that is, all light is transmitted back to the eye. Additive colors are used for lighting, video, and monitors. Your monitor, for example, creates color by emitting light through red, green, and blue phosphors.

CMYK model

The CMYK model is based on the light-absorbing quality of ink printed on paper. As white light strikes translucent inks, part of the spectrum is absorbed, while other parts are reflected back to your eyes.

In theory, pure cyan (C), magenta (M), and yellow (Y) pigments should combine to absorb all color and produce black. For this reason, these colors are called *subtractive* colors. But because all printing inks contain some impurities, these three inks actually produce a muddy brown, and must be combined with black (K) ink to produce a true black. (K is used instead of B to avoid confusion with blue.) Combining these inks to reproduce color is called four-color process printing.

The color management system in Photoshop uses International Color Consortium (ICC)-compliant color profiles to convert colors from one color space into another. A color profile is a description of a device's color space, such as the CMYK color space of a particular printer. You specify which profiles to use to accurately proof and print your images. Once you've selected the profiles, Photoshop can embed them into your image files, so that Photoshop and other applications can accurately manage color for the image.

For information on embedding color profiles, see Photoshop Help.

Before you begin working with color management, you should calibrate your monitor. If your monitor doesn't display colors accurately, color adjustments you make based on the image you see on your monitor may not be accurate. For information about calibrating your monitor, see Photoshop Help.

Getting started

First, start Photoshop and restore its default preferences.

1   Start Photoshop, and then immediately hold down Ctrl+Alt+Shift (Windows) or Command+Option+Shift (Mac OS) to restore the default preferences. (See "Restoring default preferences" on page 5.)

2   When prompted, click Yes to delete the Adobe Photoshop Settings file.

Specifying color-management settings

In the first part of this lesson, you'll learn how to set up a color-managed workflow in Photoshop. Most of the color-management controls you need are in the Color Settings dialog box.

By default, Photoshop is set up for RGB as part of a digital workflow. If you are preparing artwork for print production, however, you'll want to change the settings to be more appropriate for images that will be printed on paper rather than displayed on a screen.

You'll begin this lesson by creating customized color settings.

1   Choose Edit > Color Settings to open the Color Settings dialog box.

The bottom of the dialog box interactively describes each option.

2   Move the pointer over each part of the dialog box, including the names of areas (such as Working Spaces), the menu names, and the menu options. As you move the pointer, Photoshop displays information about each item. When you've finished, return the options to their defaults.

Now, you'll choose a set of options designed for a print workflow, rather than an online workflow.

3   Choose North America Prepress 2 from the Settings menu. The working spaces and color-management policy options change for a prepress workflow. Then click OK.

Proofing an image

You'll select a proof profile so that you can view a close onscreen representation of what an image will look like when printed. An accurate proof profile lets you proof on the screen (*soft-proof*) for printed output.

1 Choose File > Open. Navigate to the Lessons/ Lesson14 folder, and double-click the 14Start. tif file. Click OK if you see an embedded profile warning.

An RGB image of a scanned poster opens.

2 Choose File > Save As. Rename the file **14Working.tif**, keep the TIFF format selected, and click Save. Click OK in the TIFF Options dialog box.

Before soft-proofing or printing this image, you'll set up a proof profile. A proof profile (also called a *proof setup*) defines how the document is going to be printed, and adjusts the onscreen appearance accordingly. Photoshop provides a variety of settings that can help you proof images for different uses, including print and display on the web. For this lesson, you'll create a custom proof setup. You can then save the settings for use on other images that will be output the same way.

3 Choose View > Proof Setup > Custom. The Customize Proof Condition dialog box opens. Make sure Preview is selected.

4 From the Device To Simulate menu, choose a profile that represents the final output device, such as that for the printer you'll use to print the image. If you don't have a specific printer, the profile Working CMYK–U.S. Web Coated (SWOP) v2 is generally a good choice.

5 Make sure that Preserve Numbers is *not* selected.

The Preserve Numbers option simulates how colors will appear without being converted to the output device color space.

6 From the Rendering Intent menu, choose Relative Colorimetric.

A rendering intent determines how the color is converted from one color space to another. Relative Colorimetric, which preserves color relationships without sacrificing color accuracy, is the standard rendering intent for printing in North America and Europe.

Note: The Preserve Numbers option is not available when the U.S. Web Coated (SWOP) v2 profile is selected.

7 If it's available for the profile you chose, select Simulate Black Ink. Then deselect it, and select Simulate Paper Color; notice that selecting this option automatically selects Simulate Black Ink. Click OK.

Customize Proof Condition

Custom Proof Condition: Custom

Proof Conditions
Device to Simulate: Working CMYK – U.S. Web Coated (SWOP) v2
☐ Preserve Numbers
Rendering Intent: Relative Colorimetric
☑ Black Point Compensation
Display Options (On–Screen)
☑ Simulate Paper Color
☑ Simulate Black Ink

OK
Cancel
Load...
Save...
☑ Preview

▶ **Tip:** To display the document with and without the proof settings, choose View > Proof Colors.

Notice that the image appears to lose contrast. Paper Color simulates the dingy white of real paper, according to the proof profile. Black Ink simulates the dark gray that actually prints to most printers, instead of solid black. Not all profiles support these options.

Normal image

Image with Paper Color and Black Ink options selected

Identifying out-of-gamut colors

Most scanned photographs contain RGB colors within the CMYK gamut, so changing the image to CMYK mode converts all the colors with relatively little substitution. Images that are created or altered digitally, however, often contain RGB colors that are outside the CMYK gamut—for example, neon-colored logos and lights.

Before you convert an image from RGB to CMYK, you can preview the CMYK color values while still in RGB mode.

1 Choose View > Gamut Warning to see out-of-gamut colors. Adobe Photoshop builds a color-conversion table, and displays a neutral gray in the image window where the colors are out of gamut.

Because the gray can be hard to spot in the image, you'll convert it to a more visible color.

2 Choose Edit > Preferences > Transparency And Gamut (Windows) or Photoshop > Preferences > Transparency And Gamut (Mac OS).

3 Click the color sample in the Gamut Warning area at the bottom of the dialog box. Select a vivid color, such as purple or bright green, and click OK.

4 Click OK to close the Transparency And Gamut dialog box.

5 Click anywhere on the image with the Move tool. The bright, new color you chose appears instead of the neutral gray as the gamut warning color.

6 Choose View > Gamut Warning to turn off the preview of out-of-gamut colors.

Photoshop will automatically correct these out-of-gamut colors when you save the file in Photoshop EPS format later in this lesson. Photoshop EPS format changes the RGB image to CMYK, adjusting the RGB colors as needed to bring them into the CMYK color gamut.

Adjusting an image and printing a proof

The next step in preparing an image for output is to make any color and tonal adjustments that are necessary. In this exercise, you'll add some tonal and color adjustments to correct an off-color scan of the original poster.

So that you can compare the image before and after making corrections, you'll start by making a copy.

1 Choose Image > Duplicate, and click OK to duplicate the image.

2 Click the Arrange Documents button (▦) in the Application bar, and select a 2 Up layout so you can compare the images as you work.

You'll adjust the hue and saturation of the image to move all colors into gamut.

3 Select 14Working.tif (the original image).

4 Choose Select > Color Range.

5 In the Color Range dialog box, choose Out Of Gamut from the Select menu, and then click OK.

The areas that were marked as out of gamut earlier are now selected, so you can make changes that affect only those areas.

6 Click the Hue/Saturation button in the Adjustments panel to create a Hue/Saturation adjustment layer. (Choose Window > Adjustments if the panel isn't open.) The Hue/Saturation adjustment layer includes a layer mask, created from your selection.

7 Do the following:

- Drag the Hue slider until the colors look more neutral (we used -5).

- Drag the Saturation slider until the intensity of the colors looks more realistic (we used -40).

- Leave the Lightness setting at the default value (0).

8 Choose View > Gamut Warning. You have removed most of the out-of-gamut colors from the image. Choose View > Gamut Warning again to deselect it.

9 With 14Working.tif still selected, choose File > Print.

10 In the Print dialog box, do the following:

- Choose your printer from the Printer menu.

- Choose Color Management from the pop-up menu at the top of the right column.

- Select Proof to select your proof profile.

- For Color Handling, choose Printer Manages Colors.

- For Proof Setup, choose Working CMYK.

- If you have a color PostScript printer, click Print to print the image, and compare the color with the onscreen version. Otherwise, click Cancel.

Saving the image as a CMYK EPS file

You'll save the image as an EPS file in CMYK format.

1   With 14Working.tif still selected, choose File > Save As.

2   In the Save As dialog box, do the following, and then click Save:

*   Choose Photoshop EPS from the Format dialog box.

*   Under Color, select Use Proof Setup. Don't worry about the warning icon; you'll save a copy.

> **Note:** These settings cause the image to be automatically converted from RGB to CMYK when it is saved in the Photoshop Encapsulated PostScript (EPS) format.

*   Accept the filename 14Working.eps.

3   Click OK in the EPS Options dialog box that appears.

4   Save and then close the 14Working.tif and 14Working copy.tif files.

5   Choose File > Open, navigate to the Lessons/Lesson14 folder, and double-click the 14Working.eps file.

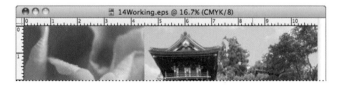

Notice in the image file's title bar that 14Working.eps is a CMYK file.

Printing

When you're ready to print your image, use the following guidelines for best results:

- Print a *color composite*, often called a *color comp*, to proof your image. A color composite is a single print that combines the red, green, and blue channels of an RGB image (or the cyan, magenta, yellow, and black channels of a CMYK image). This indicates what the final printed image will look like.

- Set the parameters for the halftone screen.

- Print separations to make sure the image separates correctly.

- Print to film or plate.

When you print color separations, Photoshop prints a separate sheet, or *plate*, for each ink. For a CMYK image, it prints four plates, one for each process color.

In this exercise, you'll print color separations.

1 With the 14Working.eps image open from the previous exercise, choose File > Print.

By default, Photoshop prints any document as a composite image. To print this file as separations, you need to explicitly instruct Photoshop in the Print dialog box.

2 In the Print dialog box, do the following:

- Choose Color Management from the pop-up menu at the top of the right column.

- Select Document.

- Choose Separations from the Color Handling menu.

- Click Print.

3 Choose File > Close, and don't save the changes.

This lesson has provided an introduction to printing and producing consistent color from Adobe Photoshop. If you're printing on a desktop printer, you can experiment with different settings to find the best color and print settings for your system. If you're preparing images for professional printing, consult with your print service provider to determine the best settings to use. For more information about color management, printing options, and color separations, see Photoshop Help.

Review questions

1 What steps should you follow to reproduce color accurately?

2 What is a gamut?

3 What is a color profile?

4 What are color separations?

Review answers

1 To reproduce color accurately, first calibrate your monitor, and then use the Color Settings dialog box to specify which color spaces to use. For example, you can specify which RGB color space to use for online images, and which CMYK color space to use for images that will be printed. You can then proof the image, check for out-of-gamut colors, adjust colors as needed, and—for printed images—create color separations.

2 A gamut is the range of colors that can be reproduced by a color model or device. For example, the RGB and CMYK color models have different gamuts, as do any two RGB scanners.

3 A color profile is a description of a device's color space, such as the CMYK color space of a particular printer. Applications such as Photoshop can interpret color profiles in an image to maintain consistent color across different applications, platforms, and devices.

4 Color separations are separate plates for each ink used in a document. Often, you'll print color separations for the cyan, magenta, yellow, and black (CMYK) inks.

INDEX

D

Default Foreground And
   Background Colors button
   212
defaults
   resetting 4, 12
   resetting colors 27
depth of field, adding 156
desaturating 264–265
deselecting 20, 71
   paths 216
Design workspace 336–337
Direct Selection tool 204,
   214, 223
discretionary ligatures 194
Dismiss Target Path button 213
displaying
   document size 117
   layers 100
   multiple documents 99
distortions, correcting 153–156
DNG file format 138
docking panels 33
document size, displaying
   117, 245
Dodge tool 144–145
dragging image files to add
   layers 108
drop shadows 90–91, 114
   layer style 186, 271
duplicating images 362

E

edges, softening 87–88
editing images
   adjusting highlights and
      shadows 149–151
   correcting distortions
      153–155
   nondestructively 168
   reducing noise 151–153
   removing red eye 151–152

editing shapes 214
Edit Plane tool 232
Elliptical Marquee tool 19, 68
   anti-aliasing and
      feathering 86
   centering selection 75
   circular selections with 72
EPS file format 364
Erase Refinements tool 167
Eraser tool 85, 119
exporting
   animations 326–329
   HTML pages 344–346
exposures, merging 139
eye icon, in the Layers panel 97

F

Favorites panel, in Bridge 15
Feather command 86
feathering 86
file formats
   from Camera Raw 138
   image quality and 251
   three dimensional 2
   transferring images between
      applications and
      platforms 138
   type 194
files
   reverting to unchanged
      version 22
   saving 22, 117–120
file size
   compressing for web 348
   flattened vs. unflattened 117
   printing 245
   reducing 117, 245–247
   with channels and layers 245
Fill Pixels option 217
fill properties, shape layer 213
Filter Gallery 260

filters 259–262
   adding clouds with 107
   improving performance 259
   overview 261
   shortcuts 261
Fit On Screen command 75
flattening layers 117–120,
   245–246
   stamping and 246
   white fill replaces
      transparency 245
focus, adjusting 156
fonts
   alternates 194
   selecting 184
foreground color 212
four-color printing 62–63, 356
fractions 194
Freeform Pen tool 201
freehand selections 80–81

G

gamut 356
   colors outside of 360–361
Gamut Warning 361–362
Geometry Options menu 205
GIF compression 344, 345
Glass filter 259
Gradient Overlay layer style 258
gradient picker 111
gradients, listing by name 111
Gradient tool 111
grid, perspective 232
guides
   adding 183, 253
   for creating slices 343
   overview 253
   Smart Guides 255

Production Notes

The *Adobe Photoshop CS5 Classroom in a Book* was created electronically using Adobe InDesign CS4. Art was produced using Adobe InDesign, Adobe Illustrator, and Adobe Photoshop. The Myriad Pro and Warnock Pro OpenType families of typefaces were used throughout this book.

References to company names in the lessons are for demonstration purposes only and are not intended to refer to any actual organization or person.

Images

Photographic images and illustrations are intended for use with the tutorials.

Lesson 4 pineapple and flower photography © Image Source, www.imagesource.com

Lesson 6 and 7 model photography © Image Source, www.imagesource.com

Typefaces used

Adobe Myriad Pro and Adobe Warnock Pro, as well as other Adobe typefaces are used throughout the lessons. For more information about OpenType and Adobe fonts, visit www.adobe.com/type/opentype/.

Team credits

The following individuals contributed to the development of this edition of the *Adobe Photoshop CS5 Classroom in a Book*:

Project Manager: Elaine Gruenke

Writer: Brie Gyncild

Illustrator and Compositor: Lisa Fridsma

Copyeditor and Proofreader: Wendy Katz

Indexer: Brie Gyncild

Cover design: Eddie Yuen

Interior design: Mimi Heft

Art Director: Andrew Faulkner

Designers: Elaine Gruenke, Megan Lee

Adobe Press Executive Editor: Victor Gavenda

Adobe Press Production Editor: Hilal Sala

Adobe Press Project Editor: Connie Jeung-Mills

Contributors

Jay Graham—began his career designing and building custom homes. He has been a professional photographer for more than 22 years, with clients in the advertising, architectural, editorial, and travel industries. He contributed the "Pro Photo Workflow" tips in Lesson 5.
http://jaygraham.com

Mark Johann—is a photographer based in San Francisco. He contributed photography for Lesson 5.
http://www.markjohann.com

Lee Unkrich—has directed major films for Pixar. His photographs appear in Lessons 9 and 14 of this book.

Special Thanks

We offer our sincere thanks to Christine Yarrow and Zorana Gee for their support and help with this project. We couldn't have done it without you!

Notes

Notes

Notes

Notes

Notes

Notes

Notes

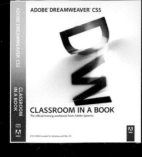

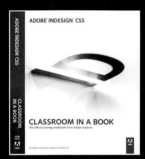

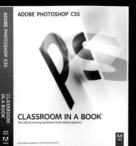

Newly Expanded LEARN BY VIDEO Series

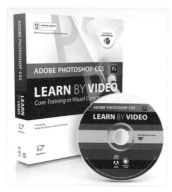

Learn Adobe Photoshop CS5 by Video:
Core Training in Visual Communication
(ISBN 9780321719805)

Learn Adobe Flash Professional CS5 by Video:
Core Training in Rich Media Communication
(ISBN 9780321719829)

Learn Adobe Dreamweaver CS5 by Video:
Core Training in Web Communication
(ISBN 9780321719812)

The **Learn by Video** series from video2brain and Adobe Press is the only Adobe-approved video courseware for the Adobe Certified Associate Level certification, and has quickly established itself as one of the most critically-acclaimed training products available on the fundamentals of Adobe software.

Learn by Video offers up to 19 hours of high-quality HD video training presented by experienced trainers, as well as lesson files, assessment quizzes and review materials. The DVD is bundled with a full-color printed book that provides supplemental information as well as a guide to the video topics.

Up to 19 hours of high-quality video training

Table of Contents never more than a click away

Watch-and-Work mode shrinks the video into a small window while you work in the software

Video player remembers which movie you watched last

Tutorials-to-Go! Transfer selected movies to your iPhone, iPod, or compatible cell phone

Lesson files are included on the DVD

Additional Titles

- **Learn Adobe Photoshop Elements 8 and Adobe Premiere Elements 8 by Video** (ISBN 9780321685773)
- **Learn Photography Techniques for Adobe Photoshop CS5 by Video** (ISBN 9780321734839)
- **Learn Adobe After Effects CS5 by Video** (ISBN 9780321734860)
- **Learn Adobe Flash Catalyst CS5 by Video** (ISBN 9780321734853)
- **Learn Adobe Illustrator CS5 by Video** (ISBN 9780321734815)
- **Learn Adobe InDesign CS5 by Video** (ISBN 9780321734808)
- **Learn Adobe Premiere Pro CS5 by Video** (ISBN 9780321734846)

For more information go to www.adobepress.com/learnbyvideo